# Clean Code with TypeScript



Elevate your TypeScript 6 skills with clean code principles and production-ready practices

**Rukevwe Ojigbo**
**Dr. Sanjay Krishna Anbalagan**

<packt>

# Clean Code with TypeScript



**Portfolio Director:** Ashwin Nair
**Relationship Lead:** Sneha Shinde
**Project Manager:** Vishnu Priya R
**Content Engineer:** Nithya Sadanandan
**Technical Editor:** Arjun Varma
**Copy Editor:** Safis Editing
**Indexer:** Hemangini Bari
**Proofreader:** Nithya Sadanandan
**Production Designer:** Alishon Falcon
**Growth Lead**: Sohini Ghosh

First published: March 2026

Production reference: 1130326

Published by Packt Publishing Ltd.
Grosvenor House
11 St Paul's Square
Birmingham
B3 1RB, UK.

ISBN 978-1-83588-956-5
www.packtpub.com

*To my mother, whose love, strength, and unwavering belief in me made this journey possible.*

*– Rukevwe Ojigbo*

*To my parents, mentors, teachers, and thinkers who shaped the way I understand systems, structure, and learning—this small contribution stands on the foundation you built.*

*To my wife, whose constant support and quiet strength inspire me to give back more to society, just as she gives so selflessly to our family every day.*

*And to my daughter, whose journey of learning to understand and respond to the world showed me what true intelligence looks like. Watching her grow changed how I think about learning itself —and ultimately how I build AI systems.*

*This book is my small tribute to all of you.*

*– Dr. Sanjay Krishna Anbalagan*

# Contributors

## About the authors

**Rukevwe Ojigbo** is a software developer with expertise in TypeScript and web and mobile applications. He has built large-scale and high-performance applications for various domains and platforms. He is currently a senior software engineer and a DevOps team member at Nationale Nederlanden, a leading insurance company. Previously, he worked as a frontend engineer at Young Capital, where he contributed to revamping the frontend architecture and design of one of the largest job boards in the Netherlands.

**Dr. Sanjay Krishna Anbalagan** is a software engineer with 15+ years of experience building large-scale frontend and full stack systems. He currently works at Amazon, focusing on generative AI applications, agent orchestration frameworks, and production-ready LLM systems. He holds a PhD in computer science from the University of Massachusetts Lowell and enjoys translating complex ideas into clear, human-centric explanations.

## About the reviewer

**Gurjit Singh** is a Berlin-based senior frontend engineer at Storyblok with 7+ years of experience building modern web applications using React, TypeScript, and Node.js. Previously at Zendesk, he contributed to AI-powered and customer-facing initiatives at scale. He led a major open source project for 5 years, growing it to 30,000+ active monthly users and collaborating with engineers from companies such as Apple and Wix. He enjoys conference speaking, sharing practical engineering insights, Indian classical music, psychology books, and traveling.

# Table of Contents

## Chapter 9: Understanding Advanced TypeScript Features 261

## Chapter 10: Setting Up Scalable TypeScript Projects 289

## Chapter 11: TypeScript in Action: Building Full Stack Applications 319

# Preface

TypeScript has become a cornerstone of modern web development, helping teams build applications that are safer, easier to maintain, and more scalable as requirements evolve. By adding strong typing and powerful tooling to JavaScript, TypeScript enables developers to catch errors earlier, communicate intent more clearly, and write code that remains reliable even as projects grow in complexity.

In this book, you will progress from TypeScript fundamentals to real-world development practices that reflect how professional teams build and maintain production systems. You will begin by learning how to set up TypeScript projects, understand essential and advanced types, and configure TypeScript effectively. From there, you will focus on writing clean functions, applying object-oriented programming principles, and organizing projects using modular, scalable structures supported by consistent tooling.

As you advance, you will learn how to test TypeScript applications with unit and integration tests, apply **Test-Driven Development** (**TDD**), and strengthen your applications through better error handling, debugging techniques, and security best practices. You will also explore performance optimization strategies and learn how design patterns can improve flexibility and maintainability in real-world code bases.

The later chapters take a hands-on, production-focused approach, guiding you through setting up scalable TypeScript environments using modern workflows such as Nx monorepos, pnpm dependency management, and automated code quality enforcement with Git hooks. You will then build a type-safe full stack application using NestJS and React, applying shared contracts to keep frontend and backend aligned. Finally, you will follow a realistic narrative where a working proof of concept evolves under changing requirements, learning how TypeScript helps prevent contract drift, protect runtime boundaries, and intentionally move failures earlier in the development lifecycle.

By the end of this book, you will have the skills to write clean, maintainable TypeScript code, architect scalable projects, and confidently apply TypeScript in real-world systems that grow, change, and evolve over time.

## Who this book is for

The book is for JavaScript developers who want to master TypeScript to build scalable and maintainable applications. Frontend, backend, and full stack developers, as well as software architects looking to leverage TypeScript for robust application design, will find practical value in this book. A basic understanding of JavaScript, including ES6+ features, functions, and asynchronous programming, is assumed. Although not required, familiarity with TypeScript fundamentals, OOP principles, and Git is helpful.

## What this book covers

*Chapter 1, Introducing TypeScript,* introduces TypeScript and explains why it has become essential for building reliable, maintainable web applications. It walks you through setting up a TypeScript project, understanding core and advanced types, and configuring `tsconfig.json` for an efficient development workflow.

*Chapter 2, Writing Clean Functions,* focuses on writing clean, maintainable TypeScript functions by applying best practices such as the single responsibility principle, avoiding side effects, and using clear function signatures. It also covers effective naming conventions and documentation techniques using TSDoc and TypeDoc to improve readability and long-term maintainability.

*Chapter 3, Object-Oriented Programming with TypeScript,* explores object-oriented programming in TypeScript, covering core concepts such as classes, inheritance, interfaces, abstract classes, and polymorphism for building scalable and reusable applications. It also highlights encapsulation and the principle of composition over inheritance to help you design cleaner, more flexible code bases.

*Chapter 4, Clean Code in TypeScript Projects,* brings together the clean code concepts from earlier chapters and applies them to building a complete TypeScript project. It focuses on structuring scalable code bases through effective folder organization, module systems, dependency management, and tooling such as linting and formatting for consistent code quality.

*Chapter 5, Testing and Test-Driven Development,* introduces a complete testing strategy for TypeScript projects, covering the fundamentals of testing along with unit and integration testing practices. It also explores **Test-Driven Development** (**TDD**) and how writing tests first can improve code quality, reliability, and overall application design.

*Chapter 6, Error Handling, Debugging, and Security Best Practices,* focuses on mastering error handling and debugging techniques to build reliable and secure TypeScript applications. It covers strategies for managing synchronous and asynchronous errors, using error types effectively, leveraging debugging tools, and applying essential security best practices.

*Chapter 7, Maximizing Performance Optimization*, explores practical techniques for optimizing the performance of TypeScript applications, from identifying bottlenecks and using profiling tools to applying proven optimization strategies. It covers approaches such as minification, tree shaking, lazy loading, and caching to help you build faster, more efficient, and cost-effective applications.

*Chapter 8, Mastering Design Patterns in TypeScript*, introduces design patterns in TypeScript and explains how they provide reusable, maintainable solutions to common software design challenges. It explores creational, structural, and behavioral patterns through practical examples, along with best practices to help you apply them effectively in real-world projects.

*Chapter 9, Understanding Advanced TypeScript Features*, explores advanced TypeScript features that help you write more flexible, scalable, and maintainable code for real-world applications. It covers generics, advanced and utility types, decorators, mapped types, and conditional types with practical examples to strengthen your expertise.

*Chapter 10, Setting Up Scalable TypeScript Projects*, shifts from TypeScript theory to real-world application by guiding you through building a production-ready development environment designed for scalability and team collaboration. It covers key architectural decisions such as monorepo versus polyrepo, setting up an Nx workspace with pnpm, and automating code quality using Git hooks for long-term maintainability.

*Chapter 11, TypeScript in Action: Building Full Stack Applications*, brings your Nx-based project to life by building a type-safe full stack application with a NestJS backend and a React frontend. It shows how shared DTOs and validated APIs help TypeScript enforce consistency across client and server, improving collaboration and reducing runtime errors.

*Chapter 12, TypeScript in Evolving Systems*, follows a real-world narrative of a full stack support chatbot that evolves from a working proof of concept into a growing system where assumptions drift and runtime failures emerge. It shows how TypeScript techniques—such as explicit contracts, runtime validation, and discriminated unions—help move errors earlier to build time, making changes safer and easier to maintain.

# To get the most out of this book

This book is designed for developers who want to write clean, scalable, and production-ready TypeScript. To get the most value from the examples and hands-on chapters, you should be comfortable with basic JavaScript concepts such as variables, functions, arrays, objects, and asynchronous programming (promises and async/await). Familiarity with ES6+ syntax (arrow functions, destructuring, modules) will also help you follow along smoothly. While prior TypeScript experience is not required, having a basic understanding of web development workflows (using the terminal, installing packages, and running scripts) will make the learning process faster and more practical.

To follow along with this book, you will need the following:

- Node.js (LTS version recommended) and npm (comes with Node.js)
- A code editor such as Visual Studio Code (recommended)
- A terminal (macOS Terminal, Windows PowerShell, or any modern shell)
- TypeScript installed either globally or as a project dependency
- A package manager such as **npm**, **pnpm**, or **Yarn** (pnpm is used in later chapters)

Some chapters include full stack and team-style workflows, so the following tools are also recommended:

- **Git** (for version control and Git hooks)
- A modern browser such as **Chrome, Firefox, or Edge** (for testing frontend behavior)

In the project chapters, you'll set up a production-ready workspace using **Nx**, configure dependencies using **pnpm**, and apply automated quality checks using tools such as **linters**, **formatters**, and **Git hooks**. Ensure you have the ability to install dependencies and run commands locally so you can experiment, break things safely, and learn by building.

## Download the example code files

This book includes a complete downloadable code bundle containing all the example projects and files used throughout the chapters. We recommend downloading the bundle so you can follow along smoothly and experiment with the examples.

Use the bundle as a practical starting point. Modify it, extend it, and apply what you learn by creating your own variations as you progress through the chapters.

**Get the code bundle**

**If you bought the book directly from Packt:**

1. Go to **packtpub.com**

2. Click your **profile picture** and select **Your Orders**
3. Find this book and click **Download Code**

**If you bought this book from Amazon or any other channel partner:**

1. Go to `packtpub.com/unlock` or scan the following QR code:

2. Search for this book
3. Sign up or log in to your free Packt account
4. Upload your proof of purchase and download the code bundle locally

**Usage note:** You're free to use and modify this code for personal learning and non-commercial projects.

## Conventions used

There are a number of text conventions used throughout this book.

`CodeInText`: Indicates code words in text, database table names, folder names, filenames, file extensions, pathnames, dummy URLs, user input, and Twitter handles. For example: "For instance, a class named `ShoppingCart` provides much more context than simply `Cart`."

A block of code is set as follows:

```
/**
 * Completes the checkout process.
 * @param discount The discount percentage to apply.
 * @returns The final total after applying the discount.
 */
checkout(discount: number): number {
  const total = this.applyDiscount(discount);
  console.log('Your total is: $' + total.toFixed(2));
  console.log('Thank you for shopping with us!');
  return total;
}
```

When we wish to draw your attention to a particular part of a code block, the relevant lines or items are set in bold:

```
/**
 * Completes the checkout process.
 * @param discount The discount percentage to apply.
 * @returns The final total after applying the discount.
 */
checkout(discount: number): number {
  const total = this.applyDiscount(discount);
  console.log('Your total is: $' + total.toFixed(2));
  console.log('Thank you for shopping with us!');
  return total;
}
```

Any command-line input or output is written as follows:

```
npm install --save-dev typedoc
```

**Bold**: Indicates a new term, an important word, or words that you see on the screen. For instance, words in menus or dialog boxes appear in the text like this. For example: "To follow along with the examples in this chapter on testing and TDD, you will need **Node.js version 20.0.0** or later and **TypeScript version 5.0** or later installed on your machine."

Note

Warnings or important notes appear like this.

Tip

Tips and tricks appear like this.

# Get in touch

Feedback from our readers is always welcome.

**General feedback**: If you have questions about any aspect of this book or have any general feedback, please email us at `customercare@packt.com` and mention the book's title in the subject of your message.

**Errata**: Although we have taken every care to ensure the accuracy of our content, mistakes do happen. If you have found a mistake in this book, we would be grateful if you reported this to us. Please visit `http://www.packt.com/submit-errata`, click **Submit Errata**, and fill in the form.

**Piracy**: If you come across any illegal copies of our works in any form on the internet, we would be grateful if you would provide us with the location address or website name. Please contact us at `copyright@packt.com` with a link to the material.

**If you are interested in becoming an author**: If there is a topic that you have expertise in and you are interested in either writing or contributing to a book, please visit `http://authors.packt.com/`.

# Free benefits with your book

This book includes free benefits designed to support your learning and help you apply what you learn effectively. Activate them now for instant access (see the *How to unlock* section for instructions).

Here's a quick overview of what you can instantly unlock with your purchase:

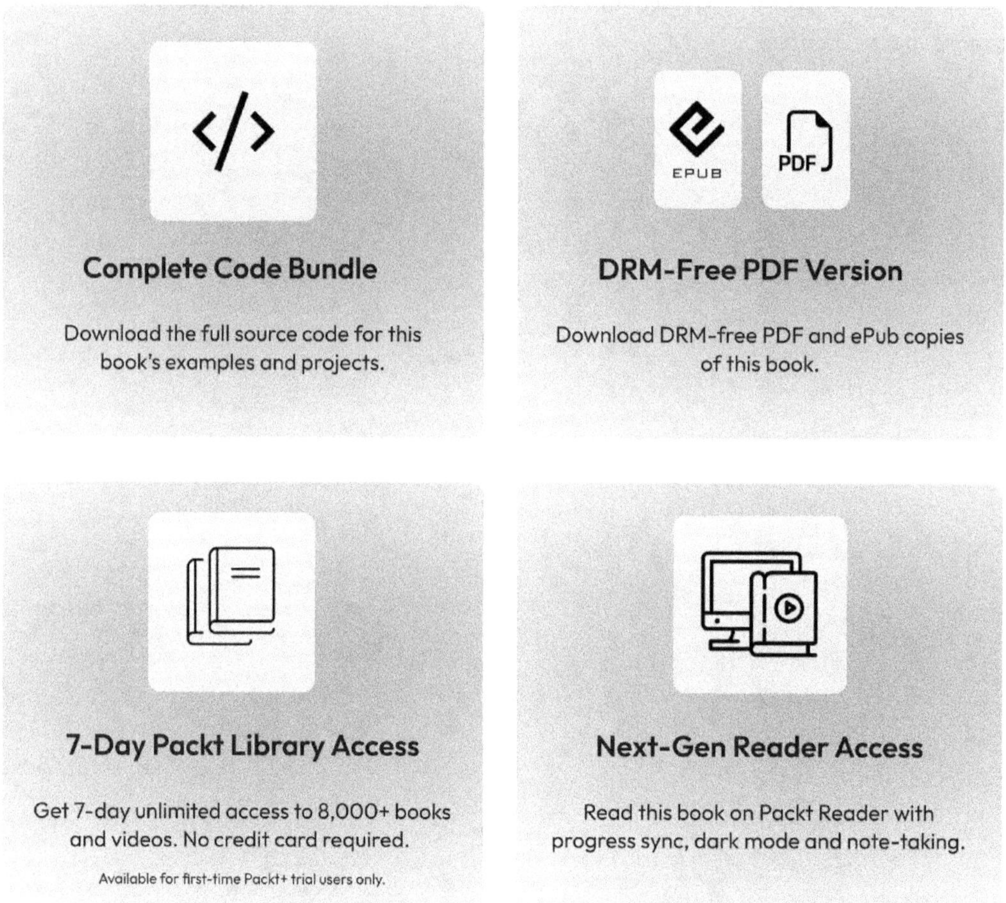

## How to unlock

Scan the QR code (or go to `packtpub.com/unlock`). Search for this book by name, confirm the edition, and then follow the steps on the page.

UNLOCK NOW

*Note: Have your invoice handy. Purchases made directly from the Packt website don't require an invoice.*

## Share your thoughts

Once you've read *Clean Code with TypeScript*, we'd love to hear your thoughts! Scan the QR code below to go straight to the Amazon review page for this book and share your feedback.

*https://packt.link/r/1835889573*

Your review is important to us and the tech community and will help us make sure we're delivering excellent quality content.

# 1

# Introducing TypeScript

In the ever-evolving world of web development, **TypeScript** has emerged as a powerful tool for creating robust, maintainable, and error-free code. In this chapter, we will explore the benefits of using TypeScript in modern web development and provide practical examples of how it can be used to enhance code quality, readability, and maintainability.

We will begin by discussing the rationale for using TypeScript and identifying scenarios where it can be most effective. Next, we will provide a step-by-step guide to setting up a basic TypeScript project and installing TypeScript. We will then dive into the foundational types of TypeScript, including strings, numbers, and Booleans, and provide practical examples of how they can be used in real-world scenarios. We will also explore more complex types, such as arrays and tuples, and discuss how they can be used to manipulate data in TypeScript.

Additionally, we will cover the use of enums for better code readability. Finally, we will introduce advanced types, such as union types and intersection types, and explain how they can be used to create dynamic and adaptable types.

As part of our comprehensive coverage, we'll walk through the most crucial aspects of the `tsconfig.json` file, providing a clear understanding of its configuration options.

By the end of this chapter, you will have a solid understanding of TypeScript and will be able to use it to write more efficient and maintainable code.

In this chapter, we're going to cover the following main topics:

- Why TypeScript
- Getting started with TypeScript
- Understanding basic types
- Working with complex types

- Mastering advanced types
- Configuring `tsconfig.json`

Note

**Your purchase includes a free PDF copy + code bundle**

Your purchase includes a DRM-free PDF copy of this book, the code bundle, and additional exclusive extras. See the *Free benefits with your book* section in the *Preface* to unlock them instantly and maximize your learning.

# Technical requirements

To maximize your engagement with this chapter and actively participate in the hands-on exercises, ensure that you have the following technical requirements:

- A basic understanding of the JavaScript programming language.
- **Node.js and npm**: Node.js must be installed on your system to execute the **TypeScript compiler** (**tsc**). You can download and install Node.js from the official website: `https://nodejs.org/en`.
- A text editor or an **integrated development environment** (**IDE**) that supports TypeScript. We recommend using **Visual Studio Code** (**VS Code**), which is a free and open source code editor developed by Microsoft. You can download VS Code here: `https://code.visualstudio.com/`. You can also use CodeSandbox to experiment with TypeScript (`https://codesandbox.io/s/vanilla-typescript-vanilla-ts`).
- **tsc**: TypeScript is a superset of JavaScript that adds optional static typing. `tsc` converts TypeScript code into JavaScript code that can run in any JavaScript environment. You can install `tsc` using `npm install -g typescript`.
- **Code repository**: You can download the example project and code for this book by following the instructions in the *Download the example code files* section in the *Preface* of this book. This chapter's code files are included in the downloadable code bundle. To clone the repository using HTTPS, you would use the following command:

```
$ git clone https://github.com/Rukeeo1/Clean-Code-in-TypeScript.git
```

With the technical prerequisites in place, you're now ready to dive into the core concepts of TypeScript. But before we begin, it's important to understand why TypeScript has become such a popular choice among developers. In the next section, we'll explore the key advantages of using TypeScript and how it enhances the development process.

# Why TypeScript?

JavaScript was originally designed as a lightweight scripting language for small browser interactions such as handling button clicks, validating forms, or adding simple UI behavior. For many years, it was never intended to manage large, long-lived applications.

As web applications grew richer and more complex, more logic moved into the browser and server-side JavaScript environments. Code bases expanded from a few scripts into hundreds of interconnected files maintained by large teams. This growth exposed several challenges: runtime errors caused by unexpected data, difficulty understanding and refactoring code safely, and limited tooling support for reasoning about large systems.

At the core of these problems was a fundamental limitation: JavaScript provides no built-in way to verify correctness before code runs. Errors are often discovered only at runtime, sometimes long after deployment.

TypeScript was created to address this gap. By adding optional static typing and improved tooling to JavaScript, TypeScript enables developers to catch errors earlier, reason about code more effectively, and scale applications with greater confidence.

## Advantages of using TypeScript

TypeScript's core feature is its static type system, which allows developers to define types for variables, function parameters, return values, classes, and namespaces. Not only do we benefit from enhanced code readability by being able to explicitly define these types, but runtime errors are reduced, and potential bugs are caught during the development phase itself. Real-world applications benefit from fewer unexpected runtime errors, leading to more reliable and stable software.

In collaborative development environments, TypeScript's type annotations serve as documentation for developers working on the same code base. Type definitions clarify the expected input and output of functions, reducing confusion and improving code comprehension. As projects grow, maintaining and extending code becomes more manageable due to the additional layer of information provided by TypeScript.

When refactoring or modifying existing code, TypeScript provides a safety net by identifying places in the code base that need to be updated due to changes in types or signatures. This minimizes the risk of introducing bugs during refactoring and encourages developers to make changes without fear of breaking existing functionality.

TypeScript's integration with modern development tools, such as VS Code, provides IntelliSense for code completion, intelligent suggestions, and real-time error checking. These features lead to faster coding, reduced cognitive load, and improved productivity for developers.

## Real-world applications of TypeScript

TypeScript is widely adopted in popular frontend frameworks and libraries such as Angular, React, and Vue.js. By adding static type checking to these frameworks, TypeScript helps developers build more reliable and maintainable applications when creating complex user interfaces, managing state, and handling data flow. TypeScript's type system provides structure and catches errors early in the development process, making frontend applications more scalable and easier to maintain.

TypeScript is not limited to frontend development. It's also gaining traction in backend development using technologies such as Node.js and Deno. The ability to define types and interfaces makes working with APIs and databases more intuitive and error-resistant.

TypeScript's type annotations ensure that requests and responses adhere to defined structures when building middleware or RESTful APIs using frameworks such as Express.js, resulting in less error-prone code and improved API documentation. Third-party libraries and modules can also benefit from TypeScript's type system, with type definitions for popular libraries available on **DefinitelyTyped**. The DefinitelyTyped repository provides type definitions for popular libraries, bridging the gap between untyped JavaScript and type-safe TypeScript projects. You can find the repository here: `https://github.com/DefinitelyTyped`.

Now that we have explored TypeScript, its rationale, and the benefits it provides, the upcoming section will guide you through the process of setting up and configuring a TypeScript project, offering a step-by-step approach for seamless implementation.

## Getting started with TypeScript: installation and project setup

Before delving into the intricacies of TypeScript, let's establish a solid foundation by installing the essential tools and configuring a basic project structure.

We will start by installing `tsc`. This can be accomplished using the following command in your terminal (either the integrated terminal in VS Code or the default one that comes with your computer):

```
$ npm install -g typescript
```

This will install `tsc` globally, allowing you to access it from anywhere on your system.

Congratulations, you just succeeded in installing TypeScript. Now, we can proceed with setting up our first TypeScript project.

To do that, follow these steps:

1. Start by creating a directory for your project. This will be the folder where all your project files will be stored. You can name it `clean-code-with-typescript` or choose a different name if you prefer. Here's how to do this in VS Code:
    1. Open VS Code.
    2. Click on **File** in the menu bar, then select **Open Folder**.
    3. In the dialog box that appears, navigate to the location where you want to create your new directory.
    4. Click on **New Folder** at the bottom of the dialog box.
    5. Enter `clean-code-with-typescript` (or your preferred name) as the name of the new folder.
    6. Click **Create**, and then **OK**.
2. Run the following command to initialize a new, empty `npm` project in your project directory (in your integrated VS Code terminal):

    ```
    $ npm init -y
    ```

This command generates a `package.json` file with default settings. The `-y` flag automatically selects default settings, skipping the interactive setup process. You can customize these settings as needed by editing the `package.json` file later. Your directory should look like *Figure 1.1*.

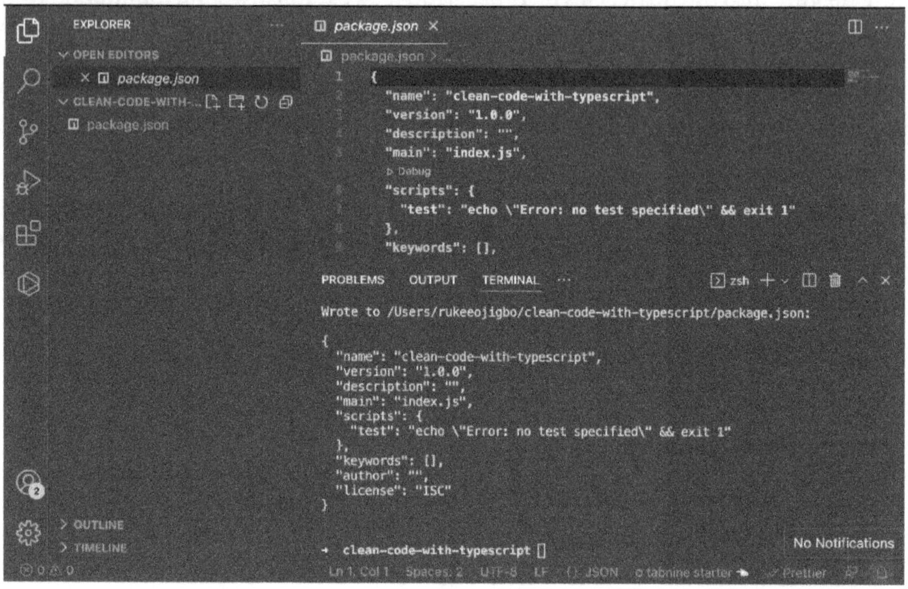


*Figure 1.1 — Generated package.json and project directory structure*

3. Install TypeScript as a development dependency in your project, with the following command:

```
$ npm install --save-dev typescript
```

If you installed TypeScript globally on your machine, then it's possible to skip this step if you are working on something basic, but it's great to do it on a project where you are collaborating with others, so that you can have the same versions, for example.

4. Create a `tsconfig.json` file by using the following command:

```
$ npm tsc --init
```

The `tsconfig.json` file contains the configuration for your TypeScript project. The preceding command should generate a file like the one in the following figure:

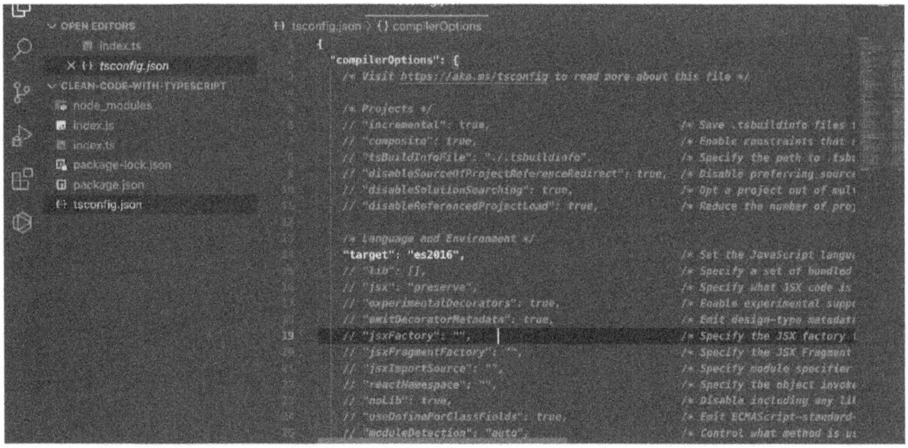


*Figure 1.2 — Generated tsconfig.json file with default settings*

5. Create your first TypeScript file and name it `index.ts`. Open a text editor and add the following content:

```
$ console.log("Hello, TypeScript!");
```

6. To compile your TypeScript code to JavaScript, run the following command in the terminal:

```
$ npx tsc
```

This will generate a JavaScript file called `index.js` in the same directory, which can be run using Node.js:

```
$ node index.js
```

You should notice the message `"Hello, TypeScript!"` printed to the console.

Congratulations! You have successfully installed TypeScript and set up a fundamental TypeScript project. The following figure gives you an overview of what the final result should look like:

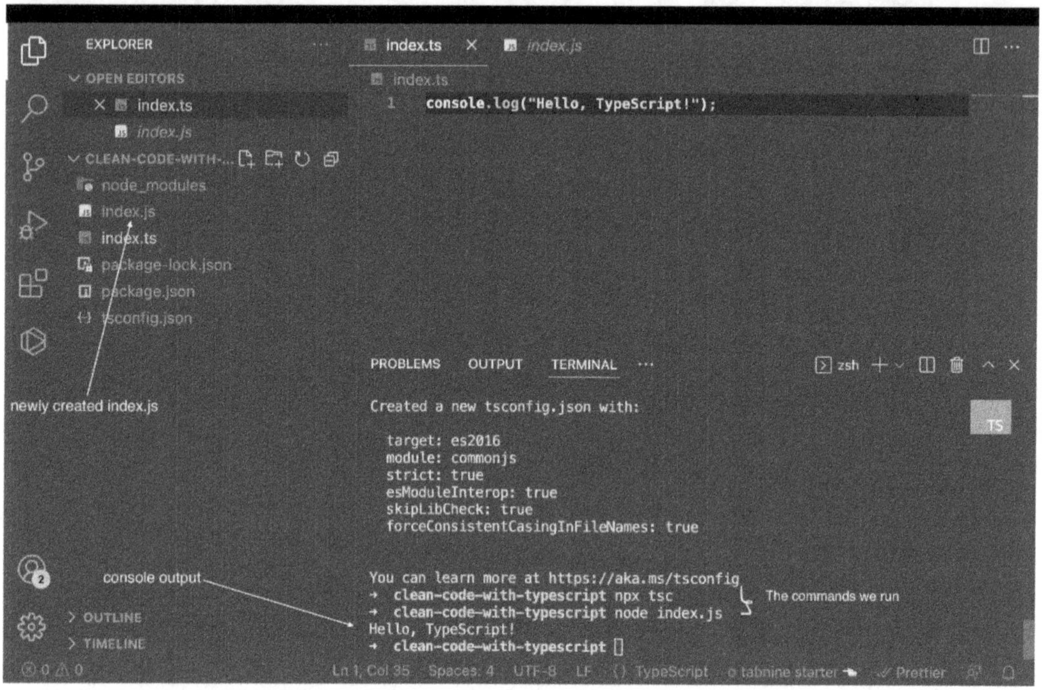


*Figure 1.3 — Result of creating and compiling the first TypeScript file (index.ts)*

Fantastic! We've created our first TypeScript project and compiled the code into JavaScript. Now, we'll continue our adventure. Before we proceed, let's discuss the `tsconfig.json` file. While we'll explore it in depth later, it's helpful to understand some of its default settings now.

Let's break down the configuration options in the `tsconfig.json` file:

- `target`: This specifies the ECMAScript version that TypeScript should aim to compile to. In this instance, we are targeting ES5, which is the fifth major version of JavaScript released in 2009. This means that TypeScript will generate JavaScript code compatible with most web browsers and Node.js installations.
- `module`: This specifies the module format for the generated JavaScript code. In this case, the module format is set to `commonjs`, which is a module format used by Node.js.

- `strict`: This activates `strict` mode, which is a set of rules that helps to improve the security and maintainability of TypeScript code. For instance, `strict` mode will prevent you from using undeclared variables or failing to close parentheses correctly.
- `esModuleInterop`: This enables compatibility with modern JavaScript features, such as the `import` and `export` keywords. This option is crucial for TypeScript to work with JavaScript libraries that utilize these newer features.
- `skipLibCheck`: This informs TypeScript to skip checking the type definitions for the TypeScript library. This is a beneficial option if you are employing a custom version of the TypeScript library. It instructs the TypeScript compiler to bypass type checking for the TypeScript library itself (the `lib.d.ts` file). This can speed up compilation times, especially in large projects with many dependencies. `skipLibCheck` should be used with care, as it potentially conceals errors within the TypeScript library or its interaction with your code.
- `allowJs`: This permits the use of JavaScript files in your TypeScript project. This can be useful if you need to include code written in JavaScript or if you want to gradually migrate your project to TypeScript.

Now that our TypeScript project is set up, let's delve deeper. In the next section, we'll explore basic types in TypeScript and begin to understand how to use them.

# Understanding basic types in TypeScript

In TypeScript, basic types serve as the building blocks for crafting meaningful data representations. They establish a shared understanding between you, the developer, and the TypeScript compiler, ensuring clarity and precision within your code.

Throughout this section, you will gain insights into the basic types in TypeScript, how to effectively utilize them in your code, and discover practical examples and use cases for each type.

## What are basic types in TypeScript?

In TypeScript, basic types are used to represent the most fundamental data types in the language. The following are the basic types in TypeScript:

- `string`: Represents a sequence of characters
- `number`: Represents a numeric value
- `boolean`: Represents a logical value that can be either `true` or `false`
- `null`: Represents a null value

- `undefined`: Represents an undefined value
- `symbol`: Represents a unique identifier

## How to use basic types in TypeScript

To use basic types in TypeScript, you can declare a variable with a specific type. Here are some examples:

- **String type**:

  ```
  let  fullName: string = "John Doe";
  ```

  **Practical example/use case**: Used to represent text data, such as names, addresses, and messages

- **Number type**:

  ```
  let age: number = 30;
  ```

  **Practical example/use case**: Used to represent numeric data, such as ages, prices, and quantities

- **Boolean type**:

  ```
  let isStudent: boolean = true;
  ```

  **Practical example/use case**: Used to represent logical data, such as whether a user is logged in or not

- **Null type**:

  ```
  let nothing: null = null;
  ```

  **Practical example/use case**: Used to represent the absence of a value

- **Undefined type**:

  ```
  let something: undefined = undefined;
  ```

**Practical example/use case**: Used to represent a variable that has not been assigned a value

- **Symbol type**:

```
let id: symbol = Symbol("id");
```

**Practical example/use case**: Used to represent a unique identifier, such as object keys

We've just listed common basic types in TypeScript. If you choose one of these variables, such as the `fullName` variable, and attempt to reassign it to a different type that doesn't match the expected type, TypeScript will show an error. For instance, in the following figure, we've tried to reassign the `fullName` variable to a number on line 4:

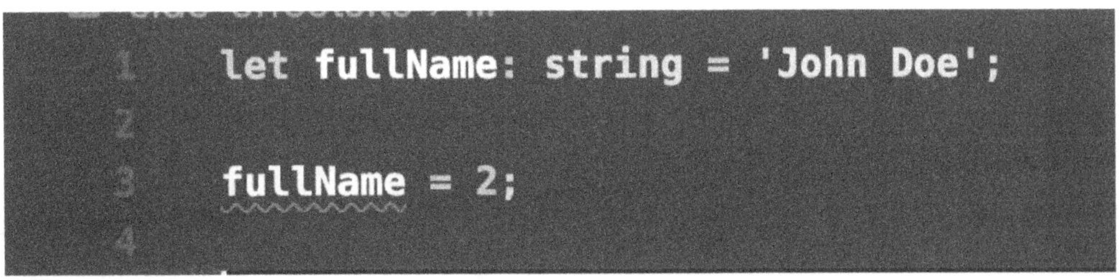


*Figure 1.4 —The squiggly red line under the fullName variable indicates a TypeScript error*

If you look closely at line 3, where the reassignment is happening, you will notice the red line. If you hover on the red line, you will notice what the issue is:

```
Error: Type 'number' is not assignable to type 'string'.
```

See the following figure for more clarity:

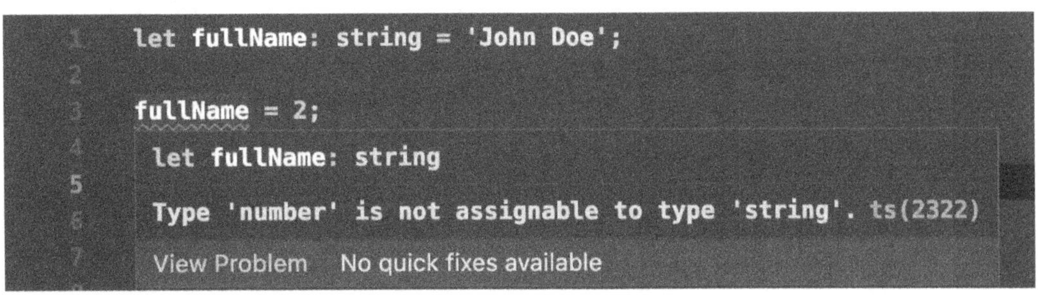


*Figure 1.5 — The error details when you hover over the fullName variable*

While this example may appear trivial, the implications become crucial in real-world scenarios. Imagine building a financial application in plain JavaScript where precise data types are essential for mathematical operations. In such scenarios, TypeScript's type checking catches potential type errors early, reducing the risk of bugs, such as unintended arithmetic operations between incompatible types (e.g., a string and a number).

## Arrays

Think of a shopping list, a sequence of items you need to buy. In TypeScript, arrays provide similar functionality, serving as ordered collections of values. Just like your list items, each element within an array can be accessed using its index position.

In the following example, we declare a `shoppingList` array with a type annotation specifying that it should contain strings. We initialize the array with some initial items – `"Apples"`, `"Bananas"`, and `"Milk"`:

```
const shoppingList: string[] = ["Apples", "Bananas", "Milk"];
```

If we attempt to add a number (123) into the `shoppingList` array using the `push` method, we get a TypeScript error:

```
"Argument of type 'number' is not assignable to parameter of type 'string'."
```

In a previous section (on types and interfaces), we discussed objects and types. As an example, we defined the `Person` type:

```
type Person = {
  name: string;
  age: number;
  greet: () => void;
};
```

Now, let's combine this `Person` type with an array to create a list of individuals, each represented by an object. For instance, we'll include two people, Alice and Bob:

```
const persons: Person[] = [
 {
   name: "Alice",
   age: 30,
   greet() {
    console.log(
`Hello, my name is ${this.name} and I'm         ${this.age} years old.`
    );
```

```
    },
  },
  {
    name: "Bob",
    age: 25,
    greet() {
     console.log(
 `Hello, my name is ${this.name} and I'm          ${this.age} years old.`);
    },
  },
];
```

In this example, we're already assembling these building blocks to create more robust and type-safe code. If you were to add a value to the `persons` array that doesn't conform to the structure defined by the `Person` type, TypeScript would raise an error.

As demonstrated earlier, we continue to reap the benefits of type inference. For instance, if we attempt to add a new `person` object to our list, TypeScript provides a helpful hint in our code editor regarding the expected property types. Take a look at the following figure:

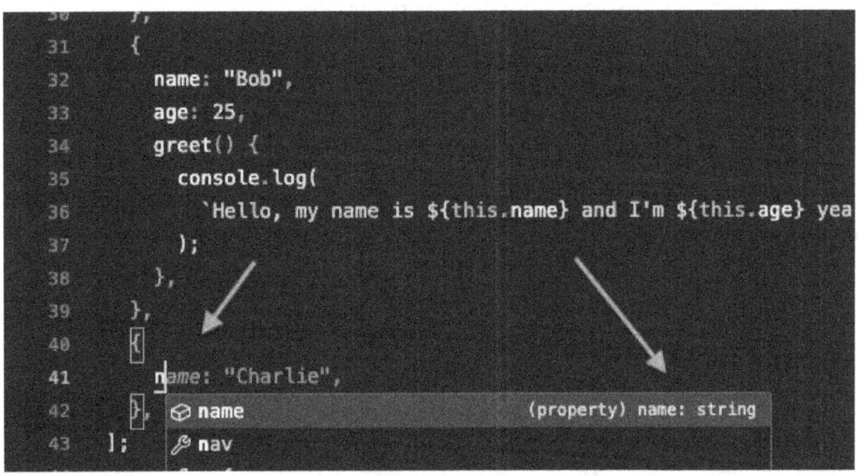


*Figure 1.9 — Code editor displaying type hints for the expected properties*

## Type inference

In the examples we've just seen regarding basic types, we explicitly specified the type of the variable. However, TypeScript's type system can infer types automatically. For instance, if we use the `fullName` variable again without explicitly specifying its type, TypeScript will still complain if we attempt to reassign the variable to a value of the `number` type:

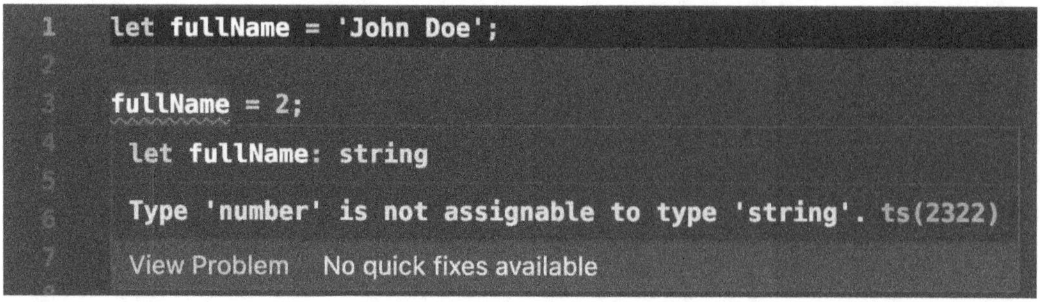


*Figure 1.6 – TypeScript inferring types, even when they are not explicitly stated*

Now that we've explored the basics of TypeScript types, let's delve into more complex types in the next section.

# Working with complex types

In the previous section, we discussed the basic types in TypeScript. In the realm of TypeScript, data representation extends beyond simple types such as strings and numbers. This section delves into objects, arrays, tuples, and enums, empowering you to structure and represent more complex data collections and enhance code readability.

We will begin with objects.

## Objects

**Objects** in TypeScript allow you to encapsulate related data and functionality into a single entity. You can define object properties and methods, providing a clear structure to your code. In the following code snippet, we have created a `person` object:

```
const person: { name: string; age: number; greet: () => void } = {
  name: "Alice",
  age: 30,
  greet() {
    console.log(
      `Hello, my name is ${this.name} and I'm ${this.age} years old.`
    );
  },
};
```

We have specified the expected structure of our object (the expected type). Let's see what happens when I remove one of the properties. Refer to the code snippet in the following figure; I have omitted the age property:

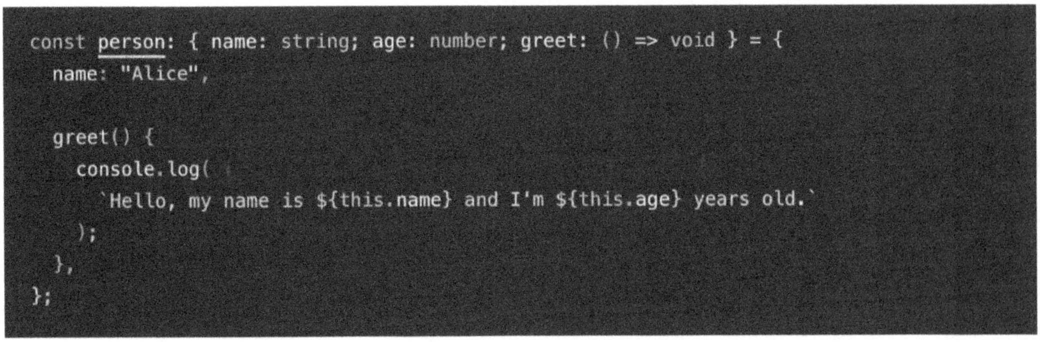


*Figure 1.7 — TypeScript error when the object contains incomplete details*

You will notice the red line under the `person` variable. If we hover over that line, we see more details about what the issue is. To get a better understanding, refer to the following figure:

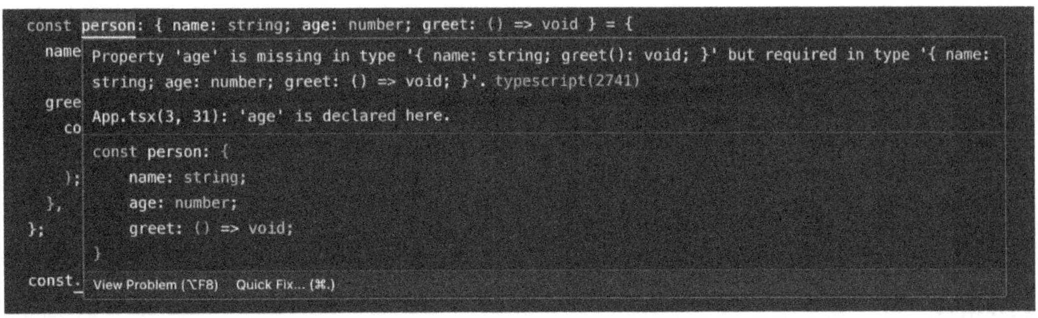


*Figure 1.8 — TypeScript shows error details when we hover over the person object*

TypeScript once again is coming in handy, highlighting errors and giving us immediate feedback.

## Types/interfaces

In the previous example, we defined the structure of an object (type) in the same line as our variable declaration. However, for improved reusability and organization, it's advantageous to extract the type definition into a separate block:

```
type Person = {
  name: string;
  age: number;
  greet: () => void
}
```

And then we can use the defined type with the object as follows:

```
const person: Person = {
  name: "Alice",
  age: 25,
  greet() {
    console.log(
      `Hello, my name is ${this.name} and I'm ${this.age} years old.`);
  },
};
```

This approach is beneficial because it enables code reuse. You can combine types to form even more complex types and reuse them across different locations in your application.

Interfaces in TypeScript serve a similar purpose to types but with additional capabilities, allowing you to define contracts for object shapes and behavior. We'll delve into interfaces in more detail later, exploring their nuances and practical applications.

```
"Argument of type 'number' is not assignable to parameter of type 'string'."
```

```
`Hello, my name is ${this.name} and I'm ${this.age} years old.`
`Hello, my name is ${this.name} and I'm ${this.age} years old.`);
```

## Tuples

Tuples are similar to arrays, but have a fixed, predefined length and specific types for each element.

Imagine modeling a product with an ID, name, and price:

```
type Product = [number, string, number];

const product: Product = [123, "T-Shirt", 19.99];
```

You can access this as a normal array, so for example, if I wanted to see the price (third element in the array or second index), I could type something like this:

```
console.log(product[2]);
```

You can see in your console or terminal that the output is as follows:

```
19.99;
```

But I declared a different variable, say `invalidProducts`, and specified its type as `Product`:

```
const invalidProduct: Product = [123, "T-Shirt"];
```

The preceding code results in a type error. See the following figure for details:

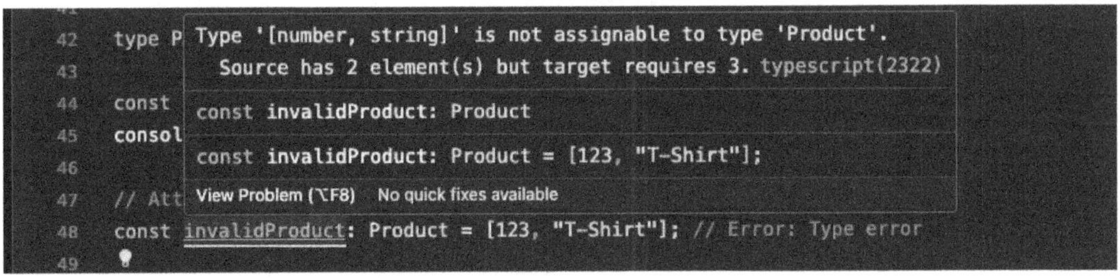


*Figure 1.10 — Code editor displaying type hints for the expected properties*

The error message states the following:

```
Type '[number, string]' is not assignable to type 'Product'.
  Source has 2 element(s) but target requires 3.
```

## Enums

Enums allow you to define named constants for a set of related values with a clear, predefined list of choices. This structure makes code more consistent and reduces the chance of invalid values.

Let's start with a simple example to demonstrate how enums work:

```
enum Direction {
  Up,
  Down,
  Left,
  Right
}

let playerDirection: Direction = Direction.Up;
console.log("Player is facing:", playerDirection);
Output: Player is facing: 0 (Up)
```

In this example, we define a `Direction` enum with four members: `Up`, `Down`, `Left`, and `Right`. By default, `Up` is assigned the value of `0`, `Down` is `1`, `Left` is 2, and `Right` is 3. We then assign

Direction.Up to a variable, playerDirection, and log its value, which outputs 0, indicating that the player is facing upward.

You can also explicitly set values for enum members:

```
enum ErrorCode {
  NotFound = 404,
  Unauthorized = 401,
  InternalServerError = 500
}

let error: ErrorCode = ErrorCode.NotFound;
console.log("Error code:", error); // Output: Error code: 404 (NotFound)
```

In this example, we define an ErrorCode enum with three members: NotFound, Unauthorized, and InternalServerError. We assign custom HTTP status code values to each member. When we assign ErrorCode.NotFound to the error variable, it holds the value of 404.

Enums are especially useful when defining functions that operate on a fixed set of values. Here is an example:

```
enum DayOfWeek {
  Sunday,
  Monday,
  Tuesday,
  Wednesday,
  Thursday,
  Friday,
  Saturday
}

function isWeekend(day: DayOfWeek): boolean {
  return day === DayOfWeek.Saturday || day === DayOfWeek.Sunday;
}

let today: DayOfWeek = DayOfWeek.Saturday;
console.log("Is today a weekend?", isWeekend(today));
```

In this example, we define a DayOfWeek enum representing the days of the week. We then define an isWeekend function that takes a DayOfWeek parameter and returns true if it is a weekend (Saturday or Sunday), and `false` otherwise. Finally, we call the function with `DayOfWeek.Saturday`, which outputs `true`.

Enums in TypeScript provide a powerful way to represent fixed sets of values. By utilizing enums effectively, you can make your code more expressive and self-documenting, leading to better overall code quality. Experiment with enums in your TypeScript projects to see how they can simplify your development process.

In this section, we've broadened our TypeScript skills by diving into objects, arrays, tuples, and enums, enhancing our ability to handle complex data. Moving forward, we'll explore advanced types such as unions, intersections, generics, and conditionals, further refining our coding capabilities.

# Mastering advanced types

In this section, you will delve deeper into TypeScript's advanced type system. You'll learn about powerful features such as union types, intersection types, generics, and conditional types. These advanced types enable you to create more flexible, dynamic, and adaptable type definitions in your TypeScript code. By mastering these concepts, you'll be equipped to handle complex scenarios and write more robust and maintainable code. Let's begin.

## Union types: the power of OR

Union types allow you to define a type that can hold values of multiple types. This flexibility is particularly useful when a function or variable can accept different types of values. Imagine representing user input that could be a string or a number:

```
type Input = string | number;

function processInput(value: Input) {
  if (typeof value === "string") {
    console.log(value.toUpperCase());
  } else {
    console.log(value.toFixed(2), "number");
  }
}
```

In the preceding code, we have defined a type called `Input` that can be either a string or a number.

We have a function that accepts this input and performs an operation depending on the value passed to the function.

Let's call the `processInput` function with a string, as follows:

```
processInput("hello");
```

The preceding call prints the capitalized string `"HELLO"` to the console.

Let's now call the `processInput` function with a number, as follows:

```
processInput(3.14121);
```

The preceding call prints the output to two decimal places: `3.14`.

Union types allow for flexible data handling and prevent runtime errors by ensuring that the assigned value matches one of the allowed types.

## Intersection types: merging strengths

In TypeScript, intersection types provide a way to merge the strengths of multiple types into a single, cohesive type. Imagine combining the properties and methods from different sources to create a more expressive type. Let's explore this concept using an example related to an organization's employees.

Suppose you're building a simple application to manage an organization's employees. Each employee has specific properties such as name, age, and a unique badge number. Additionally, they can greet others with a custom message.

Initially, you might define an `Employee` type directly, including all the necessary properties:

```
type Employee = {
  name: string;
  age: number;
  greet: () => void;
  badgeNumber: number;
};
```

However, if you look closely, some of these properties are quite familiar. The `name`, `age`, and `greet` properties are essentially the same as those in a `Person` type. Instead of duplicating ourselves, let's create a more elegant solution.

We'll create an `EmployeeBase` type that contains only the `badgeNumber` property:

```
type EmployeeBase = {
  badgeNumber: number;
};
```

Now, the magic happens. We'll combine the existing `Person` type with our `EmployeeBase` type using an intersection type:

```
type Employee = EmployeeBase&Person
```

The resulting `Employee` type inherits all properties from both the `Person` type and `EmployeeBase`. It's like merging two worlds into one!

Let's define an employee named John:

```
const john: Employee = {
  name: "John",
  age: 30,
  greet() {
    console.log(
      `Hello, my name is ${this.name} and I'm ${this.age} years old.`,
    );
  },
  badgeNumber: 2342342,
}
```

Now, John is a fully-fledged employee with all the necessary properties.

By using intersection types, we avoid redundancy and keep our code **DRY**, which stands for **don't repeat yourself**. We express relationships between types more precisely, making our code cleaner and more maintainable.

## Generics: one tool, many types

Generics in TypeScript enable you to create functions, classes, and interfaces that can work with different data types. They provide flexibility and reusability by allowing types to be specified dynamically. Let's see some applications of generics.

## Applications of generics

One of the primary uses of generics in TypeScript is to make functions more flexible and reusable. Generics allow functions to handle multiple types without needing to rewrite the same function for each type. Let's explore this with an example.

Consider a function that reverses an array. You want this function to work with any type of array (for example, string or numbers) without having to rewrite the function for each type. Here's how you can achieve this with generics:

```
function reverseArray<T>(array: T[]): T[] {
  return array.reverse();
}
```

Let's explain the preceding code block:

- **Function declaration**: We declare a function named `reverseArray`. Inside the parentheses, we use `<T>` to declare a **generic type**, `T`. This means the function can work with any type of array.
- **Function implementation**: The function takes an array of the `T` type as its parameter. `T` could represent a string, number, Boolean, and so on. It reverses the array using the `reverse()` method and returns the reversed array.

Now, let's put our function to the test. How do we do that? See the following figure:

*Figure 1.11 – TypeScript error in generic reverse array function*

Let's go over each part of the code in detail and see what's happening.

Firstly, we invoke the `reverseArray` function and specify its type, `T`, as `number`.

Then, we pass in a mixed array of numbers and strings. If you inspect closely, you will observe the red line under `"some random string"`. Let's see what the error is in the following figure:

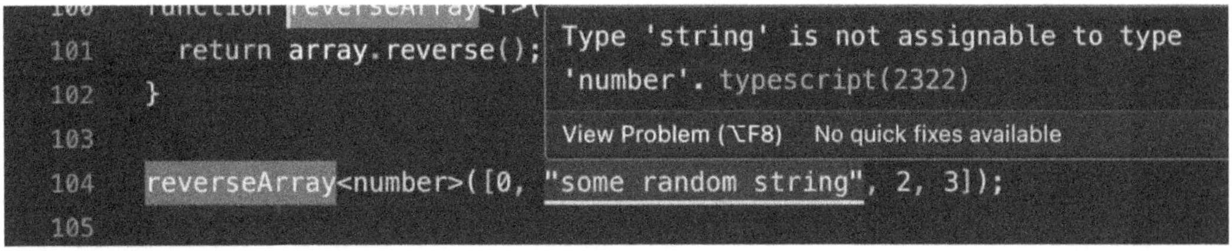


*Figure 1.12 — Error details of the generic reverse array function*

As you can see, we are dynamically specifying what the type of the array should be.

You could specify that the `reverseArray` function should accept an array of strings, as follows:

```
reverseArray<string>(['hello', 'world'])
```

Explicitly defining the type (as we've done in this case with `string`) provides several advantages. It ensures that only arrays of strings can be passed to the function, which prevents potential errors if, for example, a number is mistakenly included. Additionally, specifying the type improves code readability, making it immediately clear to other developers (or to yourself later on) what kind of data the function is intended to handle.

In essence, generics allow us to write a single function that can work with different types of arrays, making our code more flexible and reusable. We don't have to write separate functions for arrays of numbers, strings, or any other type; the same function works for all types.

At this point, you are probably wondering what happens if we fail to pass in the type. If we don't pass in a type, TypeScript infers the type from the values (an array in this case). To get a clear picture, see the following figure:

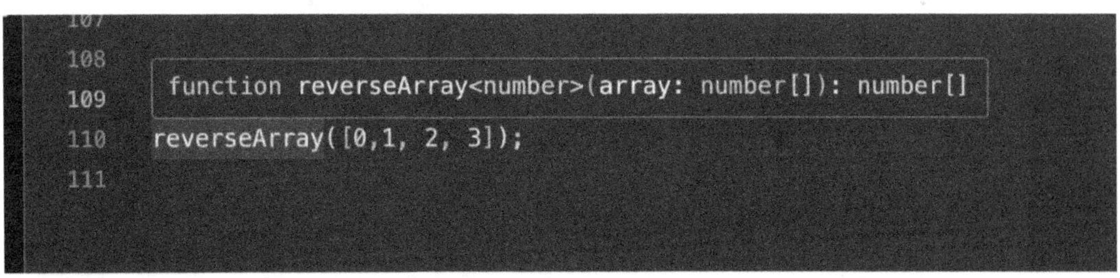


*Figure 1.13 — Demonstrating TypeScript's type inference with the reverseArray function*

In the preceding example, we have not explicitly passed in the type, yet TypeScript detects from the array passed in what the type should be—in this case, an array of numbers. Now that we understand how generic functions work, let's see how to use generics with classes.

## Generic classes: flexible object structures

We're going to illustrate this using a stack. Imagine building a `Stack` class that can hold items of any type:

```
class Stack<T> {
  private items: T[] = [];

  push(item: T): void {
    this.items.push(item);
  }

  pop(): T | undefined {
    return this.items.pop();
  }
}
```

Let's go through the code and see what it does:

- **Generic class**: We declare a class named `Stack` with a generic type, `<T>`. This `T` type acts like a placeholder, allowing the class to work with any data type.
- **Adaptable storage**: Internally, `Stack` uses an array to store items, but these items can be of the `T` type. So, `stringStack` can hold strings, and `numberStack` can hold numbers, all within the same `Stack` class.
- `push` **and** `pop` **methods**: The class provides methods such as `push` to add items and `pop` to remove them, both working seamlessly with the generic type, `T`.

Now, let's put our generic `Stack` class to use:

```
const stringStack = new Stack<string>();
stringStack.push("hello");
stringStack.push("world");
const numberStack = new Stack<number>();
numberStack.push(10);
numberStack.push(20);
```

The preceding code demonstrates how to use the generic `Stack` class with different data types:

- `const stringStack = new Stack<string>();`: Here, we're creating a new instance of the `Stack` class that will hold `string` values. The `<string>` syntax is how we specify the type for this particular `Stack` instance.
- `stringStack.push("hello");` and `stringStack.push("world");`: Here, we're using the `push` method of the `Stack` class to add the strings `"hello"` and `"world"` to `stringStack`.
- `const numberStack = new Stack<number>();`: Similar to `stringStack`, we're creating `numberStack` that will hold `number` values.
- `numberStack.push(10);` and `numberStack.push(20);`: Here, we're adding the numbers 10 and 20 to `numberStack` using the `push` method.

So, in this code snippet, we've created two stacks: one for strings and one for numbers. We've then added items to each stack using the `push` method. This demonstrates the flexibility and reusability of the generic `Stack` class, as it can handle stacks of any type.

Next, let's look at using generics with interfaces.

## Generic interfaces

In this example, we would create a generic `Car` interface that allows one of its properties to be of a dynamic type. We'll use a `type` variable to achieve this flexibility. Here's how you can define the generic `Car` interface:

```
interface Car<T> {
    make: string;
    model: string;
    year: number;
    data: T; // Dynamic property that can hold any type
}
```

Let's create some `car` objects using this generic interface:

Here's example 1 – car with string data:

```
const stringCar: Car<string> = {
    make: "Toyota",
    model: "Camry",
    year: 2022,
    data: "Some string data",
};
```

Here's example 2 – car with numeric data:

```
const numberCar: Car<number> = {
    make: "Tesla",
    model: "Model 3",
    year: 2023,
    data: 42,
};
```

Here's example 3 – car with warranty information:

```
interface WarrantyInfo {
    warrantyType: string;
    coverageMonths: number;
    expirationDate: Date;
}
const warrantyCar: Car<WarrantyInfo> = {
    make: "Chevrolet",
    model: "Cruze",
    year: 2021,
    data: {
        warrantyType: "Powertrain",
        coverageMonths: 36,
        expirationDate: new Date("2024-02-28"),
    },
};
```

In this case, `warrantyCar` represents a 2021 Chevrolet Cruze.

The `data` property contains warranty-related information, such as the warranty type, coverage duration, and expiration date.

By using generics, we've made our `Car` interface adaptable to various data types, including insurance policies, warranties, and more. TypeScript ensures type safety, allowing us to create versatile car objects.

# Understanding conditional types in TypeScript

Conditional types in TypeScript allow us to create types that adapt based on other types. They're like chameleons for our type system. This allows you to create more flexible and adaptable type definitions in your code.

The basic idea is this: you define a type with a condition. If the condition is `true`, the type resolves to one type; if the condition is `false`, it resolves to a different type.

The basic syntax of a conditional type is as follows:

```
type MyConditionalType<T> = T extends U ? X : Y;
```

Let's break down the code:

- `T`: This is like a placeholder for any type of data
- `extends U`: This checks whether `T` is the same type as `U` (or a subtype of `U`)
- `X`: If the check is `true`, the type becomes `X`
- `Y`: If the check is `false`, the type becomes `Y`

Conditional types are commonly used in scenarios where the resulting type depends on the characteristics of the input type.

Let's look at an example.

Let's say we have an `Animal` type that can be either `'cat'` or `'dog'`:

```
type Animal = 'cat' | 'dog';
```

Now, we create a `Sound` type that represents the sound each animal makes. If it's a cat, the sound is `'meow'`; if it's a dog, the sound is `'woof'`:

```
type Sound<T extends Animal> = T extends 'cat' ? 'meow' : 'woof';
```

Let's test our `Sound` type:

```
let sound1: Sound<'cat'>; // sound1 is 'meow' (because 'cat' extends 'cat')
let sound2: Sound<'dog'>; // sound2 is 'woof' (because 'dog' doesn't extend 'ca ')
```

In this example, `Sound` is a conditional type. It checks whether the `Animal` type (`T`) is `'cat'`. If it is, the sound becomes `'meow'`. Otherwise, it becomes `'woof'`.

In the next section, we are going over the `tsconfig.json` file, what it is, and how it impacts your project.

# Configuring tsconfig.json

In this section, we'll explore the critical aspects of `tsconfig.json`, the configuration file for TypeScript projects. We'll explain its importance and how it controls project behavior. You'll learn how to customize compiler options to optimize your build process and type checking. As your project grows, we'll provide tips for maintaining and expanding `tsconfig.json`.

So, what exactly is `tsconfig.json`?

`tsconfig.json` is a file that sets up your TypeScript project. It tells the TypeScript compiler which files to use and how to turn them into JavaScript. Making a `tsconfig.json` file is easy. Just run "`tsc --init`" in your project's `main` folder. This will create a `tsconfig.json` file with default settings. You can then change these settings as needed.

## Diving into compilerOptions

In your `tsconfig.json` file, the "`compilerOptions`" section provides extensive control over the compilation process. To lay a strong basis for your project, we prioritize essential compiler configurations and explain how each one affects your work. We will break this down into sections to help you understand better:

- **Essential compiler options**: These options directly influence the quality and compatibility of your generated code. They include the following:
  - `target`: Defines the ECMAScript target version for the compiled JavaScript (e.g., `es5`, `es2017`, or `esnext`). This directly affects browser compatibility and the available features in your generated code.
  - `strict`: Activates stricter type-checking rules to enhance code quality. This mode enforces more stringent checks to detect potential errors at an early stage of development.
  - `sourceMap`: Generates source maps that map the compiled JavaScript code back to the original TypeScript source code. This is crucial for easier debugging, allowing you to step through your code in the debugger and see the original TypeScript lines instead of the compiled JavaScript.

- **Module system configuration**: These options determine how modules are defined, loaded, and resolved in your project:
  - `module`: Determines the module system used in your project (e.g., `commonjs`, `amd`, or `systemjs`). This influences how modules are defined and loaded, impacting project structure and dependency management.
  - `moduleResolution`: Configures how the compiler resolves module imports. This option specifies the strategy for locating and bundling dependencies within your project.
- **Type checking**: These options enforce stricter type safety and null-checking:
  - `noImplicitAny`: Prevents variables and parameters from being implicitly assigned the any type. This enforces explicit typing, improves code maintainability, and reduces the risk of runtime errors.
  - `strictNullChecks`: Enables stricter `null` checking, differentiating between nullable and non-nullable references. This helps catch potential `null` reference errors early on.
  - `esModuleInterop`: Facilitates compatibility with CommonJS modules when using ES modules. This allows for smoother integration of different module types within your project.
- **Advanced compiler options**: Beyond the essential settings, TypeScript offers advanced options to handle specific syntaxes and provide more control over the compilation process. These options are not always required for every project, but they are essential when working with more complex setups, such as integrating external libraries, using JSX with React, or managing large code bases. Let's explore some of these advanced options and understand when and why you might need them:
  - `lib`: Includes additional library files containing type definitions for built-in objects and functionalities. This expands the available types that you can use in your project.
  - `declaration`: Generates corresponding `.d.ts` type declaration files for external modules or libraries used in your project. This aids in type checking and auto-completion for developers using those modules.
- **Build options**: These options help manage your build process and organize your project structure:
  - `compilerOptions.paths`: Allows you to define custom module resolution paths, simplifying long or repetitive `import` statements.

    - `compilerOptions.types`: Enables including or excluding specific type definitions, allowing you to control the ambient type scope available in your project. This can be useful for managing dependencies and avoiding potential conflicts.
    - `compilerOptions.baseUrl`: Sets the base directory for resolving module imports. This can be helpful for organizing projects with complex folder structures and ensuring modules are located correctly.
    - `compilerOptions.outDir`: Specifies the output directory for the compiled JavaScript files. This helps organize your build artifacts and separates compiled code from your source code.
- **Other compiler options to consider**: These options provide additional functionalities and warnings for cleaner code:
    - `allowJs`: Allows compilation of plain JavaScript files alongside TypeScript files within the same project.
    - `noUnusedLocals`: Warns about unused local variables, helping to identify potential code cleanup opportunities.
    - `noUnusedParameters`: Warns about unused function parameters, helping to promote cleaner code.
    - `preserveConstEnums`: Maintains the `const` enum behavior from older versions of TypeScript, if needed for compatibility.

Keep in mind that the configuration of your `tsconfig.json` file will vary based on your project's specific needs and preferences. By familiarizing yourself with the available options and their impact on the build process and code behavior, you can tailor `tsconfig.json` to enhance your TypeScript development experience.

In the upcoming section, we will discuss and review some highly recommended guidelines for effectively managing your `tsconfig.json` configuration file.

## Best practices for tsconfig.json maintenance

Effective management of your `tsconfig.json` file is essential for maintaining a well-structured and extensible TypeScript project. Here are some practical tips to ensure that your `tsconfig.json` file remains organized and functional:

- **Focus on essentials**: Prioritize core options for clarity and easy maintenance. Don't clutter your configuration with unnecessary settings.

- **Explain non-obvious settings**: Use clear comments to explain settings that aren't immediately self-explanatory. This aids future reference and understanding.
- **Leverage extends**: Consider extending from base configurations to inherit common settings across multiple projects. This promotes consistency and allows project-specific overrides when needed.
- **Validate with tools**: Utilize linters or dedicated validators to ensure that your `tsconfig.json` file is syntactically correct and adheres to best practices. By following these practices, you'll ensure that your `tsconfig.json` file remains clean, efficient, and scalable, contributing to a well-structured and maintainable TypeScript project.

# Summary

This chapter has equipped you with essential skills for effective TypeScript development. You've learned about the rationale for using TypeScript, including its benefits and usage scenarios. We covered the practical setup process, including installation and basic project configuration. The chapter delved into foundational types, helping you master working with strings, numbers, Booleans, and the any type. You explored working with complex types such as arrays, tuples, and enums. Additionally, the chapter introduced advanced concepts such as union/intersection types, aliases/interfaces, generics, and conditional types. As a bonus, we briefly touched on `tsconfig.json` configuration and best practices.

The next chapter focuses on writing clean and maintainable functions in TypeScript. You'll delve into the **Single Responsibility Principle** (**SRP**), function signatures, parameter types, return types, optional and default parameters, and best practices for function naming and documentation using JSDoc and TypeScript. This chapter will further enhance your TypeScript proficiency, empowering you to produce high-quality code with clarity and ease.

## Get this book's PDF copy, code bundle, and more

Scan the QR code (or go to `packtpub.com/unlock`). Search for this book by name, confirm the edition, and then follow the steps on the page.

UNLOCK NOW

*Note: Have your invoice handy. Purchases made directly from the Packt website don't require an invoice.*

# 2

# Writing Clean Functions

Functions are the building blocks of any program. They allow you to break down complex problems into smaller, simpler tasks and enable code reuse, reducing repetition. However, not all functions are created equal—some are easy to read, understand, and maintain, while others are messy, confusing, and error-prone. How can you write functions that are clean and maintainable? What are the best practices and principles for designing and documenting functions in TypeScript?

In this chapter, you'll learn how to write clean, maintainable functions by applying the **Single Responsibility Principle** (**SRP**), avoiding side effects, and using function signatures effectively. You'll also discover how to choose meaningful function names and document your code using TSDoc and TypeDoc. By understanding function signatures, such as parameter and return types, you can improve both the structure and readability of your functions. Additionally, we'll explore how to use TypeScript's type inference, optional parameters, and default values to enhance your code's clarity.

By the end of this chapter, you'll be able to write clean and maintainable functions, apply SRP, avoid side effects, understand and use function signatures, choose meaningful names, and document your functions using TSDoc and TypeDoc. We'll cover principles of clean functions, function signatures, and best practices for naming and documentation.

Specifically, this chapter will cover:

- Learning principles of clean functions
- Understanding function signatures

## Technical requirements

Before proceeding, it's essential to have a foundational understanding of TypeScript basics and its functionality. If you're new to TypeScript or need a refresher, it's recommended to familiarize yourself with its fundamental concepts (see *Chapter 1*). This includes understanding TypeScript's syntax, data types, and how it differs from JavaScript.

To get started with TypeScript, ensure you have the necessary tools and environment set up:

- A code editor or IDE (such as Visual Studio Code, IntelliJ, or Sublime Text)
- Node.js installed on your machine
- The TypeScript compiler (tsc) installed globally or locally in your project
- A basic understanding of how to create and manage TypeScript files (`.ts`) and compile them into JavaScript files (`.js`)

You can download the example project and code for this book by following the instructions in the *Download the example code files* section in the *Preface* of this book. This chapter's code files are included in the downloadable code bundle.

## Learning principles of clean functions

Imagine working on a massive building project where each brick lays haphazardly upon the last, lacking clear organization and purpose. Such a structure would be fragile, prone to crumbling under pressure. Similarly, functions written without considering clean principles can lead to tangled code that's difficult to understand, debug, and extend.

Clean functions, on the other hand, refer to functions that are well-structured, concise, and easy to understand. They act like precisely placed pillars of support, offering several advantages:

- **Easier code readability**: Clear structure and meaningful naming enhance understanding for both yourself and future collaborators
- **Reduced complexity**: Breaking down logic into focused functions prevents code bloat and simplifies maintenance
- **Enhanced reusability**: Well-defined functions can be easily integrated into different parts of your application
- **Improved testability**: Smaller, self-contained functions are easier to isolate and test thoroughly

Some of the principles for writing clean functions are the following:

- Each function should have a single responsibility, meaning that it should do one thing and do it well.
- Each function should have a clear and descriptive name that reflects its purpose and behavior.
- Each function should have a minimal and consistent number of parameters, ideally three or fewer, with each parameter well-defined and typed. If more are needed, consider grouping related parameters into an object or breaking the function into smaller parts.
- Each function should have a clear and explicit return value that is well-defined and typed.
- Each function should behave predictably and consistently, avoiding unintended effects by keeping its operations contained within its own scope.
- Each function should be documented, using comments or annotations that explain its functionality and usage.

Now that we have an overview of clean functions and their benefits, let's proceed to examine each principle in detail and see how they translate into practical applications in your code.

## Naming functions

Choosing appropriate names for functions is essential for writing readable and understandable code. Good function names improve code clarity and maintainability and make it easier for developers to understand the purpose of the code without diving into its implementation details. Here are some guidelines to effectively name your functions:

- **Use camel case**: Start function names with a lowercase letter and use uppercase letters for subsequent words (e.g., `calculateArea`, `isUserLoggedIn`). This convention is widely used in JavaScript/TypeScript and ensures consistency with variable naming.
- **Be descriptive**: Use descriptive names that accurately convey the purpose or action of the function. A function's name should provide a clear indication of what the function does without needing to read its implementation. Also, avoid using abbreviations or overly generic names (e.g., `doSomething`, `processStuff`).
- **Use verbs for actions**: Begin function names with a verb to indicate the action performed by the function. This helps in distinguishing functions from variables or other entities in the code. For example, use names such as `getUserData()` or `updateDatabase()` to clearly indicate the actions performed by these functions.

- **Consider using prefixes**: Specific prefixes can enhance clarity for certain function types – here are some examples:
    - `is`: For boolean functions (e.g., `isValid()`, `isAuthorized()`)
    - `get`: For functions that retrieve data (e.g., `getUserName()`, `getProductDetails()`)
    - `set`: For functions that set or update values (e.g., `setTheme()`, `setActiveUser()`)
- **Avoid overly long names**: While descriptiveness is important, overly long function names can be cumbersome and hinder readability. Aim for a balance between clarity and conciseness.
- **Be consistent**: Adhere to consistent naming conventions throughout your code base. Consistency in naming helps maintain readability and makes it easier for developers to understand and navigate the code base. If your team follows a specific convention, adhere to it to maintain uniformity.

By following these guidelines, you can ensure that your function names are clear, descriptive, and helpful to anyone reading or working with your code. Now that we understand the importance of naming functions properly, we will explore a fundamental principle known as the Single Responsibility Principle (SRP). This principle emphasizes that a function should have a single, well-defined purpose. We'll explore how to organize your functions following SRP principles, leading to more focused and reusable code.

## Applying the Single Responsibility Principle

The **Single Responsibility Principle** (**SRP**) is one of the most important principles of clean functions. It states that each function should have only one reason to change, meaning that it should have a single responsibility or a single task to perform. This makes the function more focused, cohesive, and modular. It also reduces the complexity and coupling of the function, making it easier to understand, test, and debug.

To apply the SRP to your functions, you should follow these steps:

1. Identify the main purpose or goal of your function and write it down in a single sentence.
2. Analyze your function and see if it does anything else besides its main purpose. If it does, consider extracting those parts into separate functions.

3. Refactor your function into multiple, smaller functions if needed. Assign each new function a clear, descriptive name that reflects its specific responsibility, as described in the preceding section.
4. Review your function and see if it still follows the SRP. If not, repeat the previous steps until it does.

Next, let's look at an example of applying the SRP to a function.

Suppose you have the following function that calculates the total price of a shopping cart, applies a discount, and prints the receipt:

```
type CartItem = {
  price: number;
  quantity: number;
};

function checkout(cart: CartItem[], discount: number) {
  let total = 0;
  for (let item of cart) {
    total += item.price * item.quantity;
  }
  total = total * (1 - discount / 100);
  console.log("Your total is: $" + total.toFixed(2));
  console.log("Thank you for shopping with us!");
}
```

This function has more than one responsibility: it calculates the *total price*, applies the *discount*, and *prints* the receipt. It also has a *vague name* that does not reflect its behavior. To make it cleaner, we can apply the SRP and extract the different responsibilities into separate functions:

```
function calculateTotal(cart: CartItem[]) {
  let total = 0;
  for (let item of cart) {
    total += item.price * item.quantity;
  }
  return total;
}

function applyDiscount(total: number, discount: number) {
  return total * (1 - discount / 100);
}
```

```
function printReceipt(total: number) {
  console.log("Your total is: $" + total.toFixed(2));
  console.log("Thank you for shopping with us!");
}

function checkout(cart: CartItem[], discount: number) {
  let total = calculateTotal(cart);
  total = applyDiscount(total, discount);
  printReceipt(total);
}
```

We've improved our code by applying the SRP principle. We broke down the `checkout` function into three separate functions: `calculateTotal`, `applyDiscount`, and `printReceipt`. Each of these functions has a clear, descriptive name and a single responsibility, making them easier to understand and test individually.

Let's check them out:

- The `calculateTotal` function iterates through each item in the cart and calculates the total price
- The `applyDiscount` function takes the total price and applies a discount
- The `printReceipt` function prints the final total and a thank-you message

Finally, we redefined the `checkout` function to use these smaller functions. This new `checkout` function is more concise and readable. It delegates tasks to the other functions, making the code more modular and testable. This approach also makes the code easier to maintain and extend, as changes to one function are less likely to impact others.

It's important to note that the SRP is not something that is TypeScript-specific but a general principle in programming. It can help you write cleaner and more maintainable code in any programming language and paradigm.

Now that we have mastered the SRP, let's look into another major aspect of clean coding: managing side effects for our TypeScript functions. To make our code predictable and easier to test, we need to have a good understanding of bad side effects and know how to avoid them. In this next section, we will find out what side effects are, why they are bad, and how we can avoid them for code integrity.

# Understanding and avoiding (bad) side effects in TypeScript functions

Side effects are any changes that a function makes to the program's state or outside environment that extend beyond its local scope. For example, a function that modifies a global variable, writes to a file, or prints to the console has side effects. These can make code unpredictable and hard to debug, as they can affect other parts of the program in hidden ways. Side effects are especially problematic when dealing with concurrency and parallelism, where multiple tasks interact with shared resources.

Concurrency and parallelism refer to different ways of handling multiple tasks, and both can lead to issues when functions share resources such as global variables. Here's a quick overview of each concept:

- Concurrency means multiple tasks are in progress around the same time but aren't necessarily executed simultaneously. For example, asynchronous functions enable tasks to overlap, even if they don't happen at the exact same moment.
- Parallelism refers to tasks executing simultaneously, often across multiple threads or processors. JavaScript itself is single-threaded, but parallelism can be achieved using Web Workers, which allow tasks to run in separate threads.

Now let's see examples of both concepts. We will look at an example for concurrency and then one for parallelism.

## Concurrency example

Imagine we have a shared global variable, `currentUser`, and a function that fetches user data and updates it:

```
let currentUser: string = 'Alice';

async function fetchUserData(userId: string) {
  const response = await fetch(`https://api.example.com/users/${userId}`);
  const data = await response.json();
  currentUser = data.name; // This updates the global variable
}
```

Now imagine we call this function twice, almost immediately after each other (concurrently).

Simulate two concurrent API calls:

```
fetchUserData('1');
fetchUserData('2');
```

In this example, if the `fetchUserData` function is called twice concurrently for two different user IDs, both fetch operations might complete at different times. This could lead to `currentUser` being set unpredictably based on which API response finishes last. The global state (`currentUser`) can end up in an inconsistent state, depending on the timing of these asynchronous operations. Now let's take a look at parallelism.

## Parallelism example

Imagine we need to process a large array of numbers by doubling each value. In a parallel environment, different parts of the array could be processed simultaneously. While TypeScript (and JavaScript) are single-threaded, parallelism can be achieved using Web Workers to perform these calculations.

For simplicity, let's assume we use a worker to process chunks of the array in parallel, rather than in the main thread. In a setup with two workers, each worker processes half of the array independently, so both parts are being processed at exactly the same time.

## Why this matters

Side effects combined with concurrency and parallelism can create multiple issues in code, especially with global state dependencies. Here's an overview of key concerns:

- **Global variable modification**: Updating global variables, as `fetchUserData` does with `currentUser`, can introduce side effects that affect other operations. In concurrent scenarios, such changes can result in an unpredictable or inconsistent program state.
- **Lack of modularity and reusability**: When functions rely on global variables, they become tightly coupled to a specific program state, making them less modular and harder to reuse elsewhere. This dependency on global state, like `currentUser`, limits the versatility of `fetchUserData`.
- **Testing difficulties**: Functions with global dependencies are harder to test in isolation, as they require specific state conditions. Testing `fetchUserData` would involve controlling the global variable `currentUser`, making it difficult to test different scenarios independently.
- **Unreliable output**: Side effects can lead to functions producing different outputs for the same inputs, based on the current global state. This lack of predictability makes debugging challenging, especially with concurrency.
- **Concurrency concerns**: In concurrent code, race conditions can occur if multiple asynchronous tasks modify the same global state. For example, if two `fetchUserData` calls overlap, the outcome may depend on the timing of each call's completion. This can lead to errors or inconsistent data.

By understanding and managing these potential issues, you can write more reliable, maintainable, and testable code in TypeScript.

Now that we've explored the potential issues with side effects, let's focus on strategies for avoiding them. By applying these techniques, you can write more reliable, maintainable, and testable code.

### How to avoid side effects

Now that we understand the problems that side effects can introduce, let's explore ways to avoid them in our code. By applying best practices, we can make our functions more predictable, easier to test, and less prone to bugs. Here are some strategies:

- **Pure functions**: Aim to write functions that don't change or depend on external states, such as global variables. These functions always produce the same output for the same inputs, making them reliable and straightforward to test.
- **Keep data immutable**: When dealing with data, consider creating new versions of objects or arrays instead of modifying existing ones directly. This ensures that the original data remains unchanged, preventing unintended side effects in other parts of the application that rely on that data.
- **Local state management**: For situations requiring state management, explore libraries designed for this purpose. These tools provide controlled and predictable ways to handle state changes within your code.

By following best practices such as avoiding side effects, using pure functions, and embracing immutability, you can write TypeScript code that's not only cleaner and more maintainable but also easier to test. In the next section, we'll dive deeper into the importance of function signatures in TypeScript code, and how they help ensure type safety and code reliability.

## Understanding function signatures

A function signature defines the structure and type information of a function, including its (inputs) parameters and return type. It serves as a blueprint for how a function should be defined and invoked. Here's what a function signature typically includes:

- **Parameter types**: The types of parameters that the function expects to receive. These types define the data that can be passed to the function when it's called.
- **Return type**: The type of value that the function is expected to return after execution. This specifies the data type of the value that the function will produce as output.
- **Exceptions**: In some cases, a function may throw exceptions. The signature can indicate which exceptions might be thrown or passed back.

Let's look at the following simple example:

```
function calculateCircleArea(radius: number): number {
  return Math.PI * radius * radius;
}
```

Let's break down the components of the code above so we can understand better:

- `calculateCircleArea` is the function name
- `(radius: number)` specifies a single parameter named `radius` of type `number`
- `: number` indicates that the function returns a value of type `number`

Function signatures are essential for type checking and ensuring type safety in TypeScript. They provide clear documentation of a function's interface, making it easier to understand how to use the function correctly. Additionally, function signatures enable TypeScript's type inference system to infer the types of function parameters and return values, aiding in catching errors early during development.

Now that we've mastered the importance of function signatures in ensuring type safety, we're ready to take our code documentation to the next level with TypeDoc. This powerful tool helps us generate comprehensive and accurate documentation for our TypeScript projects, making it easier for others (and ourselves!) to understand our code. With TypeDoc and TSDoc, we can create clear and concise documentation that saves time and reduces confusion.

## Integrating TypeDoc for comprehensive TypeScript documentation

As developers, we're not merely writing code for machines; we're crafting solutions for other developers. Clear, concise, and well-structured code is crucial, but equally important is documentation. It's the narrative that accompanies our code, providing essential context to those who come after us. Writing clean code isn't just about structure; it's about effective communication.

In the past, developers relied on tools such as JSDoc to annotate their code with comments. While helpful, JSDoc had its limitations, especially when working with TypeScript projects. Enter TSDoc – the modern solution for documenting TypeScript code. When paired with TypeDoc, they become a formidable duo for generating comprehensive documentation effortlessly.

In this section, we'll demonstrate how to use TSDoc and TypeDoc to document your TypeScript code. Let's explore how to apply these tools in a real-world scenario. Imagine building an e-commerce platform and needing a robust `ShoppingCart` class with clear documentation to ensure other developers can use it effectively. We'll define the `ShoppingCart` class, including its properties and methods, and walk through the process of annotating and documenting it using TypeDoc. This example will show you how to leverage TypeDoc's features to generate comprehensive documentation for your TypeScript code, improving maintainability and collaboration.

Here's the TypeScript code for our `ShoppingCart` example:

```
interface CartItem {
  price: number;
  quantity: number;
}

class ShoppingCart {
  private cartItems: CartItem[] = [];›

  addItem(item: CartItem): void {
    this.cartItems.push(item);
  }

  calculateTotalPrice(): number {
    let total = 0;
    for (const item of this.cartItems) {
      total += item.price * item.quantity;
    }
    return total;
  }

  applyDiscount(discount: number): number {
    const total = this.calculateTotalPrice();
    return total * (1 - discount / 100);
  }

  checkout(discount: number): number {
    const total = this.applyDiscount(discount);
    console.log("Your total is: $" + total.toFixed(2));
    console.log("Thank you for shopping with us!");
    return total;
  }
}
```

The preceding code snippet will serve as our starting point for exploring TypeDoc annotations and documentation.

The code isn't bad, but we can further improve the clarity by annotating it with TypeDoc. For instance, we could provide even more context for the `applyDiscount` method. What does `discount` represent? Is it a percentage or a fixed amount? By annotating our code, we can answer these questions directly in the source code, making it easier for others to understand and use our functions.

If you copy the code as it is now and paste it into your editor, you'll notice that hovering over one of the methods reveals limited information. While TypeScript provides some hints, such as indicating that it's a method and displaying its return type, there's a lack of detailed information.

See the following screenshot for more clarity:

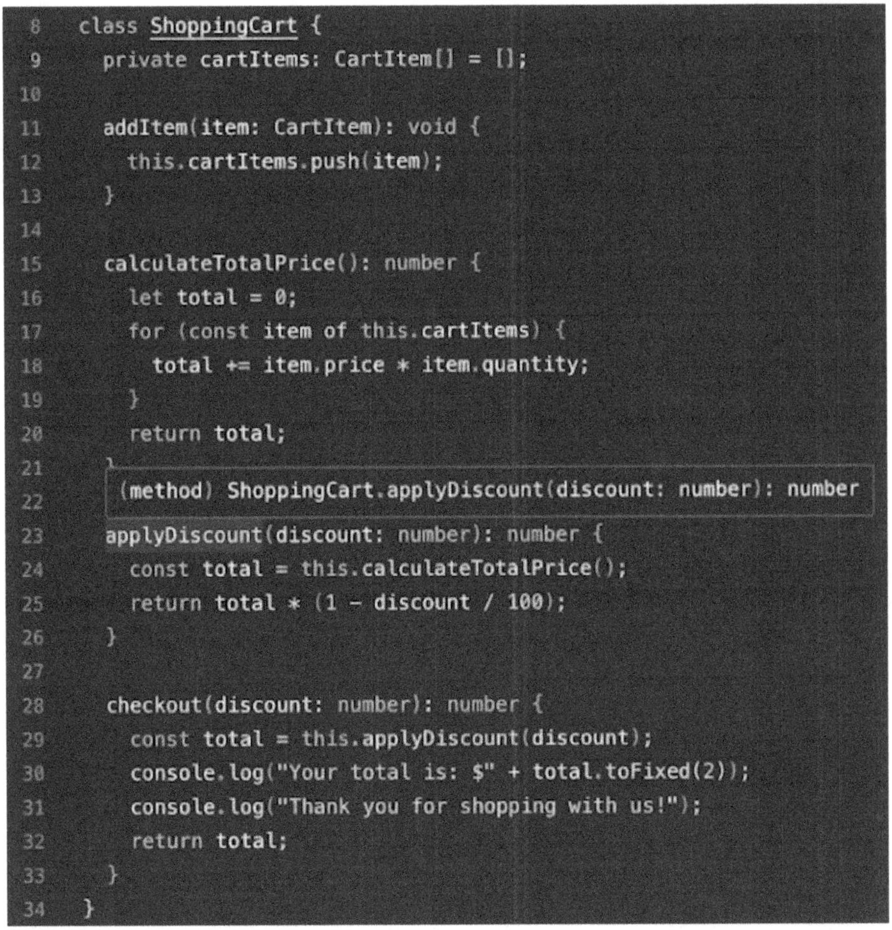


*Figure 2.1 — Showing TypeScript's feedback when we hover over the applyDiscount method*

In the next step, we start off by annotating the code with TSDoc.

TSDoc comments begin with a regular multiline comment as shown here:

```
/* ... */
```

Inside the comment block, you can add TSDoc tags to document various aspects of your code. Basic tags include the following:

- `@param`: This describes a parameter of a function or method. Here's an example:

```
/**
* Concatenates two strings.
```

```
* @param {string} firstName - The first name.
* @param {string} lastName - The last name.
*/
function getFullName(firstName: string, lastName: string): string {
  return `${firstName} ${lastName}`;
}
```

- `@returns`: This describes the return value of a function or method. Here's an example:

```
/**
* @returns {Promise<User>} A promise that resolves to the user data.
*/
async function getUserData(userId: number): Promise<User> {
  const response = await fetch(`/api/users/${userId}`);
  return response.json();
}
```

- `@remarks`: This is used to provide additional remarks or explanations about a method, class, or other code element. It is useful for sharing implementation details, design decisions, or any other relevant information. See the following example:

```
/**
* Converts a temperature from Celsius to Fahrenheit.
* @remarks The formula used for conversion is (Celsius * 9/5) + 32.
*/
function convertCelsiusToFahrenheit(celsius: number): number {
  return (celsius * 9) / 5 + 32;
}
```

- `@deprecated`: This indicates that a method or class is no longer recommended for use. It also provides information about alternative approaches or replacements and helps users transition to newer APIs. See the following example:

```
/**
* Calculates the area of a rectangle.
* @deprecated Use the `calculateRectangleArea` function instead.
*/
function getArea(width: number, height: number): number {
```

```
    return width * height;
  }
```

- `@link`: This creates hyperlinks to external resources or related documentation. It's useful for referencing specifications, related classes, or relevant websites. Here's an example: `{@link Title}`

Now, with this in mind, let's walk through the process of annotating our `ShoppingCart` class step by step:

1. **Annotating the CartItem the interface**

   ```
   /**
   * Interface representing an item in the shopping cart.
   */
   interface CartItem {
     price: number; // The price of the item.
     quantity: number; // The quantity of the item.
   }
   ```

   In the preceding code snippet, we are annotating the `CartItem` interface. A docstring comment, (`/** ... */`), describes the purpose of the interface. Each property, (`price` and `quantity`), has its type (`number`) and a brief description.

2. **Annotating the ShoppingCart class**
   Next, we annotate the `ShoppingCart` class. We make use of the `@remark` tag to provide additional information about the class:

   ```
   /**
   * Manages a shopping cart.
   * @remark The ShoppingCart class provides methods for adding items,
   calculating total prices,
   * and applying discounts. It is designed to be extensible and easy to use.
   */
   class ShoppingCart {
     private cartItems: CartItem[] = []; // Array to store cart items.

     // ... rest of the class methods
   }
   ```

3. **Annotating the addItem method**

We annotate the `addItem` method with a description and a `@param` tag to describe the parameter it accepts. In this case, we give a hint that the `item` parameter must adhere to the `CartItem` interface:

```
/**
 * Adds an item to the shopping cart.
 *
 * @param item The item to add (must conform to the CartItem interface).
 */
addItem(item: CartItem): void {
  this.cartItems.push(item);
}
```

4. **Annotating the calculateTotalPrice method**

   This annotation is similar to the preceding one; the key difference is the use of the `@returns` tag, which is used to describe the return value of a function or method:

```
/**
 * Calculates the total price of all items in the cart.
 * @returns The total price.
 */
calculateTotalPrice(): number {
  let total = 0;
  for (const item of this.cartItems) {
    total += item.price * item.quantity;
  }
  return total;
}
```

5. **Annotating the applyDiscount method**

   In the following snippet, we annotate the `applyDiscount` method with a description – a `@param` tag to describe its `(discount)` parameter. We specify that the discount is a percentage and give insight into how the calculation happens. We also use a `@returns` tag to describe its return value:

```
/**
 * Applies a discount to the total price.
 * @param discount The discount percentage (e.g., 10 for 10% off).
 * @returns The discounted total price.
 */
```

```
  applyDiscount(discount: number): number {
    const total = this.calculateTotalPrice();
    return total * (1 - discount / 100);
  }
```

6. **Annotating the checkout method**

   Finally, we annotate the checkout method with a description, a `@param` tag to describe its parameter, and a `@returns` tag to describe its return value:

```
  /**
   * Completes the checkout process.
   * @param discount The discount percentage to apply.
   * @returns The final total after applying the discount.
   */
  checkout(discount: number): number {
    const total = this.applyDiscount(discount);
    console.log('Your total is: $' + total.toFixed(2));
    console.log('Thank you for shopping with us!');
    return total;
  }
```

Congratulations – by following the preceding steps, we have successfully annotated our `ShoppingCart` class using TSDoc. Now, let's see what a difference it makes. If you observe, as shown in the following screenshot, when I hover over my `ShoppingCart` class, I get a lot more detail. At a glance, I can tell what the `ShoppingCart` class does and get an idea of what methods it provides.

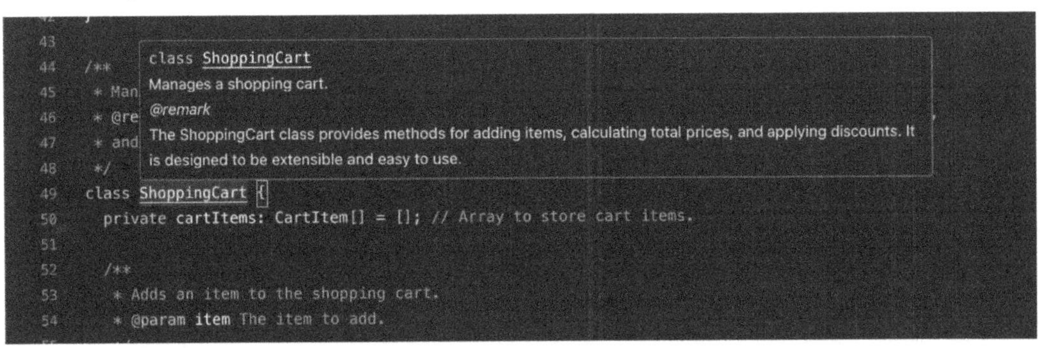


*Figure 2.2 – The shopping cart shows information about what the class does when we hover*

The steps we've implemented here provide significant advantages. As a code base expands, it's easy to lose track of the functionality of each component. This can be particularly overwhelming for newcomers to the project. However, by annotating our code as we've done, we create a self-explanatory and navigable structure that aids understanding and eases the onboarding process.

Let's also take another look at the `applyDiscount` method we spoke about previously. When we hover over the `applyDiscount` method (see the following screenshot), notice what happens:

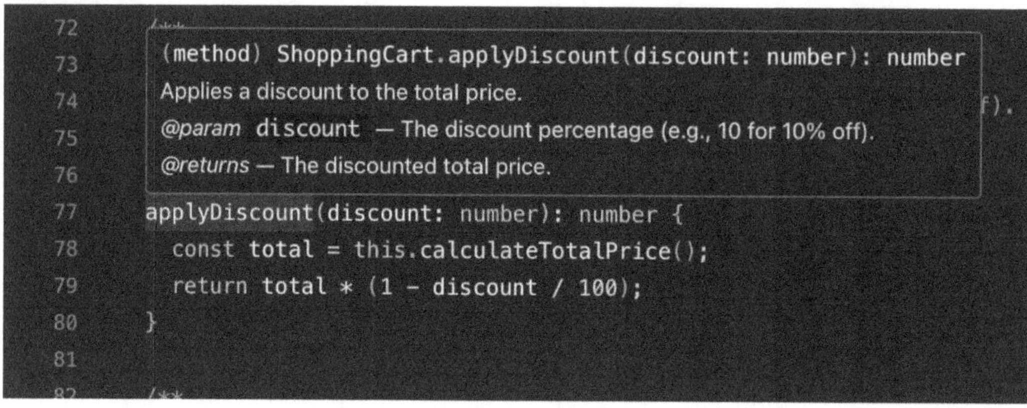


*Figure 2.3 — We can tell by merely hovering over the function what discount represents*

As seen from the preceding figure, we can now better understand what the `applyDiscount` method does and what the `discount` parameter represents, thanks to TSDoc annotations. This clarity helps us comprehend how the discount is applied.

Now that we've mastered the art of annotating our code with TSDoc, we will further expand on this knowledge in the upcoming section. We will continue using the same example and integrate it with TypeDoc. This will allow us to generate static pages, essentially transforming our code base into an easily navigable web page that serves as comprehensive documentation.

# Creating static documentation pages with TypeDoc integration

In the previous section, we added comments to our code using TSDoc. These comments act as the foundation for documentation, describing what our code does. Now, let's build on that foundation by introducing TypeDoc. TypeDoc is a popular documentation generator. It takes the comments we added in the previous section (like the ones for the `ShoppingCart` class) and transforms them into user-friendly, static web pages. In essence, TypeDoc creates an online documentation website for your code base.

This section will walk you through a step-by-step process to show you how to use TypeDoc to achieve this.

Let's do just that:

1. First, we'll install TypeDoc using the following command:

```
npm install --save-dev typedoc
```

2. Next, we'll create a `typedoc.json` file in the root of our directory and add the following code:

```
{ "theme": "default", "exclude": "node_modules/**" }
```

The `typedoc.json` file is where we keep all the configurations relating to TypeDoc on our project. To the file, we have added only a minimal setup at the moment. Let's go over what each line does:

- `theme: "default"`: This sets the documentation theme to the standard layout provided by TypeDoc, offering a clean display of information.
- `exclude: "node_modules/**"`: This instructs TypeDoc to skip processing files within the `node_modules` directory, typically containing external dependencies and irrelevant information for the documentation.

3. Now, we'll add a command to trigger the documentation process. We'll add the following script to our `package.json` file:

```
"scripts": {
  "docs": "npx typedoc ./index.ts"
},
```

Let's break down the preceding command:

- `npx`: This is a utility that comes with npm. It allows you to run packages installed locally in your project without installing them globally.
- `typedoc`: This is the actual command provided by the TypeDoc package.
- `./index.ts`: This specifies the entry point for generating documentation. In your case, it points to the `index.ts` file in your project.

Now, we can run the script using the following command:

```
npm run docs
```

The preceding command should generate a `docs` folder in your root director. See the following figure for more details:

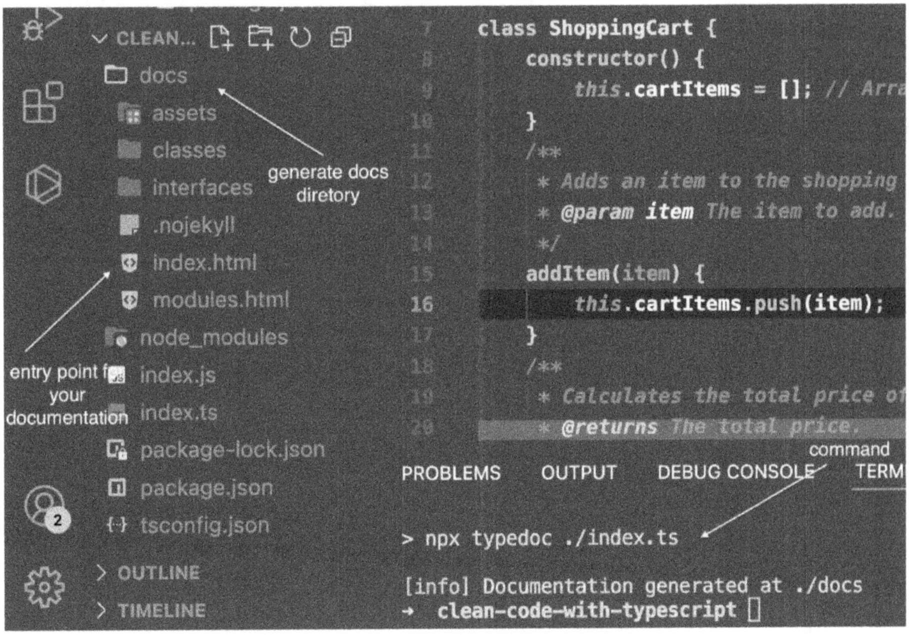


*Figure 2.4 — Screenshot showing an overview of the result after running the script to generate documentation*

The preceding figure displays the generated `docs` directory at the root of our project. This directory houses the essential static files that comprise our web-based documentation. Now, let's explore this documentation by accessing it and seeing how it appears in a web browser, giving us a firsthand look at the user-friendly interface TypeDoc has created for our code base.

Drag the `index.html` file into your browser and you should see something like this:

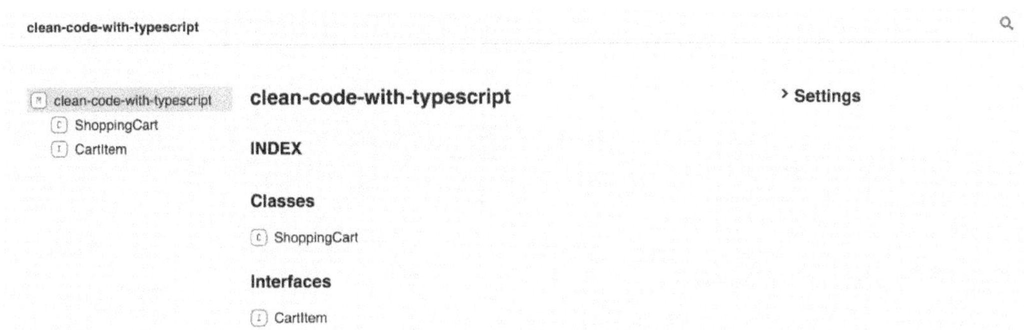


*Figure 2.5 — An overview of index.html generated by TypeDoc*

You'll see an overview of the classes/functions/interfaces you have added, which are now annotated. When you click on the shopping cart, you navigate to a page that contains details of the `ShoppingCart` class:

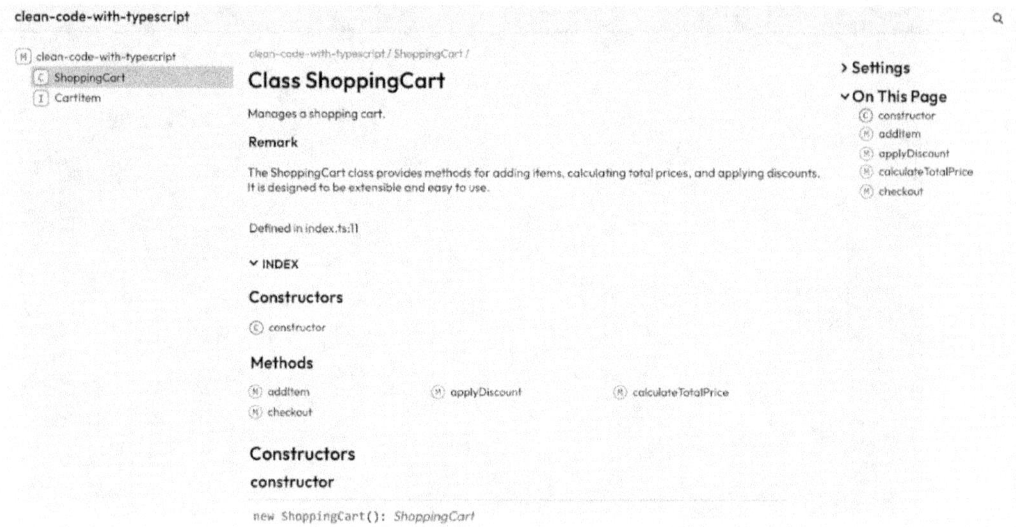


*Figure 2.6 – An overview of the ShoppingCart class*

You can scroll down to see more details about the `ShoppingCart` class or see details about a particular method. You can click on a method – for example, if we click on the `applyDiscount` method, we should see the following details:

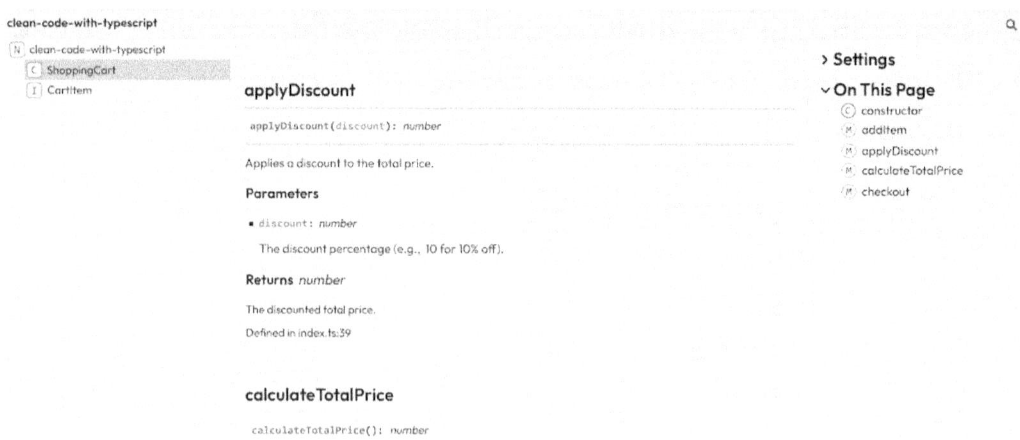


*Figure 2.7 – An overview of the applyDiscount method*

Now that we've learned how to use TSDoc comments and TypeDoc to enhance our code's clarity and generate user-friendly documentation, it's essential to establish some guidelines for commenting our code effectively. In the next section, we'll explore the importance of striking a balance between using comments and writing clean, readable code.

## Balancing comments and clean code

While using comments can greatly improve your code, it's important to note that *comments* and *documentation* are not substitutes for good, clean code. In fact, some argue that well-written code requires fewer comments. While there aren't strict rules, adhering to the principles discussed in this chapter—such as the SRP, avoiding side effects, and using proper naming—puts you on the right path.

A useful tip I learned when I started coding and first started exploring clean code principles involves what I like to call the "Stranger Test." Essentially, you should ask yourself: If someone who didn't know how to code sat in front of your computer and looked at your file, could they make a rough guess of what that code does? For instance, a class named `ShoppingCart` provides much more context than simply `Cart`. This test is a great way to ensure your code is easily understandable, even to a stranger.

# Summary

In this chapter, we delved into the fundamental principles of writing clean functions. We explored the importance of understanding function signatures and how they contribute to code readability and maintainability. Additionally, we emphasized the significance of using clear and descriptive function naming, along with proper documentation, to enhance code comprehension and collaboration within a team. By mastering these concepts, developers can produce code that is not only easier to understand but also more robust and scalable.

Looking ahead, in the next chapter, we will transition into exploring the concepts of **Object-Oriented Programming** (**OOP**) with TypeScript. We'll delve into defining classes, constructors, and inheritance, as well as diving into interfaces, abstract classes, and the principle of composition over inheritance. These topics will provide a solid foundation for building complex and flexible software structures in TypeScript.

# 3

# Object-Oriented Programming with TypeScript

Mastering **object-oriented programming** (**OOP**) is key to creating robust applications. TypeScript, with its static typing and OOP features, provides a modern way to implement these principles. In this chapter, we dive into OOP with TypeScript, explaining fundamental concepts and advanced practices for effective software design.

We'll explore classes, inheritance, interfaces, and abstract classes to understand how to structure code for reusability, flexibility, and simplicity. We'll also discuss composition over inheritance, a design principle for more manageable code bases. Through clear examples, you'll learn *how* and *why* to use these techniques for confident application in your projects.

This chapter covers the following main topics:

- Understanding the concept of OOP
- Classes, inheritance, and prototype chains for robust and flexible designs
- Encapsulation to ensure data privacy and controlled access
- Polymorphism in TypeScript OOP
- Interfaces in OOP: defining contracts and ensuring consistency
- Composition over inheritance for agile development

By the end, you'll have a strong foundation in OOP with TypeScript, making you ready to design and implement efficient, scalable code. The practices and principles discussed here will be invaluable for refining existing projects or starting new ones in the ever-changing field of software engineering.

# Technical requirements

The setup and technical requirements for this chapter are similar to the previous ones. Having TypeScript and Node.js installed will be sufficient to get started.

You can download the example project and code for this book by following the instructions in the *Download the example code files* section in the *Preface* of this book.

This chapter's code files are included in the downloadable code bundle.

# What is object-oriented programming?

In this section, we'll understand what OOP is and build a foundation for how it can be applied.

A common definition of OOP is that it is a programming paradigm. A programming paradigm is a set of principles that define how programs are written, structured, and executed. You can think of it as an overall approach or philosophy for organizing code.

From a widely accepted classification standpoint, most programming paradigms fall into two broad categories: imperative and declarative.

In imperative programming, you describe how a program should perform its tasks, step by step, by explicitly changing the program's state over time. Both procedural programming and object-oriented programming belong to this category. Procedural programming organizes code into functions or routines, while OOP organizes code into objects that combine data and behavior.

In declarative programming, you describe what the program should accomplish rather than how to do it. The underlying system determines the execution details. Examples include SQL queries and functional programming styles.

OOP, as an imperative paradigm, encourages modeling software as a collection of interacting objects. Each object represents a real-world concept, encapsulating state (properties) and behavior (methods). This approach helps make complex systems easier to understand, extend, and maintain by clearly defining responsibilities and interactions.

With this foundation in place, we'll next revisit objects and classes in TypeScript, how to define them, work with their properties, and use their methods in practice.

## TypeScript objects

**Objects** in TypeScript are collections of key-value pairs, providing a structured way to represent data and behaviors. They are fundamental building blocks in both JavaScript and TypeScript, allowing you to group related information and create more complex data structures.

In TypeScript, objects can represent real-world entities or abstract concepts, making it easier to model data in a way that aligns with your application's needs. By grouping related properties and methods within an object, you can encapsulate functionality and maintain a clear and organized code structure.

## Object literals

An object literal is the simplest and most direct way to create an object in TypeScript. It is a method of defining an object by listing its properties and their corresponding values within curly braces (`{}`). This approach is called **literal** because you are literally defining the object in place, without the need for a constructor function or a class.

## Example—the cake object

In *Figure 3.1*, we have created a sample `cake` object using an object literal; let's examine it.

*Figure 3.1 — A cake object showing key-value pairs*

In the cake object, `flavor`, `size`, and `icing` are keys, and their corresponding values are `'chocolate'`, `'medium'`, and `'vanilla'`, respectively. This example illustrates how object literals can be used to represent a real-world entity—in this case, a cake—by grouping related properties into a single, cohesive unit.

By understanding object literals, you can start creating and manipulating objects efficiently in TypeScript, laying the groundwork for more advanced concepts, such as classes, interfaces, and OOP.

In the next section, we'll explore TypeScript classes and learn how to use them to create objects.

## TypeScript classes

In the previous section, we saw how to create objects using object literals. In modern JavaScript (ES6 and beyond), and by extension TypeScript, **classes** provide a more structured way to create objects and implement OOP principles.

We define classes as a **blueprint** (**template**) for creating objects. They define the properties and methods that all objects of the given class will share. This promotes code reusability and consistency, making your code easier to understand and maintain.

Here's a step-by-step guide on creating a class in TypeScript:

1. To create a class in TypeScript, you use the `class` keyword followed by the class name and curly braces `{}`, like so:

```
class Cake {
  // Define properties and methods here
}
```

   This creates a blueprint for `Cake` objects.

2. Inside the `class` curly braces, you can define properties that represent the data an object of that class will hold. We can define properties for `flavor`, `size`, and `icing`, like so:

```
class Cake {
  flavor: string;
  size: string;
  icing: string;
}
```

3. Now, let's define methods for baking, decorating, and serving the cake:

```
class Cake {
  flavor: string;
  size: string;
  icing: string;

  bake() {
    console.log("Cake is baking in the oven!");
  }
```

```
  decorate() {
    console.log("Adding frosting and sprinkles!");
  }

  serve() {
    console.log("Slicing and serving the delicious cake!");
  }
}
```

These methods define the actions that can be performed on a `Cake` object. Next, let's add a constructor to initialize the cake's properties when creating an instance.

Without initializing these properties, the TypeScript compiler will produce an error similar to the following:

```
Property 'flavor' has no initializer and is not definitely assigned in the
constructor.
```

To resolve this, we'll define a constructor that takes arguments for `flavor`, `size`, and `icing`, and assigns these values to the corresponding properties of the class:

```
class Cake {
  flavor: string;

  size: string;

  icing: string;

  constructor(flavor: string, size: string, icing: string) {
    this.flavor = flavor;

    this.size = size;

    this.icing = icing;
  }

  bake() {
    console.log('Cake is baking in the oven!');
  }

  decorate() {
```

```
    console.log('Adding frosting and sprinkles!');
  }

  serve() {
    console.log('Slicing and serving the delicious cake!');
  }
}
```

In the preceding piece of code, we've added a constructor.

4. Next, we can use this class to create new objects (instances). To do this, we use the `new` keyword to instantiate `Cake` objects, as shown here:

```
const chocolateCake = new Cake("chocolate", "medium", "chocolate");
const redVelvetCake = new Cake("red velvet", "large", "cream cheese");6.
```

We can call the methods on the `Cake` objects we just created:

```
chocolateCake.bake(); // Output: "Cake is baking in the oven!"
redVelvetCake.decorate(); // Output: "Adding frosting and sprinkles!"
chocolateCake.serve(); // Output: "Slicing and serving the delicious cake!"
```

Now we know how to create a class in TypeScript and how we can create instances of it (objects), enabling separation of concerns and code reuse. Next, let's learn about static methods and properties in TypeScript.

## Static methods and properties in TypeScript

In the previous section, when we created our `Cake` class, we passed in values for the properties at the points where we were initializing the objects of the class. These properties, such as `flavor`, `size`, and `icing`, are unique to each object. But there are occasions where you want properties and methods that are peculiar to the class itself (parent) and not the instances (objects created from the class).

This is where **static properties and methods** come into play. Static members belong to the `Cake` class itself. You can access them directly using the class name (e.g., `Cake`), without needing to create an object first. In the following example, we will extend our `Cake` class to use some static properties and methods:

```
class Cake {
  flavor: string;
  size: string;
```

```
  icing: string;

  // Static property
  static totalCakesBaked: number = 0;

  constructor(flavor: string, size: string, icing: string) {
    this.flavor = flavor;
    this.size = size;
    this.icing = icing;
    Cake.numberOfCakes+
+; // Increment the number of cakes each time a new cake is created
  }

  // Static method
  static getTotalCakesBaked () {
    console.log(`Baked ${this.numberOfCakes} cakes in total.`);
  }

  // the other methods and properties…
}
```

In this example, `totalCakesBaked` is a static property that keeps track of the total number of `Cake` objects created. Each time a `Cake` object is instantiated, `totalCakesBaked` is incremented by 1 in the constructor (`totalCakesBaked++`).

The `getTotalCakesBaked` static method can be called directly on the `Cake` class to log the cumulative count of cakes baked. Note that within static methods, `this` refers to the class itself rather than an instance of the class. This means static properties can be accessed using `this` within static methods.

You can call the static method like this:

```
Cake.getTotalCakesBaked();
```

Static methods and properties are powerful tools for defining behavior and data that belong to the class itself, not individual instances. These are particularly useful for utility functions, counters, or any shared state or behavior. By understanding and utilizing static members effectively, you can write more structured and maintainable code.

In this section, we've reviewed how to create and instantiate classes in TypeScript, including defining properties and methods. We've also explored static properties and methods. With this foundation in TypeScript objects, classes, and properties, it's time to delve into some fundamental concepts of OOP.

Before moving on to the next section, where we'll explore inheritance and the prototype chain, a key concept in TypeScript OOP, let's take a moment to review what happens behind the scenes when we define a class in JavaScript or TypeScript.

## TypeScript classes: behind the scenes

Having learned the syntax for creating classes in TypeScript, it's crucial to peek behind the curtain to understand the underlying mechanics. We define a class like this:

```
class MyClass {}
```

TypeScript/JavaScript then performs some transformations and converts it to something like this:

```
function MyClass() {}
```

This function is known as a constructor. To illustrate, let's create a `dummy-class.ts` file. In this file, we'll define a simple `Dog` class with one method, `bark`:

```
class Dog {
  bark() {
    console.log('Woof!');
  }
}
```

When we run the `npx tsc dummy-class.ts` command, TypeScript generates the JavaScript version of the code, which we can check in `dummy-class.js`.

Here is the generated JavaScript code:

```
var Dog = /** @class */ (function () {
    function Dog() {
    }
    Dog.prototype.bark = function () {
        console.log('Woof!');
    };
    return Dog;
}());
```

Let's break down the generated code:

- **Immediately Invoked Function Expression (IIFE):**

  ```
  var Dog = /** @class */ (function () {
  ```

  This part defines an IIFE. An IIFE is a function that runs as soon as it is defined. The purpose here is to create a private scope for the `Dog` class.

- Constructor function:

  ```
  function Dog() {
  }
  ```

  Inside the IIFE, the `Dog` function is defined. This function acts as the constructor for the `Dog` class. When you create a new instance of `Dog` using `new Dog()`, this function is called to initialize the object.

- Prototype method:

  ```
  Dog.prototype.bark = function () {
          console.log('Woof!');
      };
  ```

  The `bark` method is defined on the prototype of the `Dog` constructor. This means that all instances of `Dog` will share the same `bark` method. When you call `dogInstance.bark()`, it looks up the method on the prototype chain and finds this definition.

- Returning the constructor:

  ```
  return Dog;
  }());
  ```

  The IIFE returns the `Dog` constructor function. The `Dog` function is then assigned to the `Dog` variable, making it accessible in the outer scope.

> **Note**
>
> The `class` keyword in TypeScript is syntactic sugar. It provides a more intuitive way to define object blueprints compared to raw JavaScript functions. This makes your code more readable and maintainable, especially for those familiar with OOP concepts.

Now that we understand the "secret" behind classes, we're well-equipped to explore inheritance and the prototype chain in the next section. These concepts are fundamental to object-oriented programming in TypeScript.

# Inheritance and prototype chains

**Inheritance** is a cornerstone of OOP, which allows you to create new classes (subclasses) that inherit properties and behaviors from existing classes (superclasses). This promotes code reusability and reduces redundancy in your TypeScript applications.

TypeScript, being a superset of JavaScript, uses **prototypal inheritance** behind the scenes. Prototypal inheritance differs from the classical inheritance model used in languages such as Java or C++. In prototypal inheritance, objects inherit directly from other objects. However, TypeScript provides a class-based syntax that abstracts away the prototypal nature of inheritance, making it more familiar to developers coming from classical OOP languages. Let's explore these two models to understand their differences better.

## Classical inheritance

**Classical inheritance** is used in languages such as Java and C++. Here, the inheritance hierarchy is more rigid. A subclass inherits from a superclass and has a fixed place in the inheritance tree. In classical inheritance, we have the following:

- **Subclass and superclass**: A subclass is a specialized version of its superclass, inheriting all its properties and behaviors
- **Hierarchy**: The inheritance structure is a fixed hierarchy, meaning that classes are defined and relationships are established at the time of class creation

For example, in Java, you might define classes like this:

```
class Animal {
  void makeSound() {
    System.out.println("The animal makes a sound");
  }
}

class Dog extends Animal {
  void makeSound() {
    System.out.println("The dog barks");
  }
}
```

In the preceding example, `Dog` is a subclass of `Animal`, and it overrides the `makeSound` method.

## Prototypal inheritance

Prototypal inheritance is a JavaScript runtime concept. Because TypeScript compiles to JavaScript and does not introduce a new runtime or inheritance model, all inheritance in TypeScript ultimately relies on JavaScript's prototypal inheritance.

This inheritance model is more flexible and dynamic. In prototypal inheritance, we have the following:

- **Direct inheritance**: Objects inherit directly from other objects.
- **Prototype chain**: Objects have a prototype, which is another object from which they inherit properties. This creates a chain of inheritance.
- **Dynamic relationships**: Relationships between objects can be changed dynamically at runtime.

In TypeScript, you might define classes like this:

```
class Animal {
  makeSound() {
    console.log('The animal makes a sound');
  }
}

class Dog extends Animal {
  makeSound() {
    console.log('The dog barks');
  }
}
```

Under the hood, TypeScript transforms these class definitions into JavaScript functions and prototypes, enabling prototypal inheritance:

```
function Animal() {}
Animal.prototype.makeSound = function () {
  console.log('The animal makes a sound');
};

function Dog() {}
Dog.prototype = Object.create(Animal.prototype);
Dog.prototype.constructor = Dog;
Dog.prototype.makeSound = function () {
```

```
  console.log('The dog barks');
};
```

In this example, the `Dog` constructor function's prototype is set to an object created from `Animal.prototype`, establishing the prototype chain. The `makeSound` method on `Dog.prototype` overrides the one on `Animal.prototype`.

## Key differences

When comparing classical inheritance with prototypal inheritance, there are several important distinctions to keep in mind. In the following, we outline the key differences between these two inheritance models:

- **Hierarchy**:
    - **Classical inheritance**: Fixed and rigid hierarchy. Classes are defined once, and their relationships do not change.
    - **Prototypal inheritance**: Flexible and dynamic. Objects can inherit from other objects, and these relationships can change at runtime.
- **Inheritance model**:
    - **Classical inheritance**: Classes and subclasses.
    - **Prototypal inheritance**: Objects and prototypes.
- **Method overriding**:
    - **Classical inheritance**: Methods in the subclass override methods in the superclass.
    - **Prototypal inheritance**: Methods on the prototype of a child object override methods on the prototype of a parent object.

Understanding the differences between classical and prototypal inheritance helps in effectively leveraging inheritance in your TypeScript applications. While TypeScript classes provide a familiar syntax for those coming from classical inheritance backgrounds, it's crucial to remember that they ultimately compile down to JavaScript's prototypal inheritance model. This knowledge enables you to write more flexible, dynamic, and maintainable code. So, in the next subsection, we will look into prototypes in TypeScript.

## Understanding prototypes in TypeScript

To understand prototypes in TypeScript, it helps to first understand how they work in JavaScript. TypeScript runs on top of JavaScript and uses JavaScript's object model at runtime, so the way prototypes behave is the same as it is in JavaScript.

In JavaScript, everything is an object, including functions. Every object has an internal `[[Prototype]]` reference that points to another object, called its **prototype**. That prototype can itself have another prototype, forming what is known as the **prototype chain**.

When you access a property on an object, JavaScript first looks for that property on the object itself. If it doesn't find it there, it continues searching up the prototype chain until the property is found or the end of the chain is reached.

TypeScript works with this same prototype system. It adds type information on top of JavaScript's behavior, helping you understand and validate how objects relate to each other at development time, while the actual property lookup and inheritance behavior are handled by JavaScript at runtime.

Let's see an example in the following screenshot for further details.

```
> const cake = {
    flavor: 'chocolate',
    size: 'medium',
    icing: 'vanila',
  };
<· undefined
> cake
<· ▼ {flavor: 'chocolate', size: 'medium', icing: 'vanila'} i
       flavor: "chocolate"
       icing: "vanila"
       size: "medium"
     ▶ [[Prototype]]: Object
```

*Figure 3.2: The [[Prototype]] property of objects in the browser console*

In *Figure 3.2*, we've created a simple `cake` object in our browser console. If you log the `cake` variable in the console, you will see the object details. When you look closely, you can see the `[[Prototype]]` property of the object. Every object you create has this property. When you click on the arrow, you can see more details, as shown in *Figure 3.3*:

*Figure 3.3 — Showing the details of the [[Prototype]] property of an object*

If you noticed, even the `[[Prototype]]` property has its own `__proto__`. If you click on the arrow of that `__proto__` property to see more details, you find that it also has a `__proto__`, which is null this time. For clarity, see *Figure 3.4*:

*Figure 3.4 — Showing the prototype chain of an object up to null*

Now that we've learned about the prototype chain, let's see how we can set it up ourselves.

## Setting up the prototype chain

In this section, we will look at ways in which you can set up the prototype chain in TypeScript.

## Using Object.create to set up the prototype chain

`Object.create()` is a method used to create a new object and set its prototype to an existing object. This can be useful when you want to create an object with a specific prototype. For example, `let obj = Object.create(protoObj);` creates a new object, `obj`, with its prototype set to `protoObj`.

Let's see the following example for more details:

```
const cakePrototype = {
  bake() {
    console.log('The cake is baking.');
  },
};

const chocolateCake = Object.create(cakePrototype);
chocolateCake.flavor = 'Chocolate';
chocolateCake.bake();
```

In this example, `chocolateCake` is an object that inherits from `cakePrototype`. This means `chocolateCake` can use the `bake` method defined in `cakePrototype`, demonstrating basic prototype inheritance.

## ES6 class inheritance with extends and super

With the introduction of ES6, TypeScript provided a more familiar syntax for inheritance using classes, which aligns more closely with classical programming patterns.

In ES6, we can create a class and use the `extends` keyword to create a subclass. The subclass inherits all the methods and properties of the superclass. The `super` keyword is used to call the constructor of the superclass and to access the superclass's properties and methods. Here's an example:

```
// Define the Oven class with a bake() method
class Oven {
  bake() {
    console.log('The oven is baking.');
  }
}

// Define the Cake class that extends Oven
class Cake extends Oven {
```

```
  flavor: string;
  size: string;
  icing: string;

  // Constructor for the Cake class
  constructor(flavor: string, size: string, icing: string) {
    super(); // Calls the constructor of the Oven class
    this.flavor = flavor;
    this.size = size;
    this.icing = icing;
  }

  // Additional methods specific to Cake
  decorate() {
    console.log(
      `Decorating the ${this.size} ${this.flavor} cake with ${this.icing} icing.`
    );
  }

  serve() {
    console.log(`Serving the delicious ${this.flavor} cake!`);
  }
}

// Example usage
const chocolateCake = new Cake('chocolate', 'large', 'chocolate ganache');
chocolateCake.bake(); // Inherited method from Oven
chocolateCake.decorate();
chocolateCake.serve();
```

Let's summarize the preceding code to make it clearer.

1. We define a new class, `Oven`, with a `bake` method that simulates baking functionality.
2. The `Cake` class now inherits from `Oven` by using `extends`.
3. Inside the `Cake` class constructor, we call `super()` to ensure proper initialization is inherited from `Oven`.
4. We define properties for `flavor`, `size`, and `icing` specific to `Cake` objects.

5. We add the `decorate()` and `serve()` methods to the `Cake` class, demonstrating typical actions that might be performed on a cake after baking.
6. When creating a `Cake` object (e.g., `chocolateCake`), it inherits the `bake` method from `Oven` and can use its own methods, `decorate()` and `serve()`.

The preceding setup uses class inheritance to model a real-world relationship in which a cake is a specific type of baked good that uses an oven for baking, showing how an object-oriented approach can effectively model real-world hierarchies and behaviors in software design.

In this section, we've looked at inheritance and prototype chains. We've learned about prototypes in TypeScript and how they form the backbone of TypeScript's object model. We've seen prototype-based inheritance, a way of creating objects that inherit properties and methods from other objects. We've seen how to use `Object.create` to set up the prototype chain, a mechanism for having objects inherit features from one another. And we've gone through ES6 class inheritance with the `extends` and `super` keywords, which allow a more intuitive syntax for working with prototypes and inheritance.

In the next section, we will talk about encapsulation.

# Encapsulation—protecting your cake's recipe

**Encapsulation** is a fundamental principle of OOP that involves bundling data (properties) and the methods (operations) that act on that data within a single unit, typically a class. This concept ensures that the internal representation of an object is hidden from the outside, only allowing access through a well-defined interface.

Think of encapsulation as protecting your cake's secret recipe. Just as you wouldn't want anyone to alter your cake batter without permission, in programming, you want to make sure that certain data is only accessible to specific parts of your code. This promotes data privacy and controlled access, ensuring the integrity and proper functioning of your objects.

In this section, we'll explore the importance of data privacy and how encapsulation helps achieve it. We'll delve into practical implementations, including getters and setters, which act as gatekeepers to your class's data. By understanding and applying encapsulation, you'll be able to create more secure, maintainable code.

## Getters and setters: the gatekeepers of your data

Getters and setters are special methods that provide controlled access to a class's properties.

- **Getters**: These methods allow you to retrieve the value of a property in a controlled way. You can potentially perform additional logic before returning the value, such as formatting or validation.
- **Setters**: These methods allow you to modify the value of a property in a controlled way. You can use them to enforce specific rules or data validation before assigning a new value.

Here's how you can use getters and setters in the `Cake` class:

```
class Cake {
  constructor(flavor, size, icing) {
    this._flavor = flavor;
    this._size = size;
    this._icing = icing;
  }
  get flavor() {
    // Getter for flavor property
    return this._flavor.toUpperCase();
  }
  set flavor(newFlavor) {
    // Setter for flavor property
    if (newFlavor.length < 3) {
      throw new Error('Flavor must be at least 3 characters long!');
    }
    this._flavor = newFlavor;
  }

  // other methods(decorate, serve etc).
}
const chocolateCake  = new Cake("chocolate", "medium", "vanilla");
console.log(chocolateCake .flavor); // Output: "CHOCOLATE"

chocolateCake.flavor = "ic"; // Error: Flavor must be at least 3 characters!
```

Here's a breakdown of what we did in the preceding example:

- We made the `_flavor` property private using the underscore prefix convention

- The `flavor` getter returns the flavor in uppercase
- The `flavor` setter validates the new flavor length before assigning it

In conclusion, getters and setters are powerful tools in TypeScript that allow you to control how your data is accessed and modified. They provide a layer of abstraction over your data, allowing you to enforce specific rules and perform additional logic. In our `Cake` class example, we used a getter to format the `flavor` property and a setter to validate the length of a new flavor before assigning it. This ensures that our `Cake` objects always have valid and properly formatted data.

In the next sub-section, we look at access modifiers, something else that's part of encapsulation.

## Access modifiers: controlling access to your data

Access modifiers in TypeScript are keywords that determine the visibility and accessibility of class members (properties and methods). They help enforce encapsulation by restricting access to certain parts of your code.

- `public`: The default modifier. Members with `public` can be accessed from anywhere, both inside and outside the class.
- `private`: Members with `private` can only be accessed within the class itself. This prevents external code from directly modifying these members.
- `protected`: Members with `protected` can be accessed within the class and its subclasses. This allows inheritance while still restricting external access.

Here is an example of how access modifiers would be used. We will stick with the cake example:

```
class Cake {
  private _flavor: string;
  public size: string;
  protected icing: string;

  constructor(flavor: string, size: string, icing: string) {
    this._flavor = flavor;
    this.size = size;
    this.icing = icing;
  }

  get flavor() {
    return this._flavor.toUpperCase();
```

```
  }

  set flavor(newFlavor: string) {
    if (newFlavor.length < 3) {
      throw new Error('Flavor must be at least 3 characters long!');
    }
    this._flavor = newFlavor;
  }
}
```

In the previous code, we made the `_flavor` property `private`, which means it cannot be accessed directly from outside the class. The `size` property is `public`, so it can be accessed from anywhere. The `icing` property is protected, meaning it can be accessed within the `Cake` class and any subclasses that extend `Cake`.

Now let's see what happens when we try to access the properties:

```
const chocolateCake = new Cake('chocolate', 'medium', 'vanilla');
console.log(chocolateCake.size); // Accessible
console.log(chocolateCake.flavor); // Accessible
// chocolateCake.icing = 'strawberry'; // Error: 'icing' is protected
// chocolateCake._flavor = 'strawberry'; // Error: '_flavor' is private
```

In conclusion, access modifiers are essential tools in TypeScript for controlling the visibility and accessibility of class members, enhancing encapsulation, and maintaining code integrity.

In the next section, we will delve into the concept of polymorphism. This is another fundamental concept in OOP that allows objects to take on many forms, further enhancing the flexibility and reusability of our code.

# Polymorphism in TypeScript OOP

Polymorphism, meaning *many forms*, allows objects of different classes to respond to the same method call in unique ways, making code more flexible and adaptable. For example, a `draw()` method defined in a base class, `Shape`, can be customized by subclasses such as `Circle`, `Rectangle`, and `Triangle`. Calling `draw()` on each object will execute the appropriate version for its type, enabling different behaviors from a single method call.

There are two main ways to achieve polymorphism in TypeScript: method overriding and interfaces. Let's look at these two approaches in more detail.

## Method overriding

**Method overriding** is a key aspect of polymorphism in TypeScript. It allows you to define a method in a base class and then override it in child classes to provide a more specific implementation. This enables you to write more generic code that can work with different classes.

To implement method overriding in TypeScript, follow these steps:

1. Define a base class with a method that has a general implementation.
2. Create child classes that inherit from the base class.
3. Override the method in the child class to provide a more specific implementation.

Let's see the example:

```
class PaymentMethod {
  processPayment(amount: number) {
    // This method will be overridden in each subclass
    console.log(`Processing default payment: ${amount}`)
  }
}

class CreditCard extends PaymentMethod {
  processPayment(amount: number) {
    console.log(`Processing credit card payment for amount: ${amount}`);
  }
}

class DebitCard extends PaymentMethod {
  processPayment(amount: number) {
    console.log(`Processing debit card payment for amount: ${amount}`);
  }
}

let paymentMethods: PaymentMethod[] = [new CreditCard(), new DebitCard()];

paymentMethods.forEach((paymentMethod) => paymentMethod.processPayment(100));
```

In this example, when we call `processPayment` on each item in the `paymentMethods` array, the overridden method in each subclass (`CreditCard` and `DebitCard`) is executed instead of the base class method. This demonstrates polymorphism in action, allowing each subclass to respond differently to the same method call.

Now let's look at the same example, but with interfaces.

## Interfaces

**Interfaces** in TypeScript are a very potent way to define contracts within your code. They offer a way to define a type by the shape of the data. Interfaces thus give us a chance to interact with various classes in the same way as long as they implement the same interface.

Let's see how we can implement the example in the preceding section using interfaces:

```
interface PaymentMethod {
processPayment(amount: number): void;
}

class CreditCard implements PaymentMethod {
processPayment(amount: number) {
console.log(`Processing credit card payment for amount: ${amount}`);
}
}

class DebitCard implements PaymentMethod {
processPayment(amount: number) {
console.log(`Processing debit card payment for amount: ${amount}`);
}
}

let paymentMethods: PaymentMethod[] = [new CreditCard(), new DebitCard()];

paymentMethods.forEach((paymentMethod) => paymentMethod.processPayment(100));
```

In this example, `CreditCard` and `DebitCard` are separate classes that implement the `PaymentMethod` interface. They are not related by inheritance, but they can be used interchangeably because they implement the same interface.

## Interfaces versus classes: when to use each

At this point, you've seen how interfaces and classes both enable polymorphism in TypeScript. The important question now is not what they are, but when to use one over the other.

An interface is best used when you want to define a contract, a common shape, or an API that different implementations can follow. Interfaces work especially well when multiple, unrelated classes need to expose the same behavior. Because interfaces exist only at compile time, they provide flexibility without introducing runtime coupling.

Use an interface when you want to do the following:

- Define a common shape or API
- Allow multiple unrelated classes to follow the same contract
- Enable polymorphism without enforcing inheritance
- Keep implementations loosely coupled and easy to replace

A class, on the other hand, is appropriate when you need both structure and behavior. Classes allow you to share implementation details, define constructors, and use inheritance and method overriding. They also exist at runtime, which makes them suitable when objects need to be instantiated and carry behavior.

Use a class in the following situations:

- You need shared behavior or reusable implementation
- You want to use inheritance and method overriding
- You require runtime features such as constructors or internal state
- You are creating objects that will be instantiated directly

In practice, a common and effective pattern in TypeScript is to use interfaces to define behavior and classes to implement that behavior. This approach keeps your code flexible, testable, and easier to maintain as your application grows.

With this understanding of polymorphism and abstraction, we're now ready to explore another key design decision: when to use composition and when inheritance makes sense.

# Composition over inheritance for agile development

**Inheritance** and **composition** are fundamental concepts in OOP that define relationships between classes. Inheritance establishes a "parent-child" hierarchy, where the child class inherits properties and behaviors from the parent. Composition, on the other hand, describes how an object is built from other objects.

Inheritance is useful when there is a clear **is-a** relationship between two classes. For example, a dog is a kind of animal. They share common characteristics and behaviors (such as eating and moving) that can be defined in the `Animal` class and inherited by `Dog`. This promotes code reuse and reduces redundancy.

Let's check the following code for more details:

```
class Animal {
  breathe() {
    console.log('Breathing');
```

```
  }
}

class Dog extends Animal {
  bark() {
    console.log('Barking');
  }
}

let dog = new Dog();
dog.breathe(); // Outputs: 'Breathing'
dog.bark(); // Outputs: 'Barking'
```

In the preceding example, `Dog` inherits from `Animal`, gaining its behavior while adding specific behaviors of its own, such as barking.

Composition, on the other hand, is useful when an object is made up of other objects. For example, a band is made up of a singer, a guitarist, and a drummer. In this case, it makes more sense to use composition, where `Band` has `Singer`, a `Guitarist`, and a `Drummer`.

As a rule of thumb, we prefer composition over inheritance as it is more flexible. It leads to a loosely coupled architecture with the single responsibility principle.

See the following example for more details:

```
class Band {
  singer: Singer;
  guitarist: Guitarist;
  drummer: Drummer;

  constructor() {
    this.singer = new Singer();
    this.guitarist = new Guitarist();
    this.drummer = new Drummer();
  }

  perform() {
    this.singer.sing();
    this.guitarist.playGuitar();
    this.drummer.playDrums();
  }
}
```

```
let band = new Band();
band.perform(); // Outputs: 'Singer is singing', 'Guitarist is playing guitar',
'Drummer is playing drums'
```

In the example we just considered, `Band` doesn't inherit functionalities from `Singer`, `Guitarist`, or `Drummer`. Instead, `Band` has `Singer`, a `Guitarist`, and a `Drummer`. It composes these objects and delegates specific functionalities (singing, playing guitar, playing drums) to them. This allows for greater flexibility.

You can easily change the composition of the band. Maybe it has a backup singer or a keyboard player. Composition allows for this flexibility without modifying the core `Band` functionality. Each object can be independently extended or modified without affecting the others.

By understanding and applying these concepts, you can write more flexible and maintainable TypeScript code. Remember, while inheritance can be useful in some cases, composition can often be a more powerful and flexible approach.

# Summary

This chapter provided a thorough understanding of OOP concepts as applied in modern JavaScript and TypeScript. We began with an introduction to OOP, its significance, and comparison with other paradigms. We then explored objects and methods, followed by a deep dive into classes, including their creation, instantiation, and key features such as constructors, the `this` keyword, and static properties. Throughout the chapter, we examined how TypeScript builds on JavaScript's OOP model by adding type safety and improved developer tooling.

The chapter also covered inheritance and prototype chains, encapsulation for data privacy, and polymorphism. We concluded with a discussion on composition versus inheritance, providing guidance on when to use each and the benefits of composition. The knowledge gained will enable cleaner and more maintainable TypeScript code.

In the forthcoming chapter, we will be harnessing the knowledge we've accumulated thus far. Our focus will be on its practical application within the framework of a TypeScript project. We will embark on constructing a sample project, providing us with a hands-on opportunity to implement our understanding. This will involve organizing and modularizing code and ensuring adherence to the principles we've previously discussed. This chapter promises to be an enriching journey from theoretical understanding to practical implementation.

## Get this book's PDF copy, code bundle, and more

Scan the QR code (or go to `packtpub.com/unlock`), search for this book by name, confirm the edition, and then follow the steps on the page.

UNLOCK NOW

*Note: Have your invoice handy. Purchases made directly from the Packt website don't require an invoice.*

# 4

# Clean Code in TypeScript Projects

In the previous chapters, we laid the foundation for writing clean code within the TypeScript context. We covered the installation and setup of a TypeScript project, discussed the principles of clean functions and clean code, delved into **object-oriented programming** (**OOP**), and explored documenting our code with TypeDoc and TSDoc.

In this chapter, we will advance these concepts and integrate them into a complete TypeScript project. Our focus will be on the importance of code organization, modularization, and adherence to clean code principles to create robust and scalable projects. We will examine **feature-based** versus **function-based** folder structures and provide guidance on selecting the most suitable approach for your project. Additionally, we will explore the module system, different types, and how they work. We will also dive into dependency management, comparing various systems, such as npm, Yarn, and pnpm. Finally, we will cover linting and setting up custom checks to ensure code consistency and quality.

> **Note**
>
> TypeScript configuration was discussed in detail in *Chapter 1*, and we assume familiarity with it for this project-based chapter.

Specifically, we will cover the following:

- Best practices for folder structure
- Learning module systems
- Managing dependencies in TypeScript projects
- Linting and code formatting

By the end of this chapter, you will have gained a comprehensive understanding of how to structure and organize your TypeScript projects effectively. You will learn how to manage dependencies, configure TypeScript settings, and implement tools for maintaining high code quality.

# Technical requirements

You can download the example project and code for this book by following the instructions in the *Download the example code files* section in the *Preface* of this book.

This chapter's code files are included in the downloadable code bundle.

# Best practices for folder structure

A well-organized folder structure is the backbone of a maintainable and scalable TypeScript project. It's the foundation upon which your code is built, and a good structure can make all the difference in the world. Imagine trying to find a specific file in a project with no clear organization—it's like searching for a needle in a haystack!

In any TypeScript project, a well-defined folder structure is essential for several reasons. It enhances code readability, making it easier for developers to understand the project at a glance, which is crucial in collaborative environments where multiple team members contribute to the code base. Additionally, a structured project improves maintainability, as it helps manage complexity and ensures that new features can be added without creating chaos. Lastly, a well-organized structure supports scalability, allowing the project to evolve and expand without requiring significant restructuring. By implementing a clear and logical folder structure, you'll be able to navigate your project with ease, find files quickly, and build a solid foundation for your code.

In this section, we will explore best practices for organizing your project files and directories to ensure your TypeScript project remains maintainable and scalable as it grows. First, let's look at what a standard folder structure for TypeScript projects would be.

## Standard folder structure

In a typical TypeScript project, certain directories and files are commonly used to organize code in a clear and maintainable way. While the exact structure can vary depending on the framework and tooling, the following elements are frequently seen across modern TypeScript projects.

- **src (source) directory**: The `src` directory contains all the source code files. This is where you organize your TypeScript files based on their roles and functionalities.

- **dist (distribution) directory**: The `dist` directory holds the compiled output. After the TypeScript code is transpiled to JavaScript, the files are placed here, ready for deployment.
- **config directory**: The `config` directory stores configuration files. This includes settings for tools such as webpack, Babel, or environment variables.
- **Test directory**: In modern TypeScript and React projects, tests are often colocated with the code they test (for example, `Button.test.tsx` next to `Button.tsx`). This approach aligns well with component-driven development and is supported by tools such as Vite, Next.js, Jest, and monorepo setups such as Nx or Turborepo. Some projects may still use a separate test directory, depending on team preference and tooling.
- **index.ts file**: A root-level `index.ts` file is often used for exporting modules, providing a single-entry point to your project's components.

In the preceding list, we discussed the standard folder structure in a typical TypeScript project. While this structure is common, it doesn't dictate how elements within these folders, such as UI components or services, should be organized. To address this, developers often consider two primary approaches for grouping their code into folders: **feature-based organization** and **function-based organization**. In the following sections, we will dive deeper into the specifics of these two strategies, providing a comprehensive understanding of how they can be effectively utilized in your TypeScript projects.

In addition to feature-based and function-based organization, many modern TypeScript projects adopt a **module-based architecture** as they grow in size and complexity. In this approach, code is grouped into independent modules or packages, each representing a distinct business capability, such as authentication, billing, or notifications.

This style is commonly used in monorepo setups with tools such as Yarn workspaces, Nx, or Turborepo, where each module can have its own internal structure, dependencies, and ownership boundaries. Module-based organization becomes especially valuable as teams scale, allowing different parts of the system to evolve independently while maintaining clear contracts between them.

In practice, project structure often evolves over time. Teams may start with a simple function-based or feature-based layout and gradually transition to a module-based approach as business requirements expand and code ownership becomes more distributed.

# Organizing by feature versus function

Both feature-based and function-based organization have their unique benefits and trade-offs, and understanding these differences is crucial for building a scalable, maintainable, and efficient code base. In this section, we'll delve into the core principles of both methods, exploring their advantages and disadvantages, to help you make an informed decision about which approach best suits your project's needs.

## Feature-based organization

In feature-based organization, files and directories are structured around specific features of the application. For example, you might have a directory called `cart` that contains all the files related to the shopping cart feature, including the cart component, cart service, and cart reducer.

Here are the pros and cons of feature-based organization:

First, let's look at the pros:

- **Cohesion**: Related components are grouped together, making it easier to manage specific features
- **Scalability**: Adding new features can be done without affecting other parts of the project
- **Maintainability**: Feature-related changes are easier because most relevant code lives in one place
- **Testability**: Tests can be colocated with feature code, making feature behavior easier to validate and evolve
- **Developer Experience (DX)**: Developers can navigate the code base by business capability instead of jumping across multiple layers

Here are the cons:

- **Duplication**: Common functionalities might be duplicated across different feature folders
- **Complexity**: Finding shared utilities can become difficult

## Function-based organization

In function-based organization, files and directories are organized around specific functions or layers of the application, such as components, services, and utilities. This approach groups code by what it does, rather than the feature it serves, similar to a toolbox where tools are grouped by type, regardless of the project they're used for.

For example, you might have a directory called `components` that contains all the component files, a directory called `services` for all service files, and a directory called `utils` for utility files.

Here are the pros and cons of function-based organization.

First, let's look at the pros:

- **Reusability**: Shared code is centralized, reducing duplication
- **Simplicity**: It's easier to find and manage common functionalities
- **Layered architecture**: Encourages a layered architecture, where each layer has a specific responsibility and is separated from other layers

Next, let's check out the cons:

- **Coupling**: May result in a tight coupling between layers, making it difficult to maintain and evolve the application
- **Flat directory hierarchy**: Can lead to a flat directory hierarchy, making it difficult to locate files related to a specific feature

## Hybrid approach (common in practice)

In many real-world TypeScript projects, teams use a hybrid approach. The code base is organized by feature at the top level, and within each feature, files are grouped by function or responsibility (such as components, services, or utilities). This balances feature cohesion with clear internal structure and scales well as applications and teams grow.

## Examples of both approaches

Let's consider a sample mini e-commerce project. Here's how you might organize it by feature or function:

First, let's look at a feature-based approach:

```
src/
  └─ products/
       ├─ ProductList.ts
       ├─ ProductDetail.ts
       └─ ProductService.ts
  └─ cart/
       ├─ Cart.ts
       └─ CartService.ts
  └─ users/
       ├─ UserList.ts
       └─ UserService.ts
```

In this structure, the following applies:

- The `products/` directory contains all files related to the product feature, including the product list, product details, and product service
- The `cart/` directory handles all files related to the shopping cart
- The `users/` directory contains files related to user management

Now, let's look at a function-based approach:

```
src/
  └── components/
        ├── ProductList.ts
        ├── ProductDetail.ts
        ├── Cart.ts
        └── UserList.ts
  └── services/
        ├── ProductService.ts
        ├── CartService.ts
        └── UserService.ts
```

In this structure, the following applies:

- The `components/` directory houses files for specific UI components (e.g., `ProductList.ts`, `ProductDetail.ts`, `Cart.ts`, `UserList.ts`).
- The `services/` directory includes files for backend services (e.g., `ProductService.ts`, `CartService.ts`, `UserService.ts`). These files handle business logic, data fetching, and other backend operations for different parts of the application.

This organization allows for centralized and reusable code within each functional area, promotes separation of concerns, and makes it easier to maintain and extend the application.

Now, let's look at a hybrid approach:

```
src/
  products/
    components/
      ProductList.ts
      ProductDetail.ts
    services/
      ProductService.ts
  cart/
    components/
```

```
      Cart.ts
    services/
      CartService.ts
  users/
    components/
      UserList.ts
    services/
      UserService.ts
```

This hybrid structure keeps feature-related code together, while maintaining clear separation of responsibilities within each feature.

Now that we understand the approach to organizing our project structure and its pros and cons, in the next section, we'll delve into module systems.

# Learning module systems

Modules are the building blocks of well-organized TypeScript code. They allow you to group related functions, variables, classes, and interfaces into self-contained units. Think of modules like drawers in a toolbox – each drawer holds specific tools you need for a particular task. Just like tools in a drawer have a defined purpose, modules encapsulate functionalities within your application.

## What are module systems?

In TypeScript, a module system is a way to structure and organize code by splitting it into separate files and directories, each containing related code. This helps in managing and maintaining large code bases by keeping related functionalities together and separating unrelated ones.

But why are module systems so valuable? Let's explore how they can transform your code. Module systems improve code maintainability and reuse in the following ways:

- **Encapsulation**: Keeping related code together and preventing it from interfering with other parts of the application
- **Reusability**: Allowing you to reuse code across different parts of your application or even in different projects
- **Clarity**: Making the code base easier to understand and navigate by logically grouping related functionalities

By the end of this section, you will have an understanding of how to implement module systems in TypeScript and how to use them for improved code maintainability and reuse. We will cover the basics of creating and using modules, including how to export and import functionalities between different modules.

To better understand how module systems work in TypeScript, the following subsections will walk through a practical example. We'll demonstrate how to define a simple module and integrate it into other parts of your application. By following along, you'll see how modules not only organize your code but also enhance maintainability and promote reusability.

## Defining a module

To start, we define a simple module containing a `User` class. We do this by creating a file called (`src/models/User.ts`), which encapsulates its functionality and keeps the code organized. Here's how we create it:

```
// src/models/User.ts
export class User {
    constructor(public id: number, public name: string) {}
}
```

In this example, the `User` class has a constructor that initializes the `id` and `name` properties. The `export` keyword makes the `User` class accessible to other parts of the application by allowing it to be imported where needed.

Now that we understand how to create a module, let's look a little deeper at how it helps with encapsulation and scope management in the next section.

## Encapsulation and scope management

Modules help manage scope by encapsulating code, ensuring each piece of functionality is self-contained. This prevents variables and functions from polluting the global scope, avoids potential naming conflicts, and keeps the code clean.

For instance, when importing the `User` class into another module, the encapsulation helps manage this relationship:

```
// src/services/UserService.ts
import { User } from '../models/User';

export class UserService {
getUser(id: number): User {
// Logic to retrieve user
return new User(id, 'John Doe');
```

```
}
}
```

Here, the `User` class is imported into the `UserService` module. The encapsulation ensures that the `User` class is only accessible where it is explicitly imported, maintaining a clear structure and scope within the application.

Additionally, let's see how encapsulation applies to utility functions:

```
// src/utils/MathUtils.ts
export function add(a: number, b: number): number {
return a + b;
}

export function subtract(a: number, b: number): number {
return a - b;
}
```

By encapsulating these functions within the `MathUtils` module, we prevent potential conflicts and ensure that they can be imported selectively when needed.

```
// src/app.ts
import { add, subtract } from './utils/MathUtils';

console.log(add(5, 3)); // Output: 8
console.log(subtract(5, 3)); // Output: 2
```

Now that we understand abstraction, let's move on to the next step, which involves reusability.

## Reusability—importing and using modules

Modules not only encapsulate functionality but also promote reusability by allowing you to import existing code into different parts of your application. This reduces duplication and promotes the **Don't Repeat Yourself** (**DRY**) principle.

For example, we can create a reusable logging utility:

```
// src/utils/Logger.ts
export function log(message: string): void {
console.log(`[LOG]: ${message}`);
}
```

This logging utility can then be imported into various modules across your application, improving maintainability and consistency:

```
// src/components/ComponentA.ts
import { log } from '../utils/Logger';
export function ComponentA() {
log('ComponentA initialized');
}
```

The next thing we'll explore is how modules make your code significantly easier to maintain.

## Maintainability

By organizing code into modules, you can manage and maintain your code base more effectively. Changes in one module do not affect other modules, making it easier to track bugs and implement new features.

## Scalability

As your application grows, modules make it easy to scale without disrupting existing functionality. For example, you can add a new module for handling orders in an e-commerce application without affecting the `User` or `UserService` modules. Let's see the following example:

```
// src/models/Order.ts
export class Order {
constructor(public orderId: number, public userId: number, public amount: number)
{}
}
```

This new `Order` module can be added seamlessly, demonstrating the scalability of modular code. The last thing we will look at is how organizing your code by modules can improve testing.

## Improved testing

Modules make it easier to write unit tests by allowing you to test individual pieces of functionality in isolation. For instance, you can write unit tests for the `User` class and `UserService` module separately, ensuring that each piece of functionality works as expected.

```
// src/tests/User.test.ts

import { User } from '../models/User';
```

```
test('User class should create a user with id and name', () => {
    const user = new User(1, 'Alice');
    expect(user.id).toBe(1);
    expect(user.name).toBe('Alice');
});
```

By testing the User class in isolation, you can ensure its functionality without being affected by other parts of the application.

Now that we understand what the module system is and how it improves our code, let's move on to the next section, where we will explore the various types of module systems used in TypeScript/JavaScript. We will focus primarily on the two most commonly used ones: **ECMAScript Modules** (**ES6 Modules**) and **CommonJS**. Additionally, we'll make quick references to other types of module systems, such as **Asynchronous Module Definition** (**AMD**), **Universal Module Definition** (**UMD**), and **SystemJS**.

# ES6 modules

Introduced in ES2015 (ECMAScript 6), ES6 modules provide a standardized way to organize and share code using import and export.

One key benefit of ES6 modules is tree shaking, the process of removing unused code during the build step. When code is structured as modules, bundlers can statically analyze which exports are actually used and safely eliminate the rest. Without modules, code is often bundled together in a way that makes it difficult to determine what can be removed, leading to larger and less efficient bundles.

Because ES6 modules are statically analyzed, tools such as bundlers and compilers can optimize applications ahead of time, resulting in smaller bundle sizes and better runtime performance.

Here's a simple example.

```
// utils.ts (source module)
export function formatDate(date: Date): string {
  // formatting logic
  return new Date(date).toDateString();
}
```

And here is what the consuming module looks like (`app.ts`):

```
import { formatDate } from './utils';

const formattedDate = formatDate(new Date());
console.log(formattedDate);
```

Basically, in the previous code, we use the `import` statement to bring the `formateDate` function from the `utils` module.

Now that we have an idea of ES6 modules, let's see some advantages of using ES6 modules:

- **Static imports**: ES6 modules are statically analyzed, allowing tools and compilers to optimize the code before execution
- **Browser support**: Natively supported in modern browsers
- **Tree Shaking**: Facilitates tree shaking, where unused code can be eliminated during the build process

This should give you an idea of why ES6 modules are preferred in certain cases. Now that we have an understanding of ES6 modules, the next module type we'll look at is CommonJS.

## CommonJS

CommonJS is the default module system in Node.js and is widely used in backend development. Modules are loaded dynamically at runtime using the `require` function.

To export a module in CommonJS, unlike ES6 modules that use the `export` keyword, you need to use `module.exports`. Here's an example similar to the one in the ES6 module section:

```
module.exports.formatDate = function (date) {
  // formatting logic
  return new Date(date).toDateString();
};
```

In this code, we define a `formatDate` function and export it using `module.exports`, making it available to other files. The `formatDate` function accepts a `date` parameter, applies some formatting logic, and returns the date as a string.

To use this exported function in another file, we import it using the `require` function:

```
const utils = require('./utils'); // Require the entire utils module
```

```
const formattedDate = utils.formatDate(new Date());
console.log(formattedDate);
```

In this example, we use `require('./utils')` to load the entire `utils` module. The `utils` object contains the exported `formatDate` function, which we call to format the current date. Finally, we log the formatted date to the console.

The dynamic nature of CommonJS modules, mentioned previously, offers flexibility, but makes code analysis and optimization more challenging.

Other module systems, such as AMD, SystemJS, and UMD, have been used in the past, but they are not as prevalent in modern development. As a result, we won't be diving into them in this book. In the next section, we'll focus on managing dependencies in TypeScript projects.

# Managing dependencies in TypeScript projects

In the world of software development, building applications rarely involves reinventing the wheel from scratch. We leverage the power of existing code libraries and tools; these are your dependencies. Dependencies provide essential functionalities and features that you integrate into your project, saving you time and effort.

But why do dependencies matter? Let's find out:

- **Faster development**: By utilizing pre-written, well-tested code, you don't need to build everything yourself. This accelerates development and allows you to focus on your core application logic.
- **Code quality and consistency**: Established libraries often adhere to high coding standards and best practices, improving the overall quality and maintainability of your project.
- **Community support**: Dependencies often come with a vibrant community, providing readily available documentation, tutorials, and support when you encounter issues.

As you integrate dependencies into your TypeScript project, it's crucial to understand that not all dependencies serve the same purpose. Some are used only during development, while others are necessary for your application's core functionality in production. To effectively manage and optimize your project, you need to know the difference. Let's explore the two main types of dependencies you'll encounter in TypeScript projects: development dependencies and production dependencies.

## Types of dependencies

There are two types of dependencies in a TypeScript project: development dependencies and production dependencies:

- **Development dependencies** are required for building, testing, and running your project during development but are not included in the final production build. Examples include testing frameworks (Jest), bundlers (webpack), and linters (ESLint).
- **Production dependencies** are essential for the core functionality of your application and are included when deploying your project to a production environment. Examples include web frameworks (React, Angular), data access libraries (Axios), and UI component libraries (Material UI).

Here are the common dependencies in TypeScript projects:

- **Testing frameworks**: Jest, Mocha, Jasmine, Vitest
- **Bundlers**: webpack, Rollup, Parcel
- **Linters**: ESLint, TSLint
- **Web frameworks**: React, Angular, Vue.js
- **Data access libraries**: Axios, Fetch API
- **UI component libraries**: Material UI, Ant Design, PrimeNG

We've just explored the two main types of dependencies in a TypeScript project: development dependencies, which are essential for the build and testing processes, and production dependencies, which are necessary for the application to function in a live environment. These dependencies include various tools and libraries, such as testing frameworks, bundlers, web frameworks, and more.

In the next section, we'll take a closer look at how these dependencies are managed using dependency managers in Node.js, which help automate and simplify the process of installing and maintaining the correct versions of these packages.

## Dependency managers in Node.js

Dependency managers are tools that automate the process of installing, updating, configuring, and managing the libraries and packages that a project depends on. They ensure that the right versions of dependencies are installed and help in resolving conflicts between different packages.

In the Node.js ecosystem, the most common dependency managers are npm, yarn, and pnpm. Each of these has its own set of commands for managing dependencies, but they all share some common ones.

## Overview of npm, yarn, and pnpm

In the Node.js ecosystem, there are several tools available for managing dependencies efficiently. While npm is the default package manager that comes with Node.js, alternatives such as yarn and pnpm have emerged, each offering unique features aimed at improving speed, reliability, and performance. In the following, we'll explore the key characteristics, installation steps, and basic commands for these three popular dependency managers.

- **npm (Node Package Manager)**: The default package manager included with Node.js. It offers a vast repository of public and private packages.
  *Installation*: Comes preinstalled with Node.js

  Basic commands:

  - `npm install <package-name>`: Installs a package
  - `npm uninstall <package-name>`: Uninstalls a package
  - `npm list`: Lists installed dependencies
- **Yarn**: A fast, reliable, and secure dependency manager, often considered an alternative to npm.
  *Installation*: `npm install -g yarn` (global installation)

  Basic commands:

  - `yarn add <package-name>`: Installs a package
  - `yarn remove <package-name>`: Uninstalls a package
  - `yarn list`: Lists installed dependencies
- **pnpm**: A relatively new dependency manager that focuses on performance and efficiency.
  *Installation*: `npm install -g pnpm` (global installation)

  Basic commands:

  - `pnpm add <package-name>`: Installs a package
  - `pnpm remove <package-name>`: Uninstalls a package
  - `pnpm list`: Lists installed dependencies

Here is a comparison of npm, Yarn, and pnpm:

| Aspect | npm | Yarn | pnpm |
|---|---|---|---|
| Default with Node.js | Yes | No | No |
| Installation | Comes bundled with Node.js | Installed via npm | Installed via npm |
| Dependency storage | Flat node_modules | Flat node_modules | Content-addressable store with symlinks |
| Disk space usage | Moderate | Moderate | Low (shared store across projects) |
| Install speed | Good | Faster than older npm versions | Very fast |
| Lockfile | package-lock.json | yarn.lock | pnpm-lock.yaml |
| Dependency deduplication | Partial deduplication | Better than npm | Strict and efficient |
| Monorepo support | Basic | Good | Excellent |
| Learning curve | Low | Low | Medium |
| Best suited for | Beginners, simple projects | Teams wanting stability and speed | Large projects, monorepos, performance-focused teams |

*Table 4.1 — Comparison of npm, Yarn, and pnpm*

So, how will you choose a dependency manager?

All three options are widely used and offer similar functionalities. npm is the default choice if you're starting out. Yarn is known for its speed and reliability, while pnpm focuses on performance optimizations. Consider your project needs and preferences when making a selection.

## Checking for outdated dependencies

Regularly updating dependencies ensures that your project benefits from the latest features, performance improvements, and security patches. It also helps to maintain compatibility with other packages and tools. Each dependency manager has its own built-in tool for checking outdated packages. Let's see the commands for the different dependency managers:

- **npm**: `npm outdated`
- **Yarn**: `yarn outdated`
- **pnpm**: `pnpm outdated`

These commands will scan your project's `package.json` file and identify dependencies with newer versions available in the registry. I have run the `npm outdated` command on an older project and got the result in the following screenshot:

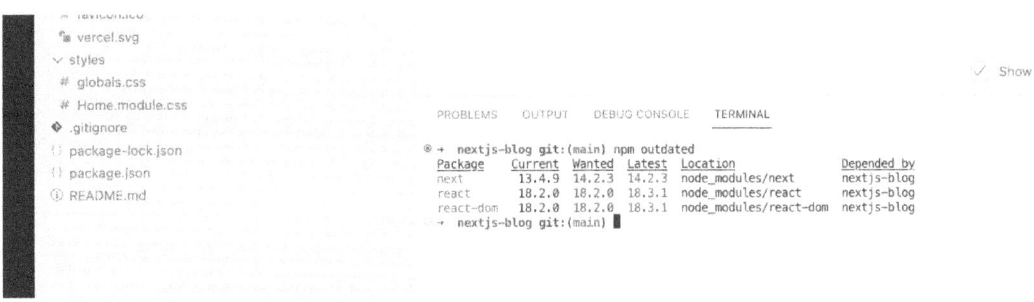


*Figure 4.1 — The result of the npm outdated command*

*Figure 4.1* displays the output of running `npm outdated`. Let's break down the columns:

- **Package**: Lists the project's dependencies, including `react` and `react-dom`
- **Current**: Shows the currently installed version of each package
- **Wanted**: Displays the desired version, which is the newest stable version compatible with the project
- **Latest**: Indicates the newest available version, which may include breaking changes
- **Depended by**: Reveals the libraries or modules within the application that rely on these dependencies

Now that we have learned how to check for outdated packages, let's look at how you update outdated packages in your project.

## Updating dependencies

When working on a project, it's important to manage and update the various libraries and packages (dependencies) your project relies on to benefit from bug fixes, security patches, and new features. However, updates can sometimes introduce changes that affect your code. To manage this, most dependencies follow a versioning system called **Semantic Versioning** (**SemVer**).

This system uses a format of `major.minor.patch` to indicate the significance of changes in a new version. Let's learn a bit more about them:

- **Major**: Introduces breaking changes that might require code modifications in your project
- **Minor**: Adds new features or functionalities while maintaining backward compatibility
- **Patch**: Fixes bugs or security vulnerabilities without introducing breaking changes

It's especially important to be cautious when upgrading to a major version. Major releases often introduce breaking changes, such as altered APIs, deprecated methods, or behavioral differences that can impact existing code. Before upgrading, it's a good practice to review release notes, test changes in a controlled environment, and update dependent code as needed to avoid unexpected issues.

Understanding SemVer is crucial when updating dependencies. It helps you anticipate potential breaking changes caused by major version bumps and plan your update strategy accordingly.

Now let's look at the relevant commands used to update dependencies for the different dependency managers:

- **npm**:
    - `npm update <package-name>`: Updates a specific package to the latest compatible version (based on the SemVer range in `package.json`)
    - `npm update`: Updates all installed dependencies to their latest compatible versions
    - `npm update <package-name>@<version>`: Updates a package to a specific version
- **Yarn**:
    - `yarn upgrade <package-name>`: Updates a specific package to the latest compatible version

    - `yarn upgrade`: Updates all installed dependencies to their latest compatible versions
    - `yarn upgrade <package-name>@<version>`: Updates a package to a specific version
    - `yarn upgrade-interactive`: Updates all packages, prompting you to confirm each upgrade before proceeding (useful for managing potential breaking changes)
- **pnpm**:
    - `pnpm update <package-name>`: Updates a specific package to the latest compatible version
    - `pnpm update`: Updates all installed dependencies to the latest compatible versions
    - `pnpm update <package-name>@<version>`: Updates a package to a specific version
    - `pnpm update --interactive`: Updates all packages, prompting you to confirm each upgrade before proceeding

Now that we understand SemVer and how packages are versioned and have seen how to update packages in our project, let's explore some strategies for safely updating dependencies. Here are some strategies for safely updating dependencies:

- **Backup and version control**:
    - Ensure your project is under version control using a system such as Git.
    - Create backups or snapshots of your project before making any updates.
- **Incremental updates**:
    - Update one dependency at a time.
    - Test thoroughly after each update to identify any issues early.
    - Review changelogs and release notes. Examine the changelogs and release notes of the dependencies you are updating.
    - Understand the changes and their potential impact on your project.
- **Testing**:
    - Run your automated test suite after each update.

This helps catch any regressions or issues introduced by the new version.

After ensuring that your dependencies are safely updated, the next step in maintaining a healthy code base is focusing on code quality and consistency. As your project grows and multiple developers contribute, it's crucial to enforce a uniform coding style and catch potential issues early. In the following section, we'll explore how tools such as ESLint, typescript-eslint, and Prettier can help achieve this by automating linting and formatting in your TypeScript projects.

# Linting and code formatting

Think of a software project as being like constructing a building. As new features and functionality are added, the code base grows. However, just like poorly laid bricks can lead to structural weaknesses, inconsistent formatting, missing best practices, and undetected errors can weaken your code base. Over time, this makes the project harder to read, debug, and maintain, especially in collaborative environments where multiple developers contribute.

To prevent these issues, developers use linting and code formatting tools. Linting acts like a quality inspector, identifying potential errors and enforcing coding standards. Code formatting ensures a consistent style, improving readability and maintainability.

In this section, you will learn how to implement code quality tools to elevate your TypeScript projects. You'll explore why linting and formatting matter, how to configure popular tools such as ESLint, typescript-eslint, and Prettier, and how to automate these processes using Git hooks. By integrating these tools into your workflow, you can write cleaner, more maintainable code and collaborate more efficiently with your team.

## Setting up ESLint

In this section, we'll walk through how to set up ESLint in a TypeScript project. ESLint helps catch errors and enforce consistent code quality. We'll go through three main steps:

### Step 1—Install ESLint and required plugins

Start by installing ESLint along with the necessary TypeScript plugins by running the following command:

```
npm install eslint @typescript-eslint/parser @typescript-eslint/eslint-plugin --
save-dev
```

These packages enable ESLint to understand TypeScript syntax and apply recommended linting rules.

## Step 2—Initialize ESLint configuration

Create an ESLint configuration file by running the following command and answering the prompts:

```
npx eslint -init
```

When you run this command, you'll be prompted to answer a series of questions to configure ESLint based on your project setup. A screenshot of this process is shown in *Figure 4.2*.

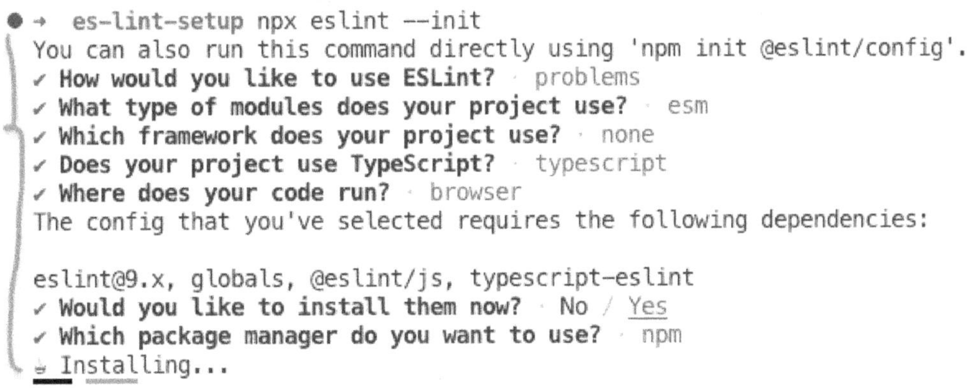


*Figure 4.2 — Showing the prompts for initializing ESLint on our project*

Here's a quick summary of the preceding screenshot.

First, we are asked, **How would you like to use ESLint?** For this question, you can choose between two options: **To check syntax only** or **To check syntax, find problems, and enforce code style.** I have picked the second option to ensure comprehensive code quality checks.

The next question is about modules: **What type of modules does your project use?** I selected **JavaScript modules (import/export)** because I want to use ES6 module syntax for my project.

After that, the next prompt asks about the framework being used by the project (React, Vue, or Angular). I chose **None of these** because this is a bare TypeScript project.

It then asks, **Does your project use TypeScript?** My answer to this question is **Yes.**

The following question is **Where does your code run?** You can choose either **Browser** or **Node** (for server-side code). I selected **Browser**, since this project runs in the browser.

Next, ESLint informs us that it needs to install additional packages based on our selected options. The prompt asks, **Would you like to install them now?** I answered **Yes**.

The final question is about our package manager: **Which package manager do you want to use?** Since I am using npm for my project, I selected **npm**.

The previous command would create an `eslint.config.mjs` file in the root directory of your project. The file holds your ESLint configuration for your project. I have added a screenshot of what the contents look like in *Figure 4.3* and added comments to the code to give more insight into what the different lines of code do:

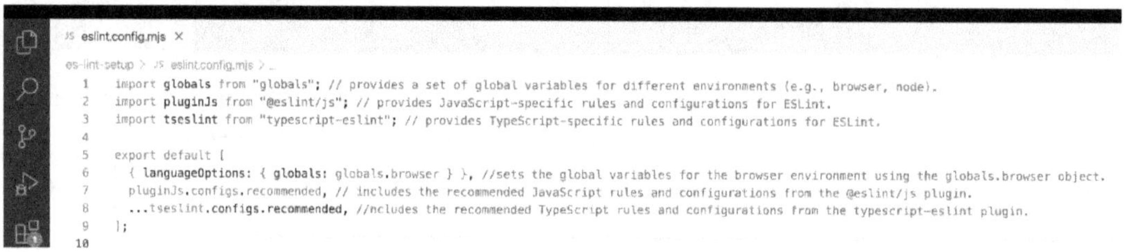


*Figure 4.3 — The generated eslint.config.mjs file*

Now that we have ESLint set up on our project, it's time to put it to the test.

## Step 3—Test ESLint with a sample code file

Now that ESLint is set up, let's test it using a small piece of TypeScript code that contains a common mistake.

Create a file named `index.ts` with the following code:

```
function greet(name: string) {
  console.log("Hello" + naame + "!");
}
```

Please refer to the following screenshot for more details.

*Figure 4.4 — index.js with the faulty greet function code*

To check if ESLint detects the issue, run the following command:

```
npx eslint *.ts
```

This command tells ESLint to lint all `.ts` files in the current directory. If configured properly, you'll see an error message in the console, as shown in the following figure:

```
⊗ → es-lint-setup npx eslint *.ts

  /Users/rukeeojigbo/clean-code-with-typescript/es-lint-setup/index.ts
    1:10  error  'greet' is defined but never used  @typescript-eslint/no-unused-vars
    1:16  error  'name' is defined but never used   @typescript-eslint/no-unused-vars

  ✖ 2 problems (2 errors, 0 warnings)
```

*Figure 4.5 — Errors found by ESLint*

Congratulations! ESLint has successfully caught the error. Your project is now equipped with basic linting.

For more details on rules and checks you can add to your project, you can refer to the documentation: `https://eslint.org/docs/latest/use/getting-started`.

In the next section, we will look at setting up Prettier, a tool that helps us ensure consistency in our code formatting.

# Prettier setup and configuration

Prettier is a popular code formatter tool that helps keep your code clean, readable, and consistent. It automatically formats your code according to a set of rules and preferences, saving you time and effort. Prettier supports a wide range of programming languages, including TypeScript, JavaScript, HTML, CSS, and many others.

In this section, we are going to look at how to set up Prettier on your project:

1. **Install Prettier**: Install Prettier along with the necessary ESLint plugin for compatibility:

   ```
   npm install prettier eslint-plugin-prettier eslint-config-prettier --save-dev
   ```

2. **Create Prettier configuration**: Create a `.prettierrc` file to define your formatting rules:

   ```
   {
     "semi": true,
     "singleQuote": true,
     "trailingComma": "all",
     "printWidth": 80
   }
   ```

3. **Integrate Prettier with ESLint**: Update `eslint.config.mjs` to include Prettier integration:

```
export default defineConfig([
{ files: ["**/*.{js,mjs,cjs,ts,mts,cts}"], plugins: { js }, extends: ["js/
recommended"] },
{ files: ["**/*.{js,mjs,cjs,ts,mts,cts}"], languageOptions: { globals:
globals.browser } },
tseslint.configs.recommended,
prettier.configs.recommended,
]);
```

4. **Format your code**: Run Prettier to format your code:

```
npx prettier --write *.ts
```

If you run this command, your code should be formatted according to the rules we set. For instance, we have specified that the code should use single quotes only; once we run the Prettier command, you will notice that all double quotes become single quotes. The same applies to spacing and other formatting rules.

# Summary

In this chapter, we explored key practices for writing clean, maintainable, and scalable code in TypeScript projects. We began by discussing best practices for structuring folders, emphasizing the importance of organizing projects in a way that promotes ease of navigation and long-term maintenance. We also delved into module systems, highlighting their role in improving code reuse and maintainability. Furthermore, we examined how to manage dependencies effectively, covering package managers, strategies for updating dependencies in large-scale projects, and the use of semantic versioning (semver) to ensure compatibility. To maintain code quality and consistency, we introduced linting and code formatting tools such as ESLint, TSLint, and Prettier. By applying these techniques, you can ensure your TypeScript code base remains efficient and easy to work with as your project grows.

In the next chapter, we will shift our focus to ensuring the quality and reliability of your code by establishing a solid testing strategy, covering essential topics such as unit testing, integration testing, and **test-driven development** (**TDD**).

## Get this book's PDF copy, code bundle, and more

Scan the QR code (or go to `packtpub.com/unlock`), search for this book by name, confirm the edition, and then follow the steps on the page.

UNLOCK NOW

*Note: Have your invoice handy. Purchases made directly from the Packt website don't require an invoice.*

# 5

# Testing and Test-Driven Development

In this chapter, we will focus on building a comprehensive testing strategy for TypeScript projects. Testing plays a vital role in software development, ensuring that your code remains reliable, maintainable, and performs well. By the conclusion of this chapter, you will gain a solid understanding of various testing types and how to implement them effectively in TypeScript. Furthermore, we will explore **Test-Driven Development** (**TDD**), a methodology that emphasizes writing tests before coding, helping to enhance both the design and quality of your applications.

In this chapter, we're going to cover the following main topics:

- Grasping the fundamentals of testing
- Understanding levels of testing in software
- Unit testing in TypeScript
- Integration testing in TypeScript
- Introducing TDD and its benefits

## Technical requirements

To follow along with the examples in this chapter on testing and TDD, you will need **Node.js version 20.0.0** or later and **TypeScript version 5.0** or later installed on your machine. Recent versions of modern testing tools, such as **Vitest**, require **Node.js 20** or newer, and using an older version may result in installation warnings or runtime errors.

You can download the example project and code for this book by following the instructions in the *Download the example code files* section in the *Preface* of this book.

This chapter's code files are included in the downloadable code bundle.

# Grasping the fundamentals of testing

In this section, we will be exploring the fundamentals of testing in software development. You will learn about the importance of testing, the different levels of testing, and their respective objectives. This knowledge will provide a solid foundation for the rest of the chapter, where we will delve into more specific testing strategies in TypeScript.

Software development often involves building complex systems with intricate functionalities. Without proper testing, it's easy for unforeseen problems to slip through the cracks. Testing helps you catch these issues before they reach production, saving time and resources in the long run. Additionally, well-written tests contribute to code maintainability, as they serve as documentation for the intended behavior of your application.

Let's look at a simple example of a function test in TypeScript:

```
function add(a, b) {
  return a + b;
}

console.log('test should run here');
// Test
console.assert(add(2, 3) === 5, 'add(2, 3) should return 5');
```

In this example, we have a basic `add` function that takes two arguments, adds them, and returns the result. The test uses `console.assert` to verify whether the `add` function behaves as expected. In this case, we expect `add(2, 3)` to return `5`. If the condition is `true`, the test passes silently. However, if the condition is `false`, the assertion fails, and an error message will be thrown, alerting us to a potential issue in the function's behavior.

For instance, let's say we modify the test as follows:

```
console.assert(add(2, 3) === 11, 'add(2, 3) should return 11');
```

The `console.assert` statement now checks whether `add(2, 3)` equals `11`, which is intentionally incorrect. When we run this code, it throws an error because the actual result of `add(2, 3)` is `5`, not `11`. The console will display the following message:

```
Assertion failed: add(2, 3) should return 11
```

In this context, the error is significant because it highlights how testing can catch unexpected issues or incorrect assumptions early in the development process. By intentionally creating a failing test, we're able to see how the `console.assert` mechanism works to flag errors. In real-world scenarios, similar tests help ensure that changes to the code don't introduce bugs or regressions. This simple example demonstrates how tests can act as safety nets, alerting developers to potential problems before they affect the end users.

# Understanding levels of testing in software

In this section, we will delve into the various levels of testing in software development. By understanding these levels, you will be able to implement a comprehensive testing strategy that ensures the reliability and performance of your applications.

Software testing is a multi-layered process designed to catch defects at different stages of development. The main levels of testing are as follows:

- Unit testing
- Integration testing
- System testing
- Acceptance testing

Each level addresses specific testing needs and plays a crucial role in ensuring software quality. While all four levels are important, in this chapter, we will focus on unit testing and integration testing. These two are foundational for catching issues early in the development process and ensuring that individual components, as well as their interactions, function correctly.

Let's start with unit testing in the next section.

# Unit testing in TypeScript

**Unit testing** is the first level of testing in software development, where individual components of the software are tested to validate that each unit performs as expected. A **unit** is the smallest piece of code that can be tested in isolation. Depending on the software and architecture, a unit might be a function, a method within a class, a class itself, or even a small module. The key idea is that a unit should be independently testable without relying on external systems or components.

This level of testing ensures that individual components of the software are reliable and function correctly, laying the foundation for higher levels of testing such as integration and system testing.

Some benefits of unit tests include the following:

- Early detection of bugs
- Simplified debugging and maintenance
- Improved code quality and reliability
- Facilitated refactoring and upgrading
- Increased developer confidence

Now that we understand the benefits of unit tests, let's take a moment to look at some common terminologies used in unit testing.

## Common terminology used in unit test/testing

As we delve into unit testing, it's essential to understand key terms that you'll frequently encounter. These terms will help you grasp how unit tests are written, executed, and organized. The following is a guide to the most commonly used unit testing terminologies:

- Test case
- Assertion
- Test suite
- Test fixture
- Mock
- Stub
- Spy

Let's explore these one after the other to get a quick insight into what they are.

### Test case

A **test case** is a scenario where you check (test) a specific unit of your code (such as a function) with a particular set of inputs (variables) to verify whether the code behaves as expected under various conditions.

For example, let's say we have a function that adds two numbers as follows:

```
function add (a: number, b: number): number {
  return a + b;
}
```

Now, we'll create two test cases to verify the behavior of the add function:

```
test('adds 2 + 2 to equal 4', () => {
// ....
```

```
});
test('adds -1 + 1 to equal 0', () => {
  // ....
});
```

Here, we've written two test cases. Basically, we are declaring what we are trying to verify. In the first test case, we are saying we want to verify that when two numbers are added, the function should return 4. In the second one, we are trying to verify that it also works well even with negative numbers: `-1 + 1` should be `0`.

Now, the test case seems more like a declaration of what we want to verify. In the next subheading, we will look at assertion, which does the actual verification.

## Assertion

An **assertion** is a statement used in testing to check whether a particular condition is true. It's like a statement that checks whether the code produces the desired result.

Continuing with the preceding example, let's add some assertions to our test cases:

```
test('adds 2 + 2 to equal 4', () => {
  expect(add(2, 2)).toBe(4); // Assertion
});
test('adds -1 + 1 to equal 0', () => {
  expect(add(-1, 1)).toBe(0); // Assertion
});
```

The `expect` function is used for asserting whether the result matches the expected output.

Now that we understand what a test case is and how to assert that the code does what it's supposed to, let's move to the next section, where we will look at mocks.

## Mock

Imagine your code interacts with a database to retrieve user information or makes an API call. In a unit test, you want to avoid actual interactions with such external systems to ensure that your tests are reliable and repeatable. This is where mocking comes in.

A **mock** object acts as a stand-in for a real object that your code interacts with. It replicates the behavior of the real object in a controlled manner, enabling you to isolate the unit under test and avoid external dependencies that might influence your test results.

Let's examine the following example:

```
async function getUserInfo(userId: string, databaseService: any): Promise<User> {
  const userInfo = await databaseService.getUserById(userId);
  return userInfo;
}
```

In this function, `databaseService` is an external dependency. During unit testing, there are two primary approaches we can take to simulate its behavior.

## Approach 1: manual mocks (dependency injection)

In this pattern, you define a mock object locally and pass it directly into your function as an argument. This is often the cleanest method because it relies on standard JavaScript objects and doesn't require any special manipulation of the module system. Here are the steps to follow:

1. **Import the function you want to test**: Before we can test anything, we must bring the function into our test file from our source code:

   ```
   import { getUserInfo } from '../src/getUserInfo';
   ```

2. **Create a mock object**: Next, we create a plain object that "mimics" our database service. We use `jest.fn()` to create a mock function that returns a successful promise with some sample data:

   ```
   const mockDatabaseService = {
     getUserById: jest.fn().mockResolvedValue({
       id: "123",
       name: "John Doe",
       email: "john@example.com",
     }),
   };
   ```

3. **Pass the mock into the function**: When we call the `getUserInfo` function this time, *we pass the mock object* as the second argument. This effectively "injects" our fake service into the function instead of using a real one:

   ```
   test("fetches user information from the database", async () => {
     const userId = "123";

     // We pass our fake mockDatabaseService directly into the function here
   ```

```
  const userInfo = await getUserInfo(userId, mockDatabaseService);

  // Assertions
  expect(userInfo.name).toBe("John Doe");
  expect(mockDatabaseService.getUserById).toHaveBeenCalledWith(userId);
});
```

Now let's take a look at the other approach.

## Approach 2: mocking imported modules

In many real-world scenarios, your function won't receive a service as an argument; instead, it will *import* that service directly into the file. To test this, you must tell your test runner to intercept that import and replace the real file with a fake version. Here are the steps:

1. **Import the modules and initialize the mock**: First, we import the modules. It is crucial to import the module you intend to mock so you can control it later in the test. Immediately after the imports, we call `jest.mock` to swap the real module for a fake implementation:

```
// Import the actual module being mocked AND the function being tested
// Import the actual module AND the function being tested
import databaseService from '../src/databaseService';
import { getUserInfo } from '../src/getUserInfo';

// Tell Jest to replace the real file with this mock implementation
jest.mock('../src/databaseService', () => ({
  getUserById: jest.fn()
}));
```

2. **Define mock behavior and run the test**: Inside the test block, we define what the mock should return for this specific scenario. Then, we call our function. Notice that we don't pass the service as an argument here—`getUserInfo` will automatically use the mocked version we set up in *step 1*:

```
test("uses a module mock to fetch data", async () => {
  // Define the return value specifically for this test
  (databaseService.getUserById as jest.Mock).mockResolvedValue({
    name: "Jane Doe"
  });

  // Call the function (it imports databaseService internally)
```

```
  const userInfo = await getUserInfo("123");

  expect(userInfo.name).toBe("Jane Doe");
});
```

3. **Verify the interaction**: Finally, because `getUserById` is now a mock function (`jest.fn()`), we can verify that our code actually interacted with the service as expected:

```
// Verify that the internal service was called with the right ID
  expect(databaseService.getUserById).toHaveBeenCalledWith("123");
```

Now that we've covered the basics of mocking and key terminology, let's move on to the next crucial aspect: **test runners**. A test runner is essential for executing and managing your unit tests. In the next section, we'll explore test runners in depth and discuss popular options in the TypeScript ecosystem.

## Test runners

Think of a test runner as the conductor of your testing orchestra. It automates running your entire test suite (collection of test cases) efficiently. Imagine manually executing each test case individually—tedious, right? Test runners streamline this process, providing clear reports on successes and failures, allowing you to focus on writing and refining your tests.

The TypeScript ecosystem offers several robust test runner options. Here are some of the most popular choices:

- **Jest**: This is a favorite choice known for its ease of use, rich features such as snapshot testing and mocking, and extensive out-of-the-box support for TypeScript
- **Mocha**: This is a flexible and lightweight option that provides a great foundation for building custom testing frameworks for complex scenarios
- **Cypress**: Primarily known for end-to-end testing, Cypress can also handle some unit testing scenarios in TypeScript applications with a UI component
- **Vitest**: Gaining popularity for its integration with the Vite build tool. Vitest offers a fast and efficient testing experience, leveraging modern JavaScript features and providing seamless compatibility with TypeScript

Since we have an overview of the common test runners, let's see how you might choose which one to use for your project:

## Choosing the right test runner

The best test runner for your project depends on your preferences, project size, and team familiarity. To make a choice, consider factors such as the following:

- **Ease of use**: How quickly can you get started and write tests?
- **Features offered**: Does it have functionalities such as snapshot testing, mocking, or code coverage?
- **Community support**: Is there a large and active community for help and resources?
- **Complexity of your testing needs**: Do you require a basic test runner or a more customizable option for intricate testing scenarios?

Vite and Vitest specifically offer an advantage for projects already using Vite for building. Their integration ensures a streamlined development workflow with fast test execution and seamless TypeScript support.

In the next subsection, we are going to walk, step by step, through how you would set up Vitest in a sample Node.js TypeScript project.

## Setting up Vitest in a Node.js TypeScript project

In this section, we'll guide you through the step-by-step process of setting up Vitest in a sample Node.js TypeScript project. You'll learn how to install the necessary dependencies, configure TypeScript, and write your first unit tests using Vitest to ensure that your project is ready for efficient testing. Let's get started:

1. **Initialize your project**: First, create a new Node.js project if you don't have one already:

   ```
   mkdir vitest-demo
   cd vitest-demo
   npm init -y
   ```

2. **Install TypeScript and Vitest**: Next, install TypeScript, Vitest, and the necessary types for Node.js:

   ```
   npm install typescript vitest ts-node @types/node --save-dev
   ```

   The command installs several packages essential for our project. First, we install TypeScript since we're building a TypeScript project and need it for compiling and type-checking our code. The `Vitest` package is our test runner, responsible for handling and executing tests. `ts-node` is included so `Vitest` can run TypeScript files directly, eliminating the need to manually compile them to JavaScript. Lastly, `@types/node` provides the necessary TypeScript definitions for Node.js, ensuring proper type support for Node's built-in modules.

3. **Configure TypeScript**: Initialize a basic TypeScript configuration by running the following command:

```
npx tsc -init
```

This command generates a `tsconfig.json` file. For a simple setup, you may not need to change much, but make sure the `tsconfig.json` includes at least the following settings:

```
{
  "compilerOptions": {
    "target": "ESNext",
    "module": "CommonJS",
    "strict": true,
    "esModuleInterop": true,
    "skipLibCheck": true,
    "forceConsistentCasingInFileNames": true,
    "types": ["node", "vitest/globals"]
  }
}
```

The key part here is `"types": ["node", "vitest/globals"]`, which ensures that Vitest's type definitions are recognized globally in your project.

4. **Create Vitest configuration**: To make sure Vitest works with TypeScript and your Node.js environment, create a `vitest.config.ts` file in the root of your project:

```
// vitest.config.ts
import { defineConfig } from 'vitest/config';

export default defineConfig({
  test: {
    globals: true,
    environment: 'node', // Running tests in a Node.js environment
  },
});
```

This configuration allows Vitest to use global functions such as `test` and `expect` without needing to import them manually in each test file. By using `ts-node`, Vitest can run TypeScript files directly, so you don't need to compile them to JavaScript first. The configuration also specifies that the tests will run in a Node.js environment, which is especially useful for server-side or utility functions. If you're testing browser-based code, such as DOM manipulation, UI behavior, or frontend utilities (e.g., with React or Vue), you can switch the environment to `jsdom` instead. Vitest supports multiple environments, so choosing the right one ensures that your tests run in a context that matches your code's runtime.

Please note, you also need to add the following to `package.json`:

```
"type": "module"
```

This tells Node.js to treat `.js` and `.ts` files as **ECMAScript Modules** (**ESM**) by default, allowing us to use `import { defineConfig } from 'vitest/config'` without errors.

5. **Write a unit test**: Now, let's write a simple test for a TypeScript function. Suppose you have a module called `square.ts`:

```
// square.ts
export function square(n: number): number {
  return n * n;
}
```

Create a test file called `square.test.ts`:

```
// square.test.ts
import { square } from './square.js';

test('calculates the square of 3 correctly', () => {
  expect(square(3)).toBe(9);
});

test('calculates the square of -4 correctly', () => {
  expect(square(-4)).toBe(16);});
```

In this file, we start by importing the `square` function from the module we want to test. Then, we use Vitest's `test` function to define two separate test cases. Finally, the `expect` function is used to verify that the `square` function produces the correct output based on the input values provided in each test case.

> **Note**
>
> You will notice we use the `.js` extension in the following code (from `'./square.js'`). This is a requirement for modern Node.js projects to ensure the runtime can find the file correctly. If you were using a frontend **bundler** (such as Vite or Webpack), these extensions are usually handled for you, but in a standard Node.js environment, being explicit is the safest approach.

6. **Add a test script to package.json**: Now, let's add a script to `package.json` to run Vitest:

```
{
  "scripts": {
  }
}
```

7. **Run the tests**: Finally, run your tests by executing the following command:

```
npm run test
```

> **Note**
>
> Vitest requires a modern version of Node.js. If you see an error such as `SyntaxError: Unexpected token '='`, ensure that you are running Node.js 20 or later. Older Node.js versions do not support some of the JavaScript features used internally by Vitest.

You should see output similar to the following figure.

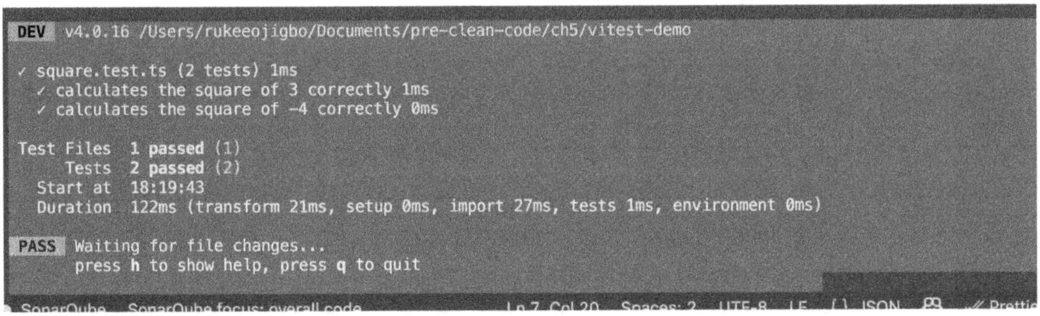


*Figure 5.1 — Successful execution of unit tests using the Vitest runner*

To better understand how to write and test a TypeScript function, let's consider a simple example. Here, we define a function called `square` that calculates the square of a given number:

```
export function square(n: number): number {
  return n * n;
}
```

The following code block shows what a unit test for the preceding function looks like:

```
// square.test.ts
import { square } from './square.js';

test('calculates the square of 3 correctly', () => {
  expect(square(3)).toBe(9);
});

test('calculates the square of -4 correctly', () => {
  expect(square(-4)).toBe(16);
});

import { square } from './square';
```

Next, we will write our first test case:

```
test('calculates the square of 3 correctly', () => {
  expect(square(3)).toBe(9);
});
```

Let's explain what we just did:

- `test`: This is a function that runs a test case. It takes two arguments: a string that describes what the test is checking, and a function that contains the test logic.
- `'calculates the square of 3 correctly'`: This is the string argument that describes what the test is checking. It's a brief description of what the test is verifying.
- `() => { ... }`: This is the function argument that contains the test logic. It's an arrow function that takes no arguments.
- `expect(square(3))`: This line calls the `square` function with the `3` argument, and then passes the result to the `expect` function. The `expect` function is a way of saying *I expect this value to be something*.
- `toBe(9)`: This line is a matcher that says *I expect the value to be equal to 9*. It's a way of specifying what you expect the result to be.

So, when you put it all together, this test is saying *I expect the square of 3 to be equal to 9*. If the `square` function correctly calculates the square of `3`, then this test will pass. If the function returns something other than `9`, then this test will fail.

Finally, we'll write our second test case:

```
test('calculates the square of -4 correctly', () => {
  expect(square(-4)).toBe(16);
});
```

Just like the previous test, this test uses the `test` function to run a test case, but this time, it passes `-4` as the input to the `square` function and expects the result to be `16`.

Now that we've understood what a unit test would look like, let's find out what the overall purpose of the test file is.

These unit tests, specifically the ones demonstrated earlier—(`test('calculates the square of 3 correctly', ...)` and `test('calculates the square of -4 correctly', ...)`)—ensure that the `square` function works correctly for both positive and negative numbers. By testing with values such as `3` and `-4`, these test cases verify that the function accurately calculates the square of any given number.

If the function passes these tests, it confirms that the implementation is correct for these specific scenarios. Conversely, if any test fails, it highlights a potential bug in the `square` function that requires further investigation.

Now that we have an overview of what a unit test is, let's move on to integration testing in the next section.

# Integration testing in TypeScript

Integration testing is a crucial aspect of the software development life cycle. In TypeScript-based applications, it plays a complementary role alongside static type checking. While TypeScript helps detect type-related errors at compile time, integration testing ensures that independently correct components interact correctly at runtime.

This section provides a comprehensive guide to integration testing in the context of TypeScript applications, covering its fundamentals, importance, common approaches, and practical implementation using popular testing tools.

## What is integration testing?

**Integration testing** is a type of testing where individual units of an application are combined and tested as a group. The main purpose of this testing is to expose faults in the interaction between integrated units. In the context of software development, a unit could be a function, a module, or a class.

When we write our code in **TypeScript**, a statically typed superset of JavaScript, we add a robust type-checking layer to our code base. This helps catch errors at compile time, making our code more predictable and easier to debug. However, type checking is not enough to ensure the correctness of our code. This is where integration testing comes into play. It helps us ensure that different units of our application work together as expected.

## Why integration testing?

Integration testing is essential for several reasons. First, it helps identify interface issues between modules. While unit tests ensure that individual components work in isolation, integration tests make sure that these components work together as expected.

For example, consider an e-commerce application. A unit test might check whether the `Add to Cart` function works correctly (i.e., it adds an item to the cart). An integration test, on the other hand, would check whether the `Add to Cart` function works correctly in conjunction with the inventory management system, ensuring that it adds an item to the cart and simultaneously updates the inventory. This highlights the need to verify how modules interact in real-world scenarios.

Additionally, integration testing verifies data flow across different components, ensuring that the output of one module is correctly passed as input to another. This is especially crucial in complex systems where data dependencies exist between modules.

Integration tests also help catch issues related to external systems or services. In many modern applications, components interact with databases, APIs, or third-party services. Integration testing ensures that these interactions function correctly under real-world conditions.

Finally, integration testing helps uncover unexpected behavior that may arise when multiple components are combined, providing a more realistic assessment of the application's functionality in its intended environment.

Now that we've learned about what integration testing is and why we need it, let's look into the types of integration testing.

# Types of integration testing

Integration testing can be performed using different approaches. The two main types are the big bang approach and the incremental approach.

Let's take a closer look at them.

## Big bang approach

The **big bang approach** involves integrating all the modules of an application at once and then conducting the tests. This approach is straightforward and doesn't require any particular order of integration for the modules.

Here are its advantages:

- It is simple to implement as there's no need for stubs or drivers (temporary modules for testing)
- It is suitable for small systems where the modules are heavily interdependent

Here are its disadvantages:

- If an issue arises, it's challenging to identify the module causing the problem due to the high degree of interconnectivity
- It requires all modules to be ready before testing can begin, which can delay the testing process

We've just learned about the big bang approach, including its advantages and disadvantages. Next, we'll explore the incremental approach to integration testing and how it differs.

## Incremental approach

The **incremental approach** involves integrating and testing two modules at a time. After testing, another module is integrated, and the testing process repeats. This approach can be further divided into three types: top-down, bottom-up, and sandwich/hybrid.

Let's delve in; we will start with the top-down approach.

## Top-down approach

In the **top-down approach**, testing starts from the top of the module hierarchy (the "parents") and moves toward the bottom (the "children"). Because the lower-level modules might not be developed yet, we use stubs to simulate their behavior. A **stub** is a temporary, simplified implementation of a module that stands in for the real one. For instance, if you are testing a high-level `Checkout` module that depends on a "tax calculator" that hasn't been built, you would use a stub that simply returns a fixed value, such as `10.00`, every time. This allows you to verify that the `Checkout` module correctly receives and displays data without needing the actual calculation logic to exist.

Here is a quick example of a stub in code:

```
// The 'TaxCalculator' isn't built yet, so we create this Stub
const taxServiceStub = {
  calculateTax: (amount: number) => {
    return 10.00; // A "canned" response regardless of the input
  }
};

// We can now test the Checkout Logic even without the real Tax engine
const total = checkout(100.00, taxServiceStub);
console.log(total); // Should be 110.00
```

Advantages of the top-down approach are as follows:

- Early discovery of high-level design issues
- Allows for early user feedback as the main functions are tested first

Here is the disadvantage:

- Requires many stubs, which can be complex to create

## Bottom-up approach

The **bottom-up approach** is the opposite of the top-down approach. Testing starts from the bottom of the module hierarchy and moves upward toward higher-level modules. Because the higher-level modules may not yet be implemented, drivers are used to simulate their behavior.

A **driver** is a temporary test module that invokes lower-level components and supplies test data to them, acting as a substitute for the real higher-level module. For example, if a database access module is ready but the service or controller that normally calls it has not yet been implemented, a driver can be written to directly call the database functions and verify their behavior.

Here is an example of a driver in code:

```
// The real Database module we want to test
import { saveToDatabase } from './dbModule.js';

// The Driver: A temporary script to "drive" data into the module
const testDriver = async () => {
  console.log("Driver starting: Testing Database Save...");
  const result = await saveToDatabase({ id: 1, title: 'Test' });

  if (result.success) {
    console.log("Success: The bottom-level module works!");
  }
};

testDriver();
```

Advantages of the bottom-up approach are as follows:

- Allows for easy fault isolation
- No need for stubs

Here are its disadvantages:

- The need for drivers can complicate the testing process
- High-level logic and data flow issues may arise late in the process

## Sandwich/hybrid approach

The **sandwich** or **hybrid approach** is a combination of the top-down and bottom-up approaches. It aims to leverage the advantages of both methods while minimizing their disadvantages.

Here are its advantages:

- Comprehensive as it tests from both the top and bottom of the module hierarchy
- Reduces the need for stubs and drivers

Here is its disadvantage:

- Can be complex to manage as it requires careful planning and coordination

Now that we know what the types of integration testing are, let's explore how to perform one. You can perform the test manually or automate it. In the next section, we will consider these two options.

# Manual integration testing versus automated integration testing

Integration testing can be performed manually or through automation, and each comes with its own set of advantages and disadvantages. This section explores the differences between manual and automated integration testing, providing insights into when and how to use each approach effectively.

## Manual integration testing

Manual integration testing involves human testers executing test cases without the assistance of automation tools. Testers manually follow the steps defined in the test cases and record the outcomes. This approach can be labor-intensive and prone to human error, but it also offers certain benefits.

Here are its advantages:

- **Flexibility**:
    - Testers can quickly adapt to new or changing requirements without needing to update automated scripts.
    - It is easier to explore edge cases or unexpected behaviors that automated tests might not cover.
- **Exploratory testing**: Testers can use their intuition and experience to explore the application in ways that are not predefined. This helps in identifying issues that might not be captured in automated tests.
- **Usability testing**:
    - Manual testing allows testers to assess the application's user interface and overall user experience.
    - Human feedback is essential for evaluating visual and interactive elements.

Here are its disadvantages:

- **Time-consuming**:
    - Manual testing is slower compared to automated testing, especially for large and complex applications
    - Repetitive test cases are tedious and time-consuming to execute manually

- **Inconsistent**:
    - Manual testing is subject to human error and inconsistencies
    - Different testers might execute the same test case differently, leading to varied results
- **Scalability**:
    - Scaling manual tests to cover extensive test suites and multiple integrations can be challenging
    - It requires significant human resources, which may not be feasible for continuous integration and deployment

So, when should you use manual integration testing? Here's when:

- **Early stages of development**: When the application is rapidly changing, and automation scripts would require frequent updates
- **Exploratory testing**: For uncovering unexpected issues and gaining insights into the application's behavior
- **Usability testing**: To evaluate the user interface and user experience aspects of the application

While manual integration testing provides flexibility and valuable insights during early development stages, it also has limitations in terms of scalability, consistency, and efficiency. As applications grow more complex and demand frequent updates, manual testing may become time-consuming and error-prone.

To address these challenges, automated integration testing can be employed to enhance speed, accuracy, and scalability. By automating repetitive test cases, testers can focus on more critical areas, and teams can ensure continuous feedback throughout the development cycle.

## Automated integration testing

Automated integration testing involves using automated tools and scripts to execute test cases. This approach helps to run tests more efficiently and consistently, providing quick feedback on the integration points of the application.

Here are its advantages:

- **Speed and efficiency**:
    - Automated tests can be executed much faster than manual tests, making them ideal for **continuous integration/continuous deployment** (**CI/CD**) pipelines
    - Automated testing allows for running a large number of test cases in a short period of time

- **Consistency and accuracy**:
    - Automated tests are executed in the same manner every time, eliminating human error and ensuring consistent results
    - Precise comparisons of expected and actual outcomes are possible
- **Reusability**:
    - Automated test scripts can be reused across different versions of the application, reducing the need for repetitive manual testing
    - Scripts can be easily modified to adapt to changes in the application
- **Scalability**:
    - Automated testing scales well, allowing for extensive test coverage without a proportional increase in resources
    - It is suitable for regression testing, where the same tests need to be run frequently

Here are its disadvantages

- **Initial setup cost**:
    - Writing and setting up automated tests requires significant initial investment in terms of time and resources
    - Skilled developers or testers are needed to write and maintain test scripts
- **Maintenance overhead**:
    - Automated tests need regular maintenance to stay in sync with the application's evolving code base
    - Outdated tests can lead to false positives or false negatives, reducing the reliability of test results
- **Limited exploratory testing**:
    - Automated tests are only as good as the scripts written; they can't explore beyond predefined scenarios
    - It may miss out on unexpected behaviors that a human tester might catch

Now, when should you employ automated integration testing? Let's find out.

Here are some scenarios in which integration testing shines:

- **Regression testing**: Regression testing is the process of rerunning previously completed tests to ensure that recent changes or additions to the code have not negatively affected the existing functionality of the system. It is typically used when new features, bug fixes, or updates are introduced to a system to verify that these modifications do not introduce new issues or regressions. Automated integration testing is indispensable in regression testing as it allows for frequent and systematic execution of test cases, ensuring that any new modifications do not disrupt or degrade the system's existing functionality.
- **CI/CD**: In a CI/CD environment, automated integration testing plays a pivotal role. It provides swift and dependable feedback on code integrations and deployments, thereby enhancing the efficiency of the development process and reducing the risk of deployment failures.
- **Large-scale and complex applications**: For applications that are extensive and intricate, manual testing can become impractical due to the sheer volume of test cases. In such scenarios, automated integration testing becomes a necessity, enabling comprehensive coverage and efficient validation of the system's integrated components.

Remember, the choice between manual and automated testing is not binary, but rather depends on the specific requirements and context of your project.

## Practical example of integration testing

In this example, we will build a simple blog application with full **CRUD** (which stands for **Create, Read, Update, Delete**) functionality and implement integration testing using **Vitest** and **Supertest**. This walkthrough covers every step, from project initialization to running the final test suite:

1. **Initialize the project**: First, create a directory for your project and initialize it:

```
mkdir blog-app
cd blog-app
npm init -y
```

   The `npm init -y` command generates a `package.json` file. Because we are using modern Node.js and Vitest, you must add `"type": "module"` to this file.

   Why `"type": "module"`? This setting tells Node.js to treat your files as ESM. Without this, you won't be able to use modern `import` and `export` statements in your `.ts` files.

2. **Install dependencies**: Next, install the production and development dependencies:

```
npm install express
npm install --save-dev typescript @types/node @types/express vitest
supertest @types/supertest
```

We install **Express** as our web framework. For development, we include TypeScript, Vitest (our test runner), and Supertest, which allow us to simulate HTTP requests against our API without needing to start a live server.

3. **Configure TypeScript**: Create a `tsconfig.json` file in the root directory. To support modern ESM rules and ensure compatibility with Node.js 20 and later, use the following configuration:

```
{
"compilerOptions": {
"target": "ESNext",
"module": "NodeNext",
"moduleResolution": "NodeNext",
"strict": true,
"esModuleInterop": true,
"skipLibCheck": true,
"outDir": "./dist",
"verbatimModuleSyntax": true
},
"include": ["src/**/*", "tests/**/*"]
}
```

4. **Create the project structure**: Organize your source code into logical layers to separate concerns:

```
mkdir src src/models src/services src/controllers src/routes tests
```

5. **Create the model**: The model defines our data structure. Create `src/models/post.ts`:

```
export interface Post {
  id: number;
  title: string;
  content: string;
}
```

```
export let posts: Post[] = [];
let currentId = 1;

// A helper to handle ID generation internally
export const getNextId = () => currentId++;
```

Let's look at what this code does:

- **The** `Post` **interface**: Defines exactly what a blog post looks like (`id`, `title`, and `content`)
- **The** `posts` **array**: Acts as our temporary database stored in the server memory
- `getNextId()`: A helper function that returns the current ID and increments it for the next post

6. **Create the service layer**: The service layer handles the business logic. Create `src/services/postService.ts`:

```
// Important: We use the .js extension for the relative import
import { type Post, posts, getNextId } from '../models/post.js';

export const getPosts = (): Post[] => posts;

export const getPostById = (id: number) => posts.find(p => p.id === id);

export const createPost = (title: string, content: string): Post => {
  const newPost = { id: getNextId(), title, content };
  posts.push(newPost);
  return newPost;
};

export const updatePost = (id: number, title: string, content: string) =>
{
  const post = getPostById(id);
  if (post) {
    post.title = title;
    post.content = content;
    return post;
  }
  return null;
};
```

```
export const deletePost = (id: number) => {
  const index = posts.findIndex(p => p.id === id);
  if (index !== -1) posts.splice(index, 1);
};
```

Let's go over the code to get a better understanding of what we just did:

- `getPosts()`: Simply returns the entire array of blog posts currently stored in our in-memory database.
- `getPostById(id)`: Uses the array `find` method to retrieve a specific post by its unique ID.
- `createPost(title, content)`: Generates a new ID using our `getNextId` helper, creates a `Post` object, and adds it to our `posts` array. Notice that we return the newly created post so the controller can send it back to the user.
- `updatePost(id, title, content)`: First, locates the existing post. If found, it updates the `title` and `content` properties directly within the array and returns the updated object.
- `deletePost(id)`: Finds the index of the post based on the ID and uses splice to remove exactly one element from that position in the array.

By separating this logic into a service layer, we ensure that our application follows the **Don't Repeat Yourself** (**DRY**). The controllers don't need to know how the data is stored or deleted; they simply tell the service what to do.

7. **Implementing the controller**: The controller handles the HTTP request/response cycle. Create `src/controllers/postController.ts`:

```
import type { Request, Response } from 'express';
import { getPosts, getPostById, createPost, updatePost, deletePost } from
'../services/postService.js';

export const getAllPosts = (req: Request, res: Response) => {
  res.json(getPosts());
};

export const getPost = (req: Request, res: Response) => {
  const post = getPostById(Number(req.params.id));
  post ? res.json(post) : res.status(404).send('Post not found');
};
```

```
export const createNewPost = (req: Request, res: Response) => {
  const { title, content } = req.body;
  res.status(201).json(createPost(title, content));
};

export const updateExistingPost = (req: Request, res: Response) => {
  const post = updatePost(Number(req.params.id), req.body.title,
req.body.content);
  post ? res.json(post) : res.status(404).send('Post not found');
};

export const deleteExistingPost = (req: Request, res: Response) => {
  deletePost(Number(req.params.id));
  res.status(204).send();
};
```

8. **Setting up routes**: Define your API endpoints in `src/routes/postRoutes.ts`:

```
import { Router } from 'express';
import { getAllPosts, getPost, createNewPost, updateExistingPost,
deleteExistingPost } from '../controllers/postController.js';

const router = Router();
router.get('/posts', getAllPosts);
router.get('/posts/:id', getPost);
router.post('/posts', createNewPost);
router.put('/posts/:id', updateExistingPost);
router.delete('/posts/:id', deleteExistingPost);

export default router;
```

In this code, we set up the routes for the blog API using the Express router. Each route is mapped to a specific controller function. The `GET /posts` route calls `getAllPosts` to retrieve all posts, while `GET /posts/:id` calls `getPost` to retrieve a post by its ID. The `POST /posts` route handles creating a new post by calling `createNewPost`. The `PUT /posts/:id` route updates an existing post with `updateExistingPost`, and the `DELETE /posts/:id` route deletes a post by calling `deleteExistingPost`. Finally, the router is exported for integration into the main application.

Finally, set up the main entry point and initialize the Express app in `src/index.ts`:

1. **Initialize the Express application**: Import express from `'express'`:

```
import postRoutes from './routes/postRoutes.js';

const app = express();

// Middleware to parse JSON request bodies
app.use(express.json());

// Connect our blog routes to the application
app.use(postRoutes);

export default app;
```

   Let's go over the code to see what it does:

   - `express()`: This initializes the Express application instance.
   - `app.use(express.json())`: This is a built-in middleware function. It tells Express to automatically parse incoming requests with JSON payloads, making the data available in `req.body`.
   - `app.use(postRoutes)`: This plugs our defined API endpoints (`GET`, `POST`, etc.) into the main application.
   - `export default app`: Instead of starting the server with `app.listen()`, we export the app instance. This is a critical step for integration testing, as it allows Supertest to start and stop the application automatically during our test runs without occupying a real network port.

   Now, with our application in place, let's add our integration test:

2. **Add the integration test**: Now, we create a single test file to ensure that all these layers work together. Create `tests/app.test.ts`.
3. **Initialize the test file and create a post**: First, we import our testing tools and the application instance. We start by testing the creation of a new blog post using the `POST /posts` endpoint. The following are the different test cases we'll use to verify each part of the blog API:

```
import { describe, it, expect } from 'vitest';
import request from 'supertest';
```

```
import app from '../src/index.js';

describe('Blog Post API Integration', () => {
  let postId: number;

  it('should create and then retrieve a blog post', async () => {
    const createRes = await request(app)
      .post('/posts')
      .send({ title: 'My Post', content: 'Integration Testing' });

    expect(createRes.statusCode).toBe(201);
    postId = createRes.body.id;
// ... The GET request verification will be added here

  })

// ... Additional test cases for Update and Delete will follow
})
```

In this block, we send a `POST` request with a title and content. The test ensures that the post is successfully created with a `201` status code. We then capture `postId` returned by the server so we can use it in subsequent tests.

4. **Retrieve the created post**: Within the same test case, we immediately verify that the post we just created can be retrieved using the `GET /posts/:id` endpoint:

```
const getRes = await request(app).get(`/posts/${postId}`);
expect(getRes.statusCode).toBe(200);
expect(getRes.body.title).toBe('My Post');
```

Here, we retrieve the post by `postId` we saved earlier. We check that the response returns a `200 OK` status code and that the title matches what we originally sent, confirming that the data successfully traveled from the controller to the service layer and back.

5. **Update an existing post**: Next, we test the `PUT /posts/:id` endpoint to verify that we can modify an existing post's data:

```
it('should update and delete the post', async () => {
    const updateRes = await request(app)
      .put(`/posts/${postId}`)
```

```
        .send({ title: 'Updated', content: 'Updated content' });

      expect(updateRes.statusCode).toBe(200);
      expect(updateRes.body.title).toBe('Updated');
  expect(res.body.content).toBe('This content has been modified.');
    });
```

This test sends a `PUT` request to update the title and content. We verify that the status code is `200` and that the response body reflects the new `Updated` title, ensuring that our service layer's update logic is working correctly.

6. **Delete the post and verify its removal**: Finally, we test the `DELETE /posts/:id` endpoint to ensure that posts can be removed, and we verify that a deleted post can no longer be retrieved:

```
  it('should delete a blog post and verify it is gone', async () => {
      // 1. Send the DELETE request
      const deleteRes = await request(app).delete(`/posts/${postId}`);
      expect(deleteRes.statusCode).toBe(204); // 204 signifies "No
  Content" (Success)

      // 2. Attempt to GET the deleted post to confirm it no longer exists
      const getRes = await request(app).get(`/posts/${postId}`);

      // The API should now return a 404 Not Found
      expect(getRes.statusCode).toBe(404);
    });
```

In this final step, we call the `DELETE` endpoint and check for a `204 No Content` status code, which signifies a successful deletion. To be absolutely sure the integration is complete, we attempt to get that same post again. We expect a `404 Not Found` status, confirming that the post has been successfully removed from our in-memory database.

Now that we've covered integration testing, let's move on to TDD. TDD is a method where you write tests before writing the actual code. This helps create clean, maintainable, and well-tested software. Let's explore the main ideas and best practices of TDD.

# Introducing TDD and its benefits

In this section, we'll dive into TDD, a development technique that reverses the typical coding process. Instead of writing code first and then creating tests afterward (as we did earlier), TDD focuses on writing the tests before the actual code. This approach helps shape the development process and ensures that functionality is tested from the very beginning. Let's explore some key aspects of TDD.

TDD involves a three-step cycle: *Red*, *Green*, and *Refactor*. Let's delve into these steps in more detail:

1. **Red**: The first step involves writing the test. You think of the expectations for the code or feature you are working on, and you write the test case for it. Think of this as your expectation of what the code should do. At this point, you run your test, and it should fail because there isn't any code yet.
2. **Green**: Once you've completed the first step, the next step involves writing just enough code to pass the test.
3. **Refactor**: Once your test passes, you can improve the code without making the test fail.

In summary, TDD is more of a philosophy that states that tests should drive your coding process. It improves how you think about the features you are working on and the code you are writing. Now, let's look at some best practices for TDD and for writing tests in general.

## Best practices for TDD in TypeScript

Implementing TDD effectively requires adhering to best practices that ensure your tests are clear, maintainable, and reliable. In this section, we'll explore key practices such as writing effective test names and descriptions, keeping tests simple and focused, and using mocking and stubbing techniques. Let's begin:

- **Writing effective test names and descriptions**: Test names should be descriptive and clearly state what functionality is being tested. A well-named test allows others to understand the purpose of the test without needing to dig into the code. For example, if you're testing a function that adds two numbers, a good test name might describe the expected behavior, such as "correctly adds two numbers."
  Here is an example of how to write a descriptive test for a simple addition function:

```
describe('Calculator', () => {
    it('correctly adds two numbers', () => {
        const result = Calculator.add(2, 3);
        expect(result).toBe(5);
```

```
    });
});
```

The code begins with a `describe` block, which groups related tests under the label `Calculator`, representing the feature being tested. Inside, the `it` block defines a specific test case with the name `correctly adds two numbers`, clearly stating the expected outcome. The test calls the `Calculator.add()` function with the arguments of `2` and `3`, and the `expect(result).toBe(5)` statement verifies that the result returned by the `add` function equals `5`. If the result matches, the test passes; otherwise, it fails. This structure ensures that the test case is both descriptive and easy to understand.

- **Keeping tests simple and focused**: Each test should focus on a single functionality. This makes it easier to identify which specific functionality is broken when a test fails. For instance, if you have a function that both adds and subtracts numbers, you should have separate tests for addition and subtraction.
  The following is an example of a test suite for a `Calculator` object using a testing framework such as Jest. This suite contains two individual tests—one for the addition functionality and another for the subtraction functionality:

```
describe('Calculator', () => {
    it('correctly adds two numbers', () => {
        const result = Calculator.add(2, 3);
        expect(result).toBe(5);
    });

    it('correctly subtracts two numbers', () => {
        const result = Calculator.subtract(5, 2);
        expect(result).toBe(3);
    });
});
```

The code defines a test suite for the `Calculator` object, grouping related tests under the label `'Calculator'` using the `describe` function. Within this suite, the `it` function specifies individual test cases, such as checking the addition functionality with `Calculator.add(2, 3)`, which stores the result in a variable. The `expect(result).toBe(5)` assertion verifies that the addition result equals `5`, indicating a passing test if `true`. Similarly, another test case checks the subtraction functionality using `Calculator.subtract(5, 2)`, with the result being verified by the `expect(result).toBe(3)` assertion. Overall, this structure allows for organized testing of specific functionalities in the `Calculator` implementation.

- **Using mocking and stubbing techniques**: Mocking and stubbing are techniques that allow you to simulate functionality. This is useful when the functionality you're testing depends on other functions or external systems. For example, if you're testing a function that fetches data from an API, you can use a mock to simulate the API response:

```
import axios from 'axios';
jest.mock('axios');

describe('ApiService', () => {
    it('fetches data from the API', async () => {
        const data = { data: { results: [1, 2, 3] } };
        axios.get.mockResolvedValue(data);

        const result = await ApiService.fetchData();
        expect(result).toEqual(data.data.results);
    });
});
```

In this code, `axios` is imported, and then `jest.mock('axios')` is used to mock the `axios` library. This means that instead of making a real API call, we simulate the behavior of the `axios.get` function. In the test, the `axios.get.mockResolvedValue(data)` method is used to simulate a successful API call that resolves with predefined data, (`{ results: [1, 2, 3] }`). The `ApiService.fetchData` function is then called, and the test verifies that it correctly returns the expected results, (`data.data.results`). This approach ensures that the test doesn't depend on external systems such as APIs, making it faster and more reliable.

- **Using the AAA pattern**: The **Arrange-Act-Assert** (**AAA**) pattern helps structure your tests in a clear and logical way, making them more readable and maintainable. The *Arrange* step sets up any necessary preconditions, the *Act* step executes the functionality you're testing, and the *Assert* step verifies that the functionality behaved as expected. Here is an example of using this pattern in a test for a `Calculator` object:

```
describe('Calculator', () => {
    it('correctly adds two numbers', () => {
        // Arrange
        const num1 = 2;
        const num2 = 3;

        // Act
        const result = Calculator.add(num1, num2);

        // Assert
        expect(result).toBe(5);
    });
});
```

  In the preceding code, the test is structured following the AAA pattern. In the *Arrange* step, the `num1` and `num2` variables are initialized with values of `2` and `3`, respectively. These values represent the input for the test. In the *Act* step, the `Calculator.add(num1, num2)` function is called, which adds the two numbers. The result of this operation is stored in the `result` variable. Finally, in the *Assert* step, the `expect(result).toBe(5)` statement checks whether the result of the addition is `5`. If the result is correct, the test passes; otherwise, it fails. This pattern keeps the test well-organized, making it easy to follow the flow of setup, execution, and validation.

- **Avoiding test interdependence**: Each test should be independent and not rely on the state set by previous tests. This ensures that tests can be run in any order and that they're not affected by side effects from other tests.
- **Testing edge cases**: Don't just test the *happy path*. Make sure to write tests for edge cases, such as invalid inputs, empty states, and extreme values. This helps ensure your code is robust and can handle unexpected situations gracefully.
- **Keeping your tests DRY**: Just like in your production code, avoid duplicating code in your tests. If you find yourself writing the same setup or assertion code in multiple tests, consider using helper functions or `before`/`after` hooks.

By following these best practices—writing clear and descriptive test names, keeping tests simple and focused, using mocking and stubbing techniques, structuring tests with the AAA pattern, avoiding test interdependence, testing edge cases, and keeping your tests DRY—you can ensure that your test-driven development process in TypeScript is both efficient and effective. These strategies will help maintain clean, reliable, and easy-to-maintain code as your project grows.

# Summary

In this chapter, we covered essential aspects of building and testing a TypeScript application. We started by setting up a TypeScript project, configuring necessary dependencies such as Jest and Supertest, and ensuring smooth integration of TypeScript and Jest for development and testing.

We then focused on writing integration tests using Jest and Supertest. To illustrate these concepts, we used an example involving an Express application to test CRUD operations. This example demonstrated best practices for organizing and testing applications with TypeScript.

By following along, you have learned how to set up a TypeScript project, define models, controllers, and routes in an Express application, and create robust integration tests to ensure that your API functions correctly.

In the next chapter, we will explore error handling and debugging with TypeScript. You will learn how to implement robust error handling, effectively debug TypeScript code, use TypeScript's type system to catch errors early, and utilize tools and techniques to improve error reporting and debugging. This will enhance your ability to maintain and troubleshoot TypeScript applications, making your code more resilient and easier to manage.

# Get this book's PDF copy, code bundle, and more

Scan the QR code (or go to `packtpub.com/unlock`). Search for this book by name, confirm the edition, and then follow the steps on the page.

UNLOCK NOW

*Note: Keep your invoice handy. Purchases made directly from the Packt website don't require an invoice.*

# 6

# Error Handling, Debugging, and Security Best Practices

Developing robust and reliable software requires mastering the art of error handling and debugging. These are the critical components of building robust TypeScript applications. Understanding how to effectively manage errors, leverage debugging tools, and implement security best practices ensures that applications are reliable, maintainable, and secure.

In this chapter, you'll learn essential techniques and strategies for handling both synchronous and asynchronous errors in TypeScript. Synchronous errors occur during the execution of a specific block of code and are thrown immediately, such as syntax errors or reference errors. Asynchronous errors, on the other hand, occur outside the main execution flow—typically in callbacks, promises, or async functions—making them more challenging to handle.

We will explore the use of different error types and learn how to utilize debugging tools to identify and resolve issues efficiently. Additionally, we will cover common error patterns and solutions, and essential security practices to safeguard your TypeScript applications.

In this chapter, we will cover the following:

- Learning strategies for error handling
- Handling synchronous errors in TypeScript
- Strategies for dealing with asynchronous errors (e.g., promises, `async`/`await`, and `try`/`catch`)
- Using error types effectively
- Debugging tools and techniques
- Common error patterns and solutions
- Security best practices in TypeScript

By the end of this chapter, you will be equipped with the knowledge to handle errors gracefully, debug effectively, and implement security measures to protect your applications.

# Technical requirements

To follow along with this chapter, you'll need the following tools installed on your system:

- Node.js (v16 or later): Required to run and compile TypeScript applications.
- TypeScript (v5 or later)
- **Visual Studio Code** (**VS Code**): Recommended editor with built-in debugging support.

You can download the example project and code for this book by following the instructions in the *Download the example code files* section in the *Preface* of this book. This chapter's code files are included in the downloadable code bundle.

The GitHub repository contains all sample projects, including examples for error handling, debugging with VS Code, source maps, breakpoints, and implementing security best practices.

# Understanding error types and patterns

Error handling is a critical part of developing reliable TypeScript applications. Before diving into how to handle errors, it's essential to first understand the different types of errors you might encounter and recognize common patterns that can lead to these errors. By doing so, you'll be better equipped to identify, debug, and resolve issues efficiently. Let's break down this heading into two key components: introducing error types and common error patterns.

## Introducing error types

Errors in programming are generally classified into three main categories: syntax errors, runtime errors, and logical errors. These types are common across most programming languages.

In TypeScript, additional error types arise due to its unique features. These include type errors, compilation errors, and errors specific to asynchronous or synchronous operations. Understanding these categories is essential for diagnosing and resolving issues in your code effectively. Let's go over them one after the other.

### Syntax errors

**Syntax errors** are mistakes in the code that violate the rules of the TypeScript language, such as mismatched parentheses or invalid function names. These errors prevent your code from compiling, and the TypeScript compiler catches them during the compilation process. Let's see an example and how you would identify and solve them:

Missing a closing parenthesis:

Consider the following line of code:

```
const x = 2;
  if (x > 5 { console.log("x is big");}
```

Do you notice anything wrong? Well, if you copy that into a random TypeScript file, for example, an `index.ts` file, you should see a red squiggly line, as shown in the following figure:

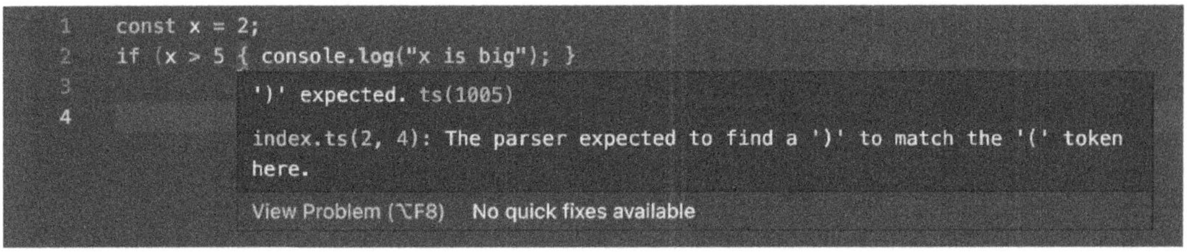


*Figure 6.1 — VS Code editor highlighting a syntax error with a red squiggly line under the problematic code, displaying the hover tooltip: ')' expected ts(1005)*

What's wrong? In the previous code, we have a condition that checks whether x is greater than 5. However, we are missing the closing parenthesis. This is immediately apparent because the editor (e.g., VS Code) highlights the issue with a red squiggly line under the curly braces. When we hover over the red line, we can see the following error message:

```
')' expected ts(1005)
```

Additionally, if you check your terminal while running `npx tsc --w`, you'll see more details about the error. This is because the missing parenthesis causes a syntax error, which prevents TypeScript from compiling the code, as shown in the following figure:

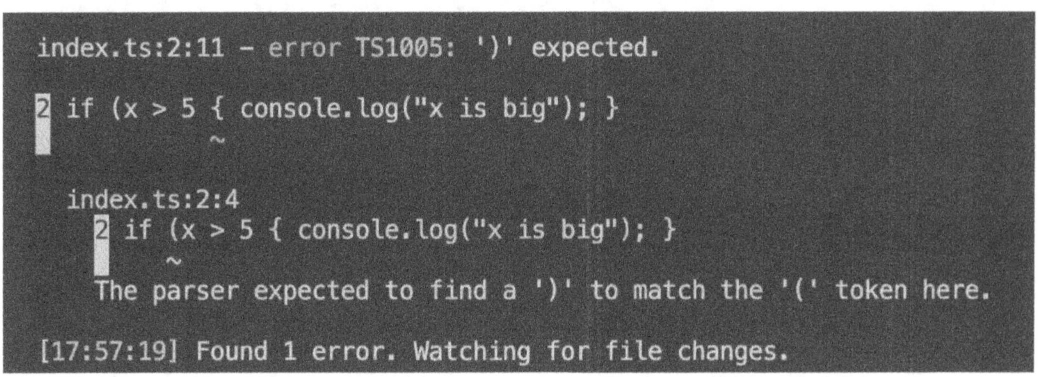


*Figure 6.2 — Terminal output from the TypeScript compiler showing error TS1005 for a missing closing parenthesis in index.ts, including line references and parser details*

Now that we know what syntax errors are, let's look at how to identify and fix them.

Syntax errors are typically highlighted in modern code editors (such as VS Code), making them easy to spot. These errors prevent your code from compiling, and most editors display error messages or underline the problematic code.

To resolve them, carefully review the error messages provided by the TypeScript compiler or your editor. These messages often include details about the issue and its location.

Here's what the correct code looks like:

```
const x = 2;
if (x > 5) {
  console.log("x is big");
}
```

If we copy that and paste it into our editor, the error should be gone. See the following figure:

*Figure 6.3 — VS Code editor displaying the corrected code with the missing parenthesis added, showing no red squiggly lines indicating a successful syntax fix*

Now that we've fixed the error as shown in the preceding figure, you notice that the red squiggly line is gone. If we proceed to check out the terminal, we would see that the code compiles successfully and there are no errors, as seen in the following figure:

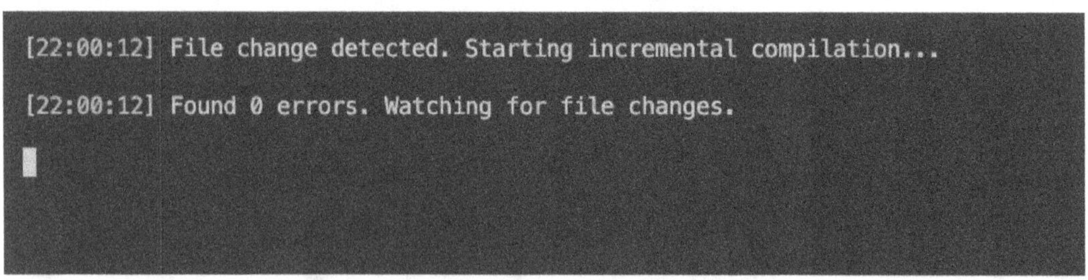


*Figure 6.4 — Terminal output after fixing the syntax error, showing successful compilation with zero errors and ongoing file change monitoring*

What you just saw with syntax errors stopping the code from compiling is one of the beauties of TypeScript, as it helps us catch bugs early. Now that we know about syntax errors, let's jump to the next subsection, where we will look at type errors.

## Type errors

**Type errors** occur when a value is used in a way that is incompatible with its declared or inferred type. Unlike syntax errors, type errors do not break the structure of your code, but they violate the rules of how values are supposed to behave. One of TypeScript's greatest strengths is that it detects these issues during compilation, allowing you to fix them before the program runs.

Let's look at some common examples of type errors and how to resolve them:

- **Assigning incompatible types**: Assigning a value of one type to a variable expected to hold another type can lead to type errors:

  ```
  let num: number = 42;
  num = "Hello"; // Error: Type 'string' is not assignable to type 'number'.
  ```

  To fix this, simply assign a value that matches the declared type:

  ```
  num = 24; // Correctly assigning a number to a variable of type 'number'
  ```

- **Calling a method that doesn't exist on a type**: Another common type error occurs when calling a method that does not exist on the given type:

  ```
  let user: string = "John";
  user.push("Doe");
  ```

  In the preceding code, we are trying to call the `push` method on a variable of the `string` type. However, `push` is not a method on the `string` type; it's a method on the `array` type. As a result, you will get an error:

  ```
  // Error: Property 'push' does not exist on type 'string'
  ```

  Here, `push()` is an array method, not a string method. Since `user` is declared as a string, TypeScript correctly reports an error.

  To resolve this, ensure that the variable is declared with the appropriate type:

  ```
  let user: string[] = ["John"];
  user.push("Doe"); // Correct usage
  ```

By declaring `user` as an array of strings (`string[]`), we can safely use array methods such as `push()`.

- **Accessing a property on a value that is potentially null or undefined**: TypeScript also warns you when a value might not exist at runtime:

```
interface User {
  firstName: string;
  lastName?: string;
}

// Simulated API call that may return a user or null
function fetchUserFromAPI(): User | null {
  return Math.random() > 0.5 ? { name: "Rukee", lastName: "Doe" } : null;
}
const user = fetchUserFromAPI();
console.log(user.firstName); //  Error: Object is possibly 'null'
```

Because `user` may be `null`, TypeScript prevents direct property access. You must first check that the value exists:

```
if(user) {
console.log(user.firstName);
}
```

Or you can use optional chaining:

```
console.log(user?.firstName);
```

Both approaches ensure that you only access properties when the value is defined.

Type errors are typically easy to spot because modern editors highlight them instantly using visual indicators such as red squiggly lines. The TypeScript compiler also provides detailed error messages explaining what went wrong and where.

To resolve type errors effectively, you can do the following:

- Review compiler or editor messages carefully
- Ensure that variable, parameter, and return types match their intended values

- Use type guards (`typeof`, `instanceof`, or custom checks) when working with union or unknown types
- Enable strict mode in your TypeScript configuration for stronger guarantees

Type errors are especially valuable because they catch problems before your code runs. This shifts failures earlier in the development cycle, making them easier and cheaper to fix.

Now that we've seen how TypeScript catches mistakes before execution, let's move on to runtime errors—issues that only appear when your program actually runs.

## Runtime errors

**Runtime errors** occur when your code is syntactically correct and passes TypeScript's static type check, but an issue arises during the execution of the program. These errors are often related to unexpected runtime conditions, rather than simple type mismatches.

TypeScript can prevent many common mistakes at compile time. However, it cannot eliminate all runtime failures—especially when working with dynamic data, external APIs, user input, or values that are typed loosely (for example, using any or type assertions).

Common causes of runtime errors include the following:

- Accessing a property on `undefined` or `null`
- Assuming that external API responses conform to a specific structure
- Performing operations on unexpected values
- Bypassing type safety using any or forced type assertions

Let's see some examples:

```
type User = {
  name: string;
};

function greet(user: User) {
  console.log(user.name.toUpperCase());
}

// Simulating external or unsafe input
greet(undefined as any); // Compiles, but throws at runtime
```

Although this code compiles, it fails at runtime because `undefined` does not have a `name` property.

This example highlights an important distinction: static type checking improves safety, but it cannot guarantee correctness when runtime assumptions are violated. When dealing with external APIs or untrusted input, additional validation is necessary to ensure reliability.

Now that we know what runtime errors are, let's look at how to identify and fix them.

### How to identify and resolve runtime errors

Unlike syntax errors, runtime errors will only appear when you run your application. These errors are typically logged to the console and can cause your program to crash or behave unpredictably. To resolve runtime errors, you'll need to debug your code by using tools such as breakpoints, console logs, or debuggers. These tools help trace the execution flow and pinpoint where the error occurs, allowing you to fix the issue and prevent it from affecting your program's functionality.

This section covered runtime errors, their identification, and their resolution. You learned how to use debugging techniques to trace and correct runtime issues in your applications.

Next, we will explore logical errors—errors that affect the correctness of your program's output despite no syntax or runtime issues.

## Logical errors

These occur when the code runs without crashing but produces incorrect results due to flaws in the logic. **Logical errors** are the trickiest to identify because they occur when your code runs without any syntax or runtime errors but doesn't produce the expected outcome.

Let's see some examples:

- **Incorrectly calculating a value**:

  ```
  let total = price - discount * quantity; // Incorrect calculation
  ```

  In this example, the error occurs because the calculation doesn't account for the correct order of operations. The subtraction and multiplication need to be grouped properly to get the intended result. The correct approach would be as follows:

  ```
  let total = (price - discount) * quantity; // Correct calculation
  ```

- **Misusing conditionals**:

  ```
  if (a = b) { // Incorrect use of assignment operator
      // Some code
  }
  ```

In this example, the error occurs because the single equals sign (=) is used for assignment, not comparison. This will always evaluate to `true` (or the assigned value), not the intended comparison. The correct approach should be as follows:

```
if (a == b) { // Correct use of equality operator
    // Some code
}
// or
if (a === b) { // Correct use of strict equality operator
    // Some code
}
```

## How to identify and resolve logical errors

Logical errors are challenging because they don't produce error messages. To identify them, you must test your code thoroughly and compare the actual output against what you expect. Look for discrepancies by examining how your code handles various inputs, especially **boundary values**—the smallest and largest valid inputs in a range. These values often reveal hidden flaws in logic that typical test cases might miss. For example, if a function accepts ages between 18 and 65, testing with 17, 18, 65, and 66 helps ensure the logic correctly handles the limits.

Once identified, resolve the error by carefully analyzing the faulty logic. Use test cases, particularly edge cases, to validate your corrections. To prevent these errors proactively, consider adopting **test-driven development** (**TDD**), where you write tests before the code. This approach forces you to think about the desired outcomes and logic upfront, significantly reducing the chance of logical errors.

Let's go over a quick example.

Consider a TypeScript function designed to calculate the average of an array of numbers:

```
function calculateAverage(numbers: number[]): number {
let sum: number = 0;
for (let i: number = 0; i <= numbers.length; i++) {
sum += numbers[i];
}
return sum / numbers.length;
}
```

When testing this function with `calculateAverage([1, 2, 3, 4])`, you expect an average of `2.5`, but get `NaN`. To identify the issue, you review the logic and add debugging logs as follows:

```
function calculateAverage(numbers: number[]): number {
let sum: number = 0;
for (let i: number = 0; i <= numbers.length; i++) {
console.log(`Index: ${i}, Value: ${numbers[i]}`); // Debugging
sum += numbers[i];
}
console.log(`Sum: ${sum}, Length: ${    ${numbers.length}`);
return sum / numbers.length;
}

const averageResult = calculateAverage([1, 2, 3, 4]);
console.log(averageResult,'this is average result')
```

Running this with `[1, 2, 3, 4]` logs an undefined value at index 4, revealing that the loop iterates one step too far (`i <= numbers.length` includes an out-of-bounds index). See the following figure for reference:

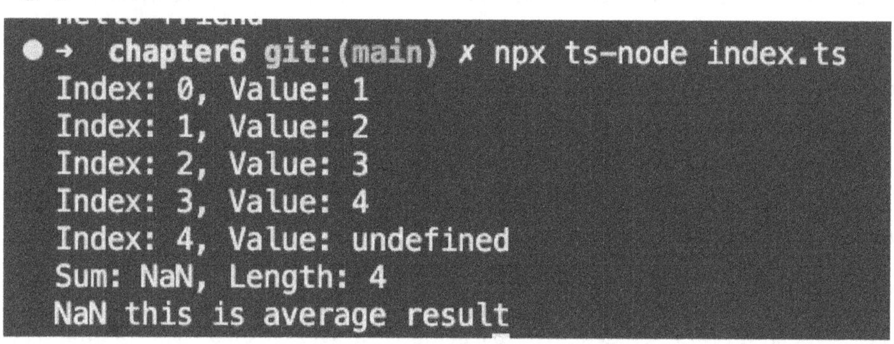


*Figure 6.5 — Debugging logs from a TypeScript function with a logical error, showing an undefined value at index 4 due to an off-by-one loop condition when calculating the average of [1, 2, 3, 4]*

The correct logic should use `i < numbers.length`. See the correct full code here:

```
function calculateAverage(numbers: number[]): number {
if (numbers.length === 0) return 0; // Handle edge case
let sum: number = 0;
for (let i: number = 0; i < numbers.length; i++) {
sum += numbers[i];
}
```

```
return sum / numbers.length;
}
```

In the preceding example, we demonstrated how debugging combined with TypeScript's type safety and attention to edge cases can help resolve logical errors and improve code reliability.

Now, you have learned about logical errors and strategies for identifying and correcting them. Logical errors require careful code review, testing, and consideration of edge cases to resolve, as they often do not produce explicit error notifications. TypeScript's type system can also help by catching potential issues during development.

# Handling errors in TypeScript

With a clear understanding of the different error categories, this section explores practical strategies for managing them effectively. The goal is to ensure that errors don't negatively impact the user experience by breaking functionality or preventing proper use of your application—even when things don't go as planned.

To keep things structured, we'll approach error handling from two key angles:

- **Synchronous errors**: Issues that occur during sequential code execution, such as logic or type-related problems
- **Asynchronous errors**: Challenges that arise from operations running independently, such as API calls or timers

We'll explore both approaches in depth, starting with strategies for handling synchronous errors.

## Synchronous error handling

In JavaScript and TypeScript, code execution is typically synchronous, meaning the syntax parser starts at the top of a module (such as `index.js`) and reads the code line by line, executing each statement in sequence. This linear flow is predictable, but it also means that if something goes wrong along the way—such as a bad calculation or an invalid value—it can break the entire program unless it's handled properly.

Errors in synchronous code can happen at any point, from simple logic bugs to unexpected input values. That's why it's important to have clear strategies in place to catch and manage them—preventing crashes and ensuring that your application stays stable and user-friendly.

In this section, we'll explore the following:

- What synchronous errors are

- Why they occur
- How to handle them effectively using `try-catch` blocks and input validation

## What are synchronous errors?

Synchronous errors happen during the execution of synchronous code—code that runs line by line, in the order it's written. These errors typically arise from incorrect logic, faulty assumptions, or unexpected input data. If not handled properly, synchronous errors can cause your application to fail or produce incorrect results.

To demonstrate, let's take a look at a small web-based application powered by **TypeScript** ( as shown in the following figure). It performs a very simple operation: calculating the square of a number.

*Figure 6.6 — Basic HTML structure for a square calculator app, featuring an input field for number entry, a Calculate Square button, and a result display area, linked to a JavaScript file for functionality*

You enter a number, click on the **Calculate Square** button, and the app displays the square of the number.

Here's the basic HTML structure that powers our frontend:

```
<!DOCTYPE html>
<html lang="en">
<head>
<meta charset="UTF-8" />
<title>Synchronous Error Handling</title>
</head>
<body>
<h2>Calculate the square of:</h2>
<input type="text" id="numberInput" placeholder="Enter a number" />
<button onclick="handleCalculation()">Calculate Square</button>
<p id="result"></p>
<script src="script.js"></script>
</body>
</html>
```

Nothing too fancy—just an input field, a button, and a paragraph to show the result. Now, let's see what the TypeScript code that powers our web app looks like. In the `script.ts` file, we have the following code:

```
function calculateSquare(input: string): number {
  const num = parseFloat(input);
  if (isNaN(num)) {
    throw new Error("Please enter a valid number.");
  }
  return num * num;
}

function handleCalculation(): void {
  const inputValue = (document.getElementById("numberInput") as
HTMLInputElement).value;
  const resultEl = document.getElementById("result") as HTMLParagraphElement;

  const result = calculateSquare(inputValue);
  resultEl.style.color = "green";
  resultEl.textContent = `Square: ${result}`;
}
```

In our `script.ts` file, we have two functions, `handleCalculation()` and `calculateSquare()`. Let's get a quick overview of what they do:

- `handleCalculation`: Grabs the input value from the DOM and passes it to the `calculateSquare` function. It also updates the result display.
- `calculateSquare`: Takes a number, checks whether it's valid, and returns its square, or throws an error if invalid.

When we enter a valid number, say 5, we get a result of 25, displayed in green. Everything works perfectly! See the following figure:

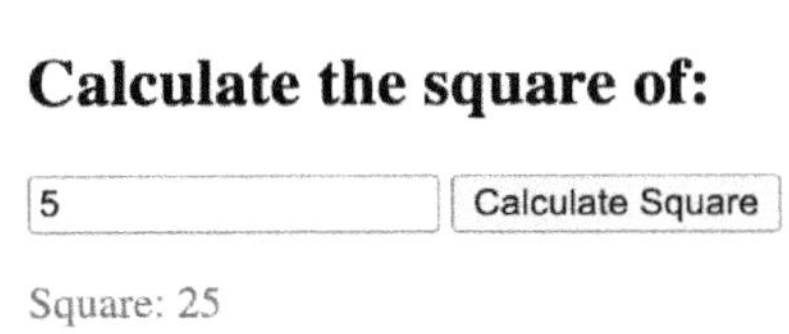


*Figure 6.7 – Calculate Square app working as expected*

But what could go wrong? Well, for numeric inputs, the code works exactly as expected. However, if a user enters a non-numeric value, such as text, they won't see any result in the browser. The app seems to have crashed. If we inspect the console (using Chrome DevTools), we can see what happened, as shown in the following figure:

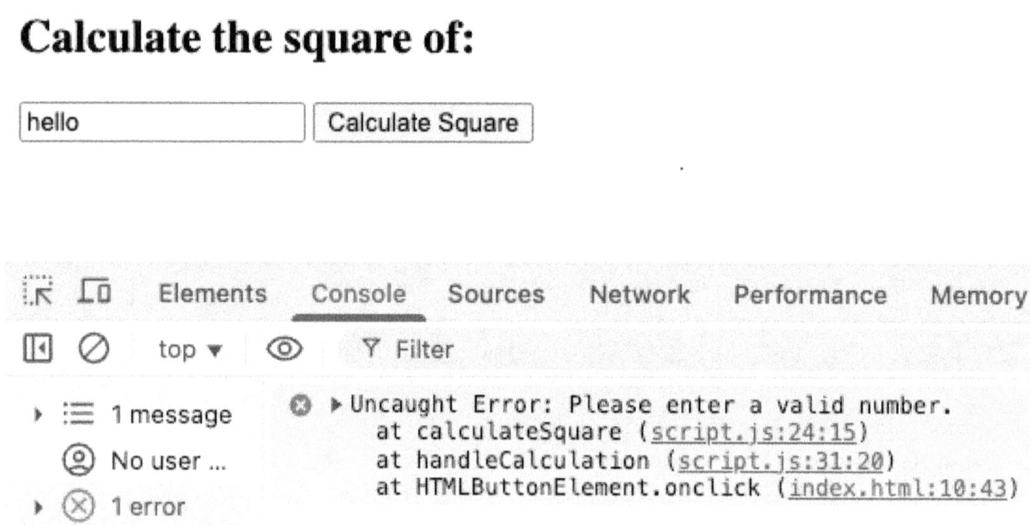


*Figure 6.8 — Displaying an error message in the browser console for invalid input*

In the console, we find the following error message: `Please enter a valid number`.

This error is thrown by the `calculateSquare()` function. Because the code is running synchronously, once the error is thrown, **execution stops immediately**, and the part of the code that updates the result is never reached. While this is a trivial example, in a real-world application, this kind of behavior could be disastrous.

In web applications—just like with products such as shoes, furniture, or cars—user experience is everything. Crashes like this could hurt your brand's reputation and negatively impact your company's revenue.

Let's see how we can fix this problem and improve error handling by introducing something called a `try-catch` block.

## Fixing the issue with try...catch

In the previous example, our Calculate Square application crashed due to a synchronous error caused by invalid text input.

In this section, we'll resolve the issue by using a `try-catch` block to handle potential errors gracefully. The solution involves updating the `handleCalculation()` function as follows:

```
function handleCalculation(): void {
  const inputValue = (document.getElementById("numberInput") as
HTMLInputElement).value;
  const resultEl = document.getElementById("result") as HTMLParagraphElement;

  try {
    const result = calculateSquare(inputValue);
    resultEl.style.color = "green";
    resultEl.textContent = `Square: ${result}`;
  } catch (error: unknown) {
    resultEl.style.color = "red";
if (error instanceof Error) {
      resultEl.textContent = error.message;
    } else {
      resultEl.textContent = "An unexpected error occurred.";
    }
  }
}
```

Before checking it in the browser, let's quickly go over what we changed.

First, we introduced a `try { } catch (error) { }` block. Inside the `try` block, we call the `calculateSquare()` function and proceed to update the UI with the result if everything goes well. This is where you handle your main logic.

However, if something goes wrong—such as when the input is not a number and `calculateSquare()` throws an error—the execution jumps into the `catch` block. Inside the `catch` block, we now handle the error by displaying a user-friendly error message in red. In more advanced applications, you might also log these errors to a monitoring service such as Sentry or Datadog for further analysis.

Now, when we return to our app and test it, the following happens:

- Entering a valid number still works exactly as before
- Entering invalid text now displays a clear error message, instead of crashing the app

The user sees immediate feedback, and the experience remains smooth and professional. See the following figure:

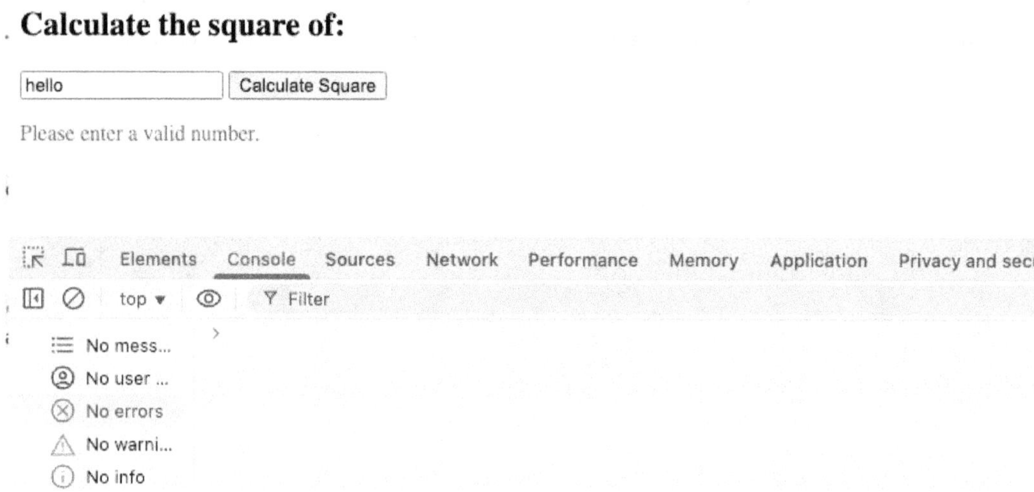


*Figure 6.9 – Displaying a clear error message as feedback to the user when a text is entered*

In the previous example, we explored synchronous errors—their nature, impact on your application, and how to handle them using a `try-catch` block.

In the next subsection, we'll build on this by discussing input validation, a proactive technique to prevent synchronous errors before they occur.

## Validating input data

Another essential strategy for handling synchronous errors is validating input data before using it in your functions or calculations. Input validation ensures that the data your functions receive meets the expected criteria, reducing the likelihood of errors.

Continuing with our example, we will now extend the `handleCalculation` function as follows:

```
function handleCalculation(): void {
const inputValue = (document.getElementById("numberInput") as
HTMLInputElement).value;
const resultEl = document.getElementById("result") as HTMLParagraphElement;

// Input validation
if (!inputValue) {
 resultEl.style.color = "red";
 resultEl.textContent = "Input cannot be empty.";
 return;
}
```

```
if (!/^-?\d*\.?\d*$/.test(inputValue)) {
 resultEl.style.color = "red";
 resultEl.textContent = "Please enter a valid number.";
 return;
}

// Try-catch for main logic
try {
 const result = calculateSquare(inputValue);
 resultEl.style.color = "green";
 resultEl.textContent = `Square: ${result}`;
} catch (error: any) {
 resultEl.style.color = "red";
 resultEl.textContent = error.message;
}
}
```

In the updated code, we introduced two new validation checks using simple `if` conditions.

The first check verifies whether the input field is empty. If it is, the user immediately sees an error message—`Input cannot be empty`. The `return` statement ensures that the function exits early and does not proceed any further:

```
if (!inputValue) {
  resultEl.style.color = "red";
  resultEl.textContent = "Input cannot be empty.";
  return;
}
```

The second check validates the format of the input using a regular expression:

```
if (!/^-?\d*\.?\d*$/.test(inputValue)) {
  resultEl.style.color = "red";
  resultEl.textContent = "Please enter a valid number.";
  return;
}
```

This regular expression ensures that the supplied input is a valid number—it allows for optional negative signs and decimal points, covering a broad range of numeric inputs.

Of course, we keep the `try-catch` block as a fallback to catch any unexpected errors that might still occur during the actual calculation process.

Why is this approach better?

We want to catch issues as early as possible, before they propagate into larger problems. Early validation greatly improves user experience by giving instant feedback and preventing application crashes.

While our example is simple, imagine real-world applications: think about a signup form that collects a user's email or age, or a financial app that processes transaction amounts. Allowing users to enter anything without validation could lead to serious errors—even security vulnerabilities. Proper input validation isn't just about avoiding bugs; it also helps protect applications from risks such as **cross-site scripting** (**XSS**) attacks.

In short, good input validation is one of the first lines of defense for building stable, secure, and user-friendly applications.

So far, we've explored the concept of synchronous errors—errors that happen during the step-by-step execution of our code. We showed the dangers of unhandled synchronous errors, introduced a `try-catch` block to handle them, and took things a step further by adding input validation. We used a simple, practical example to make these concepts clear.

In the next section, we'll move on to errors in asynchronous code—where things don't happen immediately, and errors become a bit trickier to catch.

# Asynchronous error handling

Asynchronous programming is a powerful tool in TypeScript that allows your application to perform multiple tasks at once, such as fetching data from an API, reading files, or interacting with a database, without blocking the main execution thread. However, handling errors in asynchronous code can be more complex than in synchronous code. This section will guide you through the key concepts and techniques you need to manage asynchronous errors effectively.

We will explore what asynchronous errors are, why they occur, and the best practices for handling them using promises, `async/await` syntax, and other essential techniques. By the end of this section, you'll have a solid understanding of how to keep your asynchronous code resilient and error-free.

# What are asynchronous errors?

Asynchronous errors happen when tasks take time to complete and don't run in the main thread. While waiting for these tasks to finish, the program continues doing other things. Examples include fetching data from the internet, reading files, or setting timers.

Because these operations are not completed instantly, the errors they produce might not occur at the same time as the function call. This delayed error occurrence makes it necessary to handle errors differently than in synchronous code.

Here is an example of asynchronous code:

```
function fetchData(url: string): Promise<void> {
  return fetch(url)
    .then(response => response.json())
    .then(data => {
      console.log(data);
    })
    .catch(error => {
      console.error("An error occurred:", error);
    });
}

fetchData("https://api.example.com/data");
```

In this example, the `fetch` function is an asynchronous operation. If something goes wrong (e.g., the network is down or the URL is incorrect), an error might occur, but only after the `fetch` request is initiated.

Handling asynchronous errors is crucial because it does the following:

- **Ensures application stability**: Proper error handling prevents your application from crashing when an asynchronous operation fails
- **Improves user experience**: Users receive meaningful feedback when something goes wrong, instead of being left with a frozen or unresponsive application
- **Facilitates debugging**: Identifying and managing errors in asynchronous code makes it easier to diagnose issues during development

Without proper error handling, your asynchronous code could fail silently, leading to hard-to-trace bugs and poor user experience.

In the next subsection, we will look at strategies for handling asynchronous errors.

## Strategies for handling asynchronous errors

Let's explore the three primary strategies for managing errors in asynchronous code: using promises, using `async`/`await` syntax, and applying best practices for robust error handling.

## Handling errors with promises

**Promises** are a fundamental tool in JavaScript and TypeScript for working with asynchronous operations. A promise represents a value that may not be available yet but will be resolved in the future. Every promise starts in a *pending* state and then settles into either *fulfilled* (successful operation) or *rejected* (operation failed).

There are three main methods you can use to handle the results and errors of a promise:

- `then()`: Used to handle successful results of a promise
- `catch()`: Used to handle errors or rejections from a promise
- `finally()`: Used to execute code after the promise is settled, regardless of the outcome

Let's look at an example of handling errors with promises, to demonstrate the concepts we just shared:

```
function fetchData(url: string): Promise<void> {
  return fetch(url)
    .then(response => {
      if (!response.ok) {
        throw new Error("Network response was not ok");
      }
      return response.json();
    })
    .then(data => {
      console.log("Data fetched successfully:", data);
    })
    .catch(error => {
      console.error("An error occurred:", error.message);
    })
    .finally(() => {
      console.log("Fetch operation completed.");
    });
}
```

Let's explain the preceding code:

- **Error propagation**: If an error occurs during the `fetch` operation or when processing the response, it is propagated through the chain and caught in the `catch` block
- **Graceful recovery**: The `finally` block ensures that certain cleanup actions can be performed, regardless of whether the operation succeeded or failed

Here are the benefits of using promises for error handling:

- **Chained execution**: Promises allow you to chain multiple asynchronous operations together and handle errors at any point in the chain
- **Error propagation**: Errors can be caught and managed effectively, preventing them from disrupting the entire application flow
- **Readability**: Promises make it easier to follow the logic of asynchronous operations by clearly separating success and error paths

## Handling errors with async/await

The `async/await` syntax offers a modern, cleaner way to work with asynchronous code. It allows developers to write asynchronous functions that look and behave like synchronous code, making them easier to read and maintain—without sacrificing the benefits of non-blocking execution.

When working with `async/await`, there are three key elements that help manage asynchronous operations and handle potential errors effectively:

- `async`: A keyword used to declare an asynchronous function, allowing the use of `await` within it
- `await`: A keyword used to pause the execution of an `async` function until the promise is resolved
- `try-catch`: Blocks that wrap `await` calls to catch and handle errors that may occur during asynchronous execution

Let's look at an example of handling errors with `async/await`:

```
async function fetchData(url: string): Promise<void> {
  try {
    const response = await fetch(url);
    if (!response.ok) {
      throw new Error("Network response was not ok");
    }
    const data = await response.json();
    console.log("Data fetched successfully:", data);
  } catch (error) {
    console.error("An error occurred:", error.message);
  } finally {
    console.log("Fetch operation completed.");
  }
}
```

```
fetchData("https://api.example.com/data");
```

Let's explain the preceding code:

- **Synchronous-like flow**: The `await` keyword allows the asynchronous code to be written in a way that looks synchronous, making it easier to follow and understand
- **Error handling with `try/catch`**: Just like in synchronous code, errors can be caught using a `try/catch` block, making the error handling process intuitive and straightforward
- **Final actions with `finally`**: The `finally` block ensures that any necessary cleanup or final actions are performed after the asynchronous operation is completed

Here are the benefits of using `async/await` for error handling:

- **Improved readability**: The code is easier to read and write, resembling synchronous code while maintaining asynchronous behavior
- **Centralized error handling**: Errors are handled in a familiar way using `try/catch`, making the code base more consistent
- **Less boilerplate**: `async/await` reduces the need for chaining `.then()` and `.catch()`, simplifying the code

While promises and `async/await` are JavaScript features, TypeScript introduces additional compile-time safety when working with errors. One important difference is how errors are typed inside a `catch` block.

You might wonder why TypeScript does not simply assume that every caught value is an instance of `Error`, especially if your project follows good practices and always throws proper `Error` objects.

Inside your own code base, you can absolutely enforce a convention like this:

```
throw new Error("Something went wrong");
```

However, JavaScript does not restrict what can be thrown. Any value can be used with `throw`, including the following:

```
throw "Something went wrong";
throw 404;
throw { code: 500, message: "Server error" };
```

In real-world applications, many asynchronous operations involve third-party libraries, browser APIs, database drivers, or external services. You do not control how those systems throw errors. A library might throw a string, a plain object, or some other unexpected value.

Because JavaScript allows any value to be thrown, TypeScript cannot safely assume that a caught value has a message property or any specific structure. For this reason, the `error` variable inside a `catch` block is typed as `unknown`.

This design encourages safer error handling. Before accessing properties such as `message`, you must first verify the shape of the value:

```
catch (error: unknown) {
  if (error instanceof Error) {
    console.error("Error message:", error.message);
  } else {
    console.error("Unexpected error value:", error);
  }
}
```

Even if your own project standardizes error creation, you cannot guarantee how external dependencies behave. By treating errors as unknown, TypeScript helps you write defensive, reliable code at system boundaries—especially in asynchronous operations that involve APIs or third-party services.

## Best practices for robust asynchronous error handling

In addition to using promises and `async/await`, there are several best practices you should follow to ensure that your asynchronous error handling is robust and reliable:

- **Always handle errors**: Never leave a promise or `async` function without error handling. Use `catch()` with promises or `try/catch` with `async/await` to manage errors.
- **Use `finally` for cleanup**: If you need to perform cleanup actions (e.g., closing a connection or releasing resources), use the `finally` block to ensure that it happens regardless of success or failure.
- **Graceful degradation**: When an error occurs, your application should fail gracefully, providing useful feedback to the user and preventing the entire application from crashing.

- **Centralized error logging**: Consider implementing a centralized error logging mechanism that collects and logs all errors, making it easier to monitor and debug issues.
- **Timeouts and retry logic**: For network requests or other potentially slow operations, implement timeouts and retry logic to handle temporary failures or network issues.

Handling asynchronous errors effectively is crucial for building reliable and user-friendly TypeScript applications. By using promises and `async/await`, along with best practices for error handling, you can ensure that your asynchronous code is resilient, easy to manage, and less prone to unexpected failures. With these strategies in place, your applications will be better equipped to handle the complexities of modern asynchronous operations.

In the next section, we will explore debugging tools and techniques, which will help you identify and resolve errors more efficiently in both synchronous and asynchronous code.

# Debugging tools in TypeScript

**Debugging** is the process of finding and fixing errors in your code. There are several tools and techniques that make this process easier and more effective. These tools let you inspect program state, follow the flow of execution, and catch problems before they make it to production.

Some of the most commonly used debugging tools are the following:

- **Editor debuggers**: Most modern editors and IDEs include built-in debuggers that allow you to step through code, inspect variables, evaluate expressions, and observe execution flow. In this book, we use VS Code for demonstrations, but the same concepts apply to other editors.
- **Browser DevTools**: Modern browsers provide powerful developer tools for inspecting runtime behavior, network activity, performance, and console output. When working with frontend TypeScript applications, these tools are essential for diagnosing issues in real time.
- **Source maps**: Source maps bridge compiled JavaScript and original TypeScript files, allowing you to debug your application as if it were running the original TypeScript source.
- **Breakpoints**: When running code inside a debugger, breakpoints pause execution at specific lines so you can inspect program state and understand how execution reached that point.
- **Console logs**: Simple `console.log()` statements help trace values and execution flow. Although basic, they remain one of the fastest ways to investigate issues.

These tools work best when used together, giving you a complete picture of your application's behavior. Let's start by looking at source maps.

## Working with source maps

TypeScript code compiles to JavaScript, which can make debugging challenging without source maps. Source maps (`.js.map` files) link the compiled JavaScript back to your original TypeScript code, allowing debuggers to display and interact with your TypeScript files directly. To enable source maps, configure your `tsconfig.json` file as follows:

1. **Enable source maps in** `tsconfig.json`: In your project root, add (or update) a `tsconfig.json` file to include the `sourceMap` option:

   ```
   {
     "compilerOptions": {
       "target": "ES6",
       "module": "commonjs",
       "outDir": "./dist",
       "sourceMap": true
     }
   }
   ```

   This tells the TypeScript compiler to generate `.map` files alongside your compiled JavaScript.

2. **Create a simple example file**: Let's add a minimal `index.ts` file:

   ```
   function greet(name: string): string {
     return `Hello, ${name}!`;
   }

   const message = greet("Alice");
   console.log(message);
   ```

3. **Compile the code**: Run the TypeScript compiler:

   ```
   npx tsc
   ```

This will generate the following files in the `dist/` folder:

```
dist/
  index.js
  index.js.map
```

4. **Inspect the output**: First, check the `index.js` file (compiled JavaScript):

```
function greet(name) {
    return `Hello, ${name}!`;
}
const message = greet("Alice");
console.log(message);
//# sourceMappingURL=index.js.map
```

Take note of the final line, `//# sourceMappingURL=index.js.map`. It tells the debugger that a source map exists. See the following figure for a reference to what the source map looks like:

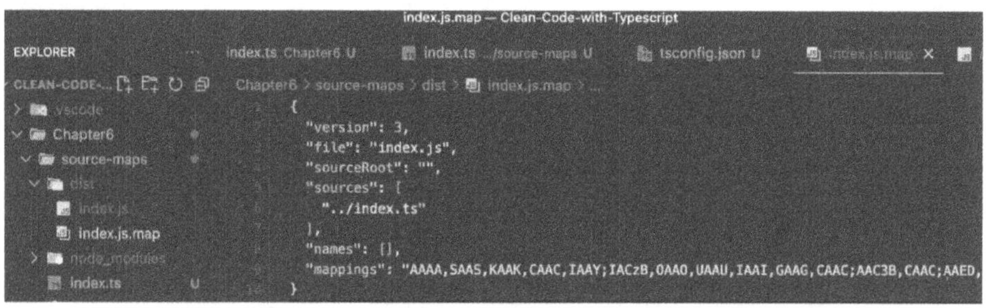


*Figure 6.10 — Displaying the contents of the generated source map file*

5. **Debug with source maps**: Now that we have our source maps in place, any breakpoints you add in VS Code will map directly to your TypeScript source instead of the compiled JavaScript. This means you can debug in the code you actually wrote, making the process smoother, clearer, and much more natural.

## Using the VS Code debugger

The VS Code debugger is a powerful tool integrated directly into your development environment. It provides a visual way to debug your TypeScript code by allowing you to pause execution, inspect variables, and step through your program.

We're focusing on the VS Code debugger because this book uses VS Code as the primary editor. The same debugging concepts (such as setting breakpoints, stepping through code, and inspecting variables) apply in most modern editors, even if the setup steps differ slightly.

We'll continue working with the same `index.ts` file we created in the source maps example. This way, you can see how the debugger builds on top of the setup you already have.

To use the VS Code debugger, we will go over the following steps.

## Step 1: Create a launch configuration

Before you can start debugging, you need to tell VS Code how to run your program. This is done through a configuration file called `launch.json`.

Open the **Run and Debug** view in VS Code (click the *play* icon with a bug on the sidebar, or press *Ctrl* + *Shift* + *D*/*Cmd* + *Shift* + *D* on macOS):

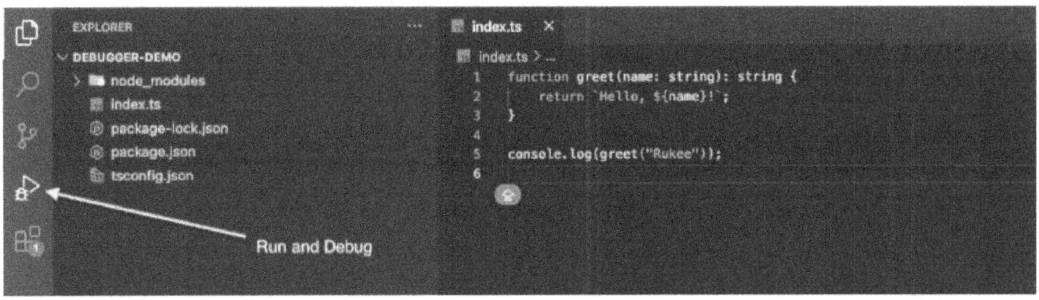


*Figure 6.11 — The Run and Debug icon in the VS Code sidebar, used to open the Run and Debug view (Ctrl + Shift + D/Cmd + Shift + D on macOS)*

Click **create a launch.json file**:

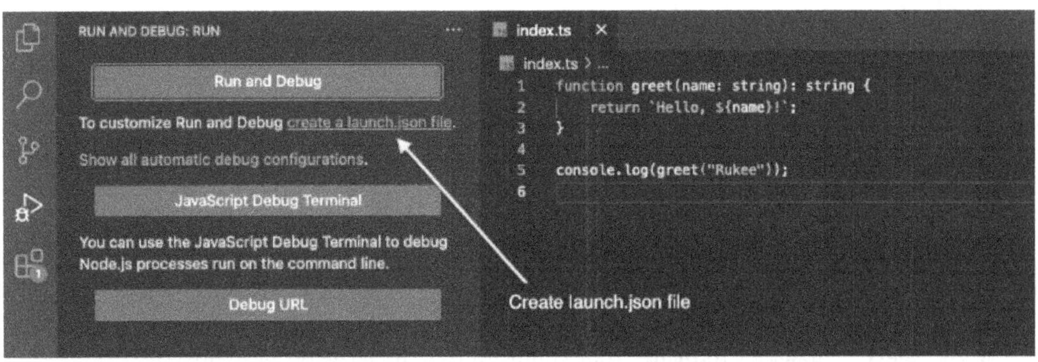


*Figure 6.12 — The create a launch.json file option in VS Code's Run and Debug view, used to configure debugging settings*

Choose **Node.js** as the environment:

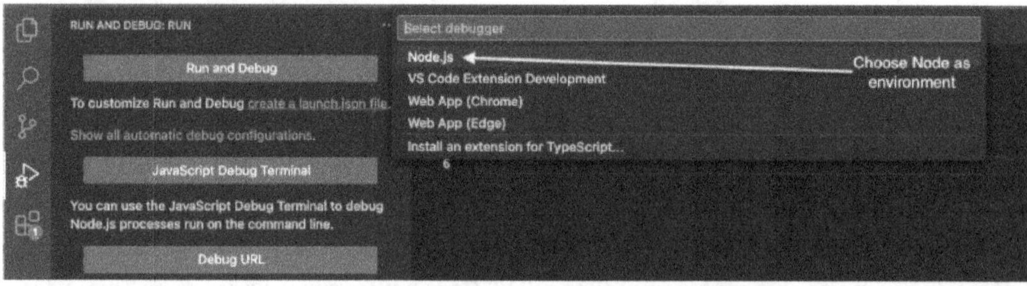


*Figure 6.13 – Selecting Node.js as the debugging environment in VS Code after clicking create a launch.json file to configure the debugging settings for a Node.js application*

Following the instructions in this step, as shown in the preceding figure, will generate a `launch.json` file in your `.vscode` folder. It contains configurations that tell the debugger how to launch and manage your program. The file content should look like this:

```
{
// Use IntelliSense to learn about possible attributes.
// Hover to view descriptions of existing attributes.
// For more information, visit: https://go.microsoft.com/fwlink/?linkid=830387
"version": "0.2.0",
"configurations": [
{
"type": "node",
"request": "launch",
"name": "Launch Program",
"skipFiles": ["<node_internals>/**"],
"program": "${workspaceFolder}/Chapter6/source-maps/dist/index.js",
"outFiles": ["${workspaceFolder}/**/*.js"]
}
]
}
```

Here is an explanation of the key configuration options:

- `"type": "node"`: Specifies that you're debugging a Node.js application
- `"request": "launch"`: Indicates that you want to launch the program instead of attaching to a running process
- `"name": "Launch Program"`: A label for this debug configuration

- "skipFiles": ["<node_internals>/**"]: Skips debugging Node.js internal files for clarity
- `"program": "${workspaceFolder}/index.ts"`: Specifies the entry TypeScript file to debug
- `"outFiles": ["${workspaceFolder}/**/*.js"]`: Points to the compiled JavaScript output files

Congratulations, you just set up the VS Code debugger and are now ready to start debugging. In the next step, we will see how to add breakpoints to your code and use the debugger to step through it for deeper insight.

## Step 2: Add a breakpoint

In the previous step, we created a launch configuration and set up the debugger. In this step, we are going to add a breakpoint. A breakpoint tells the debugger where to pause execution:

1. Open your `index.ts` file.
2. Click in the **gutter** (the area to the left of the line numbers) on the line where you want to pause.
3. A red dot appears, marking the breakpoint.

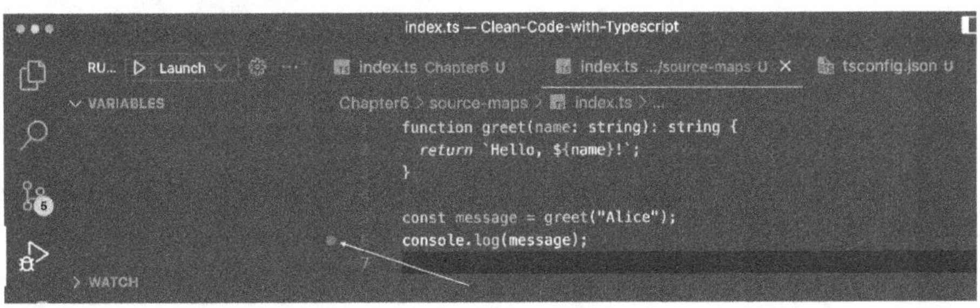


*Figure 6.14 — The figure shows a breakpoint added to the console.log(message); line in index.ts, allowing inspection of the greeting variable during debugging*

Now that we have our breakpoint in place, let's start debugging in the next step.

## Step 3: Start debugging

Now, you're ready to run the debugger:

1. Go back to the **Run and Debug** view.
2. Select your configuration (**Launch Program**).
3. Click the green **Start Debugging** button or press *F5*.

   The program runs and pauses at your breakpoint. From here, you can do the following:

   - **Inspect variables**: Hover over a variable or check the **Variables** pane
   - **Step over** (*F10*): Run the next line of code

- **Step into** (*F11*): Enter into a function call
- **Step out** (*Shift* + *F11*): Exit the current function
- **Continue** (*F5*): Resume execution until the next breakpoint

See the following figure for details:

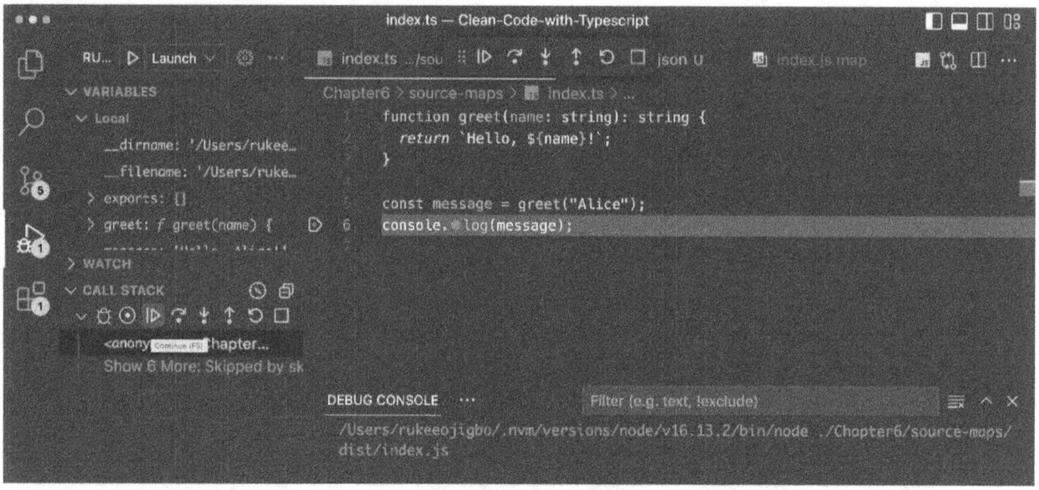


*Figure 6.15 — VS Code debugging interface showcasing variable inspection in the Variables pane, along with controls for step over (F10), step into (F11), step out (Shift + F11), and continue (F5) during a debugging session*

When you hit the *play* button or *F5*, execution resumes, and you can see the result in **DEBUG CONSOLE**, as shown here:

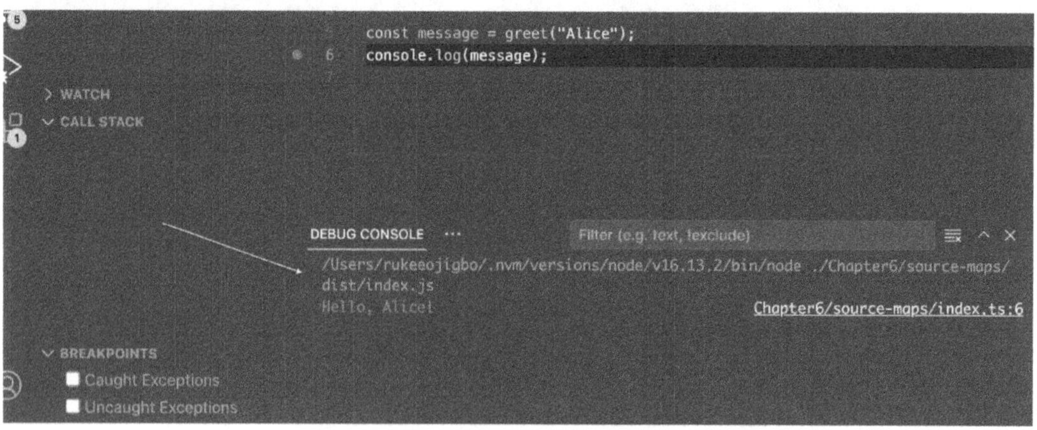


*Figure 6.16 — Advanced breakpoint usage*

VS Code also provides **advanced breakpoint options** that let you debug more efficiently. If you right-click on the gutter (the space to the left of the line numbers), instead of immediately adding a regular breakpoint, you'll see a menu of options as in the following screenshot:

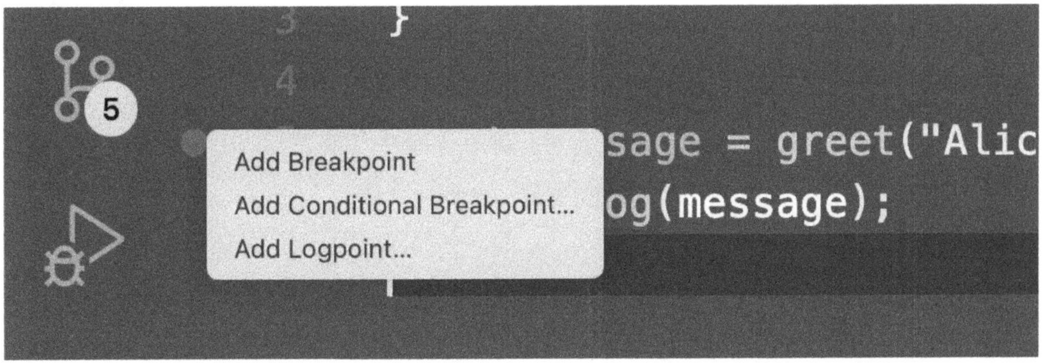


*Figure 6.17 — Breakpoint menu in VS Code showing Add Breakpoint, Add Conditional Breakpoint, and Add Logpoint options*

Let's go over each briefly:

- **Line breakpoints**: These are the most common type of breakpoint, where you click next to a line number in your code to set a breakpoint. The debugger will pause execution when it reaches that line. We've seen this already.
- **Conditional breakpoints**: These allow you to pause execution only if a certain condition is met, such as when a variable reaches a specific value. Here is an example:

```
count > 10
```

  This ensures that the program only stops when `count` is greater than `10`.

- **Logpoints**: These are like breakpoints, but instead of pausing execution, they log a message to the console without stopping your code. This is useful for quick checks without interrupting your flow. Here is an example:

```
Greeting value: {message}
```

  These are useful when you want quick feedback without interrupting the program.

Here's how you can use breakpoints effectively:

- **Isolate issues**: Set breakpoints around the code where you suspect an issue might be occurring. Step through the code to see how variables change and how the logic flows.
- **Combine with `watch` expressions**: Use breakpoints in conjunction with `watch` expressions to monitor specific variables or expressions as you step through your code.

Let's see an example:

```
function processData(data: number[]): number[] {
  let processedData = data.map(num => num * 2);
  return processedData;
}

let result = processData([1, 2, 3]);
console.log(result); // Expected output: [2, 4, 6]
```

By setting a breakpoint on `let processedData = data.map(num => num * 2);`, you can pause the execution and inspect the `data` array and the `processedData` array, ensuring that your transformation logic is working correctly.

## Leveraging console logs

While more advanced debugging tools, such as the VS Code debugger, are powerful, console logs remain a simple yet effective method for debugging. They allow you to output information to the console at runtime, helping you track the flow of your application and inspect values at specific points in your code.

There are two ways of using `console.log`:

- **Basic usage**: You can insert `console.log()` statements in your code to print out the values of variables, the results of expressions, or messages indicating that a certain part of the code has been reached
- **Debugging specific issues**: You can use `console.log()` to verify that your code is reaching the expected lines or to check the values of variables at different stages of your program

Let's see an example:

```
function calculateDiscount(price: number, discount: number): number {
  console.log("Original price:", price);
  console.log("Discount percentage:", discount);
```

```
    let finalPrice = price - (price * (discount / 100));
    console.log("Final price after discount:", finalPrice);

    return finalPrice;
  }

  calculateDiscount(100, 20);
```

In this example, `console.log()` statements are used to print out the original price, discount percentage, and the final price after the discount is applied. This helps you verify that your discount calculation is correct.

Here are the advanced console methods:

- `console.error()`: Use this to output error messages to the console, typically in red text, which makes it clear that something went wrong
- `console.warn()`: Use this to output warnings that something might not be working as expected, but isn't necessarily breaking the code
- `console.table()`: This method is useful for logging arrays or objects in a tabular format, making it easier to visualize the data

Here are the best practices with console logs:

- **Remove before production**: Console logs should be removed or minimized in production code, as they can clutter the console and potentially expose sensitive information.
- **Use sparingly**: While useful, console logs can become overwhelming if overused. Use them strategically to debug specific issues and remove them once the issue is resolved.

Mastering debugging tools and techniques is crucial for becoming a proficient TypeScript developer. By effectively using tools such as the VS Code debugger, source maps, breakpoints, and console logs, you can identify and fix issues more efficiently, leading to cleaner, more reliable code. Practice these techniques regularly to build your confidence and improve your problem-solving skills in real-world development scenarios.

Now that you know how to debug effectively, the next step is learning how to secure your TypeScript applications against common vulnerabilities.

# Security best practices in TypeScript

Security is a crucial aspect of software development, especially in TypeScript applications that handle sensitive data, user input, and interact with external services. Adopting security best practices helps you build applications that are not only functional but also resilient against common security threats. This section provides a comprehensive guide to understanding the importance of security in TypeScript and practical strategies to implement robust security measures.

In this section, we will cover the following key topics:

- Introduction to security practices
- Input validation and data sanitization
- Secure coding techniques
- Error handling with security in mind
- Managing sensitive data

By the end of this section, you will be able to apply these best practices in your TypeScript projects, ensuring that your applications are protected against vulnerabilities and security breaches.

## Introduction to security practices

Security practices in TypeScript aim to protect your application from malicious attacks, data breaches, and other vulnerabilities. As a developer, understanding the importance of security ensures that your application remains safe and trustworthy for users.

Let's delve deeper into why security matters:

- **Protecting user data**: Applications often handle sensitive information such as user credentials, personal data, and payment details. A lack of security measures can expose this data to unauthorized access.
- **Preventing attacks**: Common security threats such as XSS, SQL injection, and other code injection attacks can compromise your application. Implementing security best practices helps mitigate these risks.
- **Maintaining trust and compliance**: Security breaches can damage your reputation and result in non-compliance with regulations such as **GDPR**. A secure application maintains user trust and meets legal standards.

When building secure applications, it's important to keep in mind the three fundamental security goals:

- **Confidentiality**: Ensuring that data is only accessible to those authorized to view it
- **Integrity**: Preventing unauthorized modifications to data
- **Availability**: Ensuring that your application is available and accessible when needed, without being compromised by attacks

These principles, often called the **CIA triad**, form the foundation of every security practice you'll apply in your TypeScript projects.

In the next section, we will look at input validation and data sanitization.

# Input validation and data sanitization

User input is one of the biggest sources of security risks. Attackers often exploit unchecked input to inject malicious scripts (XSS) or manipulate database queries (SQL injection). By validating and sanitizing input, you ensure that your application only processes safe and expected data.

## Input validation

**Input validation** is the process of checking user inputs to ensure they meet the expected format, type, and constraints before processing them in your application.

Validating inputs helps prevent attackers from injecting malicious code or unexpected data that can cause your application to behave unpredictably.

Here are the types of input validation:

- **Client-side validation**: Performed in the browser, this provides immediate feedback to the user but is not a substitute for server-side validation, as it can be bypassed
- **Server-side validation**: This is the primary defense line, as it ensures that data meets expected criteria before being processed by the server

Here are the best practices for input validation:

- **Whitelist validation**: Only allow specific inputs that are known to be safe, such as known formats for email addresses or specific allowed characters
- **Use regular expressions**: Regular expressions can be used to define acceptable input patterns, ensuring that the data matches the required format
- **Limit input length**: Restrict input lengths to prevent buffer overflow attacks or overly large submissions that could crash your application

Let's see an example of input validation in TypeScript:

```
function validateEmail(email: string): boolean {
  const emailRegex = /^[^\s@]+@[^\s@]+\.[^\s@]+$/;
  return emailRegex.test(email);
}

if (!validateEmail(userInputEmail)) {
  throw new Error("Invalid email format.");
}
```

In this example, an email validation function checks whether the user input conforms to the expected email pattern. If not, an error is thrown, preventing the invalid data from being processed further.

## Data sanitization

**Data sanitization** involves cleaning or filtering user inputs to remove potentially harmful elements, such as script tags in HTML.

Sanitization helps ensure that inputs do not contain harmful code that could be executed by your application.

Here are the sanitization techniques:

- **Escape special characters**: Convert special characters (<, >, ", and ') into safe representations to prevent them from being executed as code
- **Remove unwanted elements**: Strip out potentially dangerous content, such as HTML tags or SQL keywords, that could be used for injections

Here is an example of data sanitization in TypeScript:

```
function sanitizeInput(input: string): string {
  return input.replace(/[<>"'();]/g, ""); // Removes potentially harmful
characters
}

const sanitizedUserInput = sanitizeInput(userInput);
```

This is what's happening in the preceding code:

- The `sanitizeInput` function uses a regular expression to remove characters such as <, >, ", ', (, ), and `;`, which are often used in malicious inputs such as XSS attacks

- It returns a cleaned version of the input string, helping reduce the risk of executing harmful code
- The sanitized input is then stored in `sanitizedUserInput`

In real-world applications, you'd typically use a validation and sanitization library such as Zod (`https://github.com/colinhacks/zod`) or Joi (`https://joi.dev/`) for a more robust and maintainable approach—especially when handling complex user input or validating structured data.

# Secure coding techniques

Writing secure code is critical to building robust applications. Secure coding techniques involve designing your code to minimize vulnerabilities and protect against common attack vectors such as XSS, SQL injection, and data exposure.

This section covers key practices for writing secure TypeScript code, including input validation, error handling, and sensitive data management.

Here are the key secure coding practices:

- **Avoid using** `eval()`: The `eval()` function executes a string as code, which can be exploited to run malicious code. Avoid using it or restrict its usage to safe inputs only.
- **Use TypeScript's type system**: Leverage TypeScript's strong typing to reduce errors and prevent type-related vulnerabilities. For instance, use specific types instead of any to avoid unexpected values.
- **Implement secure defaults**: Set secure defaults for all configuration options, such as using HTTPS for network communication and requiring strong passwords for authentication.

Let's see an example of secure coding in TypeScript:

```
function getUserData(id: number): string | null {
  if (typeof id !== 'number' || id <= 0) {
    return null; // Reject invalid inputs early
  }
  // Proceed with fetching user data
}
```

In the preceding example, the function validates the `id` parameter before doing anything else. It checks two things:

- The `id` type must be a number. This prevents unexpected values such as strings, objects, or malicious payloads from being used.
- The value of `id` must be greater than zero. This ensures that the input falls within an acceptable range, rejecting invalid or nonsensical values.

If either check fails, the function immediately returns `null` instead of processing the input. This "fail fast" approach stops invalid data from propagating deeper into the system, where it could cause errors, data corruption, or open the door to injection attacks.

Here are some additional secure coding considerations:

- **Handle sensitive data carefully**: Avoid logging sensitive information such as passwords or tokens
- **Use parameterized queries**: When interacting with databases, always use parameterized queries to prevent SQL injection

Now that we understand data sanitization, it's time to explore error handling. In this section, we'll look at how to handle errors securely.

# Error handling with security in mind

Error handling plays a crucial role in security. Poorly managed errors can expose sensitive information, such as stack traces or database queries, to potential attackers.

Here are the secure error handling best practices:

- **Generic error messages**: Always display user-friendly messages that do not reveal internal details. Avoid exposing stack traces or database errors directly to users.
- **Log errors securely**: Log errors in a secure location, accessible only to authorized personnel, and avoid logging sensitive data.
- **Graceful degradation**: Ensure that your application continues to function in a limited capacity even if an error occurs, without exposing critical data.

Let's see an example of secure error handling:

```
try {
  // Code that might throw an error
} catch (error) {
  console.error("An error occurred. Please try again later."); // User-friendly
message
```

```
    logError(error); // Detailed logging in a secure location
}
```

Let's break down this example:

- The `try` block contains the code that might throw an error.
- The `catch` block catches any errors that occur and executes the code within it.
- `console.error("Sorry, something went wrong. Please try again later.");` displays a friendly, generic error message to the user. This message doesn't reveal any internal details about the error.
- `logError(error);` logs the detailed error information in a secure location, such as a server-side log file or a logging service. This allows developers to troubleshoot the issue without exposing sensitive information to the user.

This approach balances usability and security. Users see a safe message, while developers still get the information needed to debug and maintain the application.

## Managing sensitive data

Handling sensitive data securely is a fundamental aspect of application security. Ensuring that data is stored, transmitted, and processed securely helps prevent unauthorized access.

Here are the key practices for managing sensitive data:

- **Use encryption**: Encrypt sensitive data both at rest and in transit to protect it from unauthorized access. Encryption converts data into an unreadable format that can only be accessed with the correct decryption key, making it secure from unauthorized access :
    - When storing user passwords, always hash them (e.g., using **bcrypt**) instead of saving them as plain text
    - For data transmission, use **HTTPS** to ensure that data is encrypted while traveling between the client and server
- **Secure API keys and credentials**: Store API keys, tokens, and credentials securely, using environment variables or secure storage solutions instead of hardcoding them in your code.
  Let's see an example of how you can securely store your keys using environment variables, in a `.env` file:

  ```
  API_KEY=your_secret_key_here
  ```

Access them in your TypeScript application like this:

```
const apiKey = process.env.API_KEY;
```

This way, your keys remain secure and aren't exposed in your code base.

- **Implement access controls**: Restrict access to sensitive data based on roles and permissions, ensuring that only authorized users can access it.
  For example, use **role-based access control** (**RBAC**) to define who can access certain parts of your application. For instance, only admins should have access to user management functions.

  Implement middleware that checks a user's role before allowing access:

  ```
  function isAdmin(req, res, next) {
    if (req.user.role !== 'admin') {
      return res.status(403).send('Access Denied');
    }
    next();
  }
  ```

  In this example, the `isAdmin` middleware function checks whether the user's role is `'admin'` before allowing access to the next route or controller. Here's how it works:

  - `req.user.role`: This checks the user's role, which is assumed to be stored in the `req.user` object
  - `if (req.user.role !== 'admin')`: If the user's role is not `'admin'`, the function returns a `403` Forbidden response with the message `'Access Denied'`
  - `next()`: If the user's role is `'admin'`, the function calls the `next()` function to allow the request to proceed to the next route or controller

  This approach ensures that only users with the appropriate permissions can access sensitive data or functionality, safeguarding your application against unauthorized access.

Implementing security best practices in TypeScript is essential to building applications that are resilient against threats. By focusing on input validation, data sanitization, secure coding, error handling, and proper management of sensitive data, you can significantly reduce the risk of security vulnerabilities in your applications. These strategies will help you create robust, secure TypeScript applications that protect both your data and your users.

## Summary

In this chapter, we explored the crucial aspects of error handling, debugging, and security best practices in TypeScript. We began by understanding various error types—syntax, runtime, and logical errors—and examined common error patterns and strategies to manage them effectively. This foundational knowledge equipped us with the skills to identify and address errors efficiently in any TypeScript application.

We then delved into synchronous and asynchronous error handling, highlighting practical techniques such as `try-catch` blocks for synchronous errors and using promises and `async/await` for managing asynchronous errors. We emphasized the importance of proper error handling to create resilient applications that can gracefully recover from unexpected issues.

Next, we covered debugging tools and techniques, focusing on how to effectively use the VS Code debugger, source maps, breakpoints, and console logs. Mastering these tools enhances your ability to troubleshoot and resolve issues swiftly, ultimately improving the reliability of your code.

Finally, we discussed security best practices in TypeScript, highlighting the importance of input validation, data sanitization, and secure coding techniques to protect applications from common vulnerabilities. We also covered how to handle sensitive data securely, including the use of encryption, secure storage of credentials, and implementing access controls.

By mastering these concepts, you are now equipped to handle errors gracefully, debug effectively, and implement security measures to safeguard your TypeScript applications, making them more robust, maintainable, and secure.

Looking ahead, in the next chapter, we will shift our focus to performance optimization.

## Get this book's PDF copy, code bundle, and more

Scan the QR code (or go to `packtpub.com/unlock`). Search for this book by name, confirm the edition, and then follow the steps on the page.

UNLOCK NOW

*Note: Keep your invoice handy. Purchases made directly from the Packt website don't require an invoice.*

# 7

# Maximizing Performance Optimization

In this chapter, we will discuss various techniques and strategies to optimize the performance of TypeScript applications. You will learn techniques for identifying bottlenecks, profiling tools, and implementing code optimization strategies such as minification, tree shaking, lazy loading, and caching. The goal is to equip you with actionable strategies that can be applied in real-world scenarios to enhance the efficiency of the applications. Performance optimization is crucial not just for improving user experience but also for reducing resource consumption, which can lead to cost savings.

Here is what you will learn as part of this chapter:

- Understanding the importance of performance optimization
- Identifying performance bottlenecks
- Performance-enhancing techniques

By the end of this chapter, you will have a solid understanding of how to maximize the performance of TypeScript applications, ensuring that your projects are not only functional but also efficient.

## Technical requirements

You can download the example project and code for this book by following the instructions in the *Download the example code files* section in the *Preface* of this book.

This chapter's code files are included in the downloadable code bundle.

# Understanding performance optimization

Performance optimization is a key part of building TypeScript applications that are reliable and scalable. As your code base grows and your app handles more features, users, and data, its real-world performance becomes just as important as the features it provides. Optimization isn't only about speed; it's about keeping your application responsive, efficient, and cost-effective.

In this section, we'll look at why performance optimization matters, how it affects both users and developers, and the core principles behind building high-performing TypeScript applications. Understanding these ideas early will help you make smarter architectural decisions and write code that scales smoothly.

## Why performance optimization matters

When you build a TypeScript application, your main goal is to create something that works efficiently and provides a smooth experience for users. However, even if your app functions correctly, it might not be optimized to give a great user experience. A slow application can frustrate users, cause high bounce rates, and even lead to lost revenue.

Performance optimization ensures that your TypeScript applications run fast, respond quickly, and use fewer system resources. This is especially important as applications grow in complexity, handle more users, and process large amounts of data.

Here are some key reasons why optimizing performance is crucial:

- **Improves user experience**: Users expect applications to load quickly and respond instantly. Research supports this strongly. For example, Google's data shows that increasing page load time from 1 second to 3 seconds raises the likelihood of users bouncing by 32% (`https://majordigital.com/articles/website-speed-impacts-your-bottom-line`). In an e-commerce context, studies show that even 100 ms of additional latency can reduce conversion rates by 2–7%, depending on the application (`https://www.researchgate.net/publication/319449830_The_Impact_of_Web_Pages'_Load_Time_on_the_Conversion_Rate_of_an_E-Commerce_Platform`).
  Imagine opening an online store and waiting 10 seconds for a product page to load. Most users would close the tab and look elsewhere. Performance optimization helps prevent this by making sure your application responds as quickly as possible.
- **Reduces resource consumption**: Optimized applications use less CPU, memory, and network bandwidth. This is important for the following reasons:
  - It improves battery life for mobile users

  - It reduces hosting costs for businesses
  - It allows applications to scale efficiently without needing expensive upgrades

  For example, a poorly optimized function running in the background could unnecessarily consume memory, making the entire app sluggish. By improving efficiency, you ensure that only necessary resources are used.

- **Boosts search engine ranking (SEO)**: Google and other search engines prioritize fast websites. If your application is slow, it might not rank well in search results, making it harder for people to find your site. Faster websites generally receive more traffic and engagement.
- **Enhances scalability**: As more users access your application, performance issues become more noticeable. A well-optimized application can handle thousands of users efficiently without slowing down or crashing.
  For example, an unoptimized database query might work fine with 10 users but become a huge problem when 10,000 users are making the same request at the same time. Optimizing code ensures smooth performance even under heavy load.
- **Saves development and maintenance time**: Fixing performance problems early prevents major issues later. If you wait until users start complaining, solving the problem might require rewriting large parts of the code. Good performance practices help developers avoid technical debt and maintain the application more easily.

## Common causes of poor performance in TypeScript applications

To improve performance, you need to know what slows applications down. Some common reasons include the following:

- **Too many re-renders**: In frameworks such as React, unnecessary re-renders can slow down applications
- **Inefficient loops and recursive functions**: Loops that perform unnecessary calculations or iterate over large datasets can slow execution
- **Large bundle sizes**: If your app loads too much JavaScript at once, it takes longer to start
- **Unoptimized API calls**: Making too many API requests or fetching large amounts of unnecessary data can slow down performance
- **Memory leaks**: Not properly cleaning up event listeners, variables, or references can cause the app to use more and more memory over time

## Code example: comparing iteration patterns

To understand how coding patterns influence both performance and readability, let's compare two approaches to summing numbers in an array. Here is the traditional loop example:

```
function sumWithForLoop(numbers: number[]): number {
  let total = 0;

  for (let i = 0; i < numbers.length; i++) {
    total += numbers[i];
  }

  return total;
}

const nums = Array.from({ length: 1000000 }, (_, i) => i);

console.time("For Loop Sum");
console.log(sumWithForLoop(nums));
console.timeEnd("For Loop Sum");
```

The `for` loop performs a straightforward iteration. It directly accesses array elements and updates the accumulator. In many JavaScript engines, this approach is highly optimized and can be faster than higher-order methods for large datasets. Here is an example using the `reduce()` function:

```
function sumWithReduce(numbers: number[]): number {
  return numbers.reduce((acc, num) => acc + num, 0);
}

console.time("Reduce Sum");
console.log(sumWithReduce(nums));
console.timeEnd("Reduce Sum");
```

The `reduce()` method provides a more declarative and expressive way to perform the same operation. Instead of manually managing an index and an accumulator, the logic is expressed in a functional style.

## Performance versus readability

Although `reduce()` can produce cleaner and more expressive code, it is not necessarily faster. In fact, traditional `for` loops may outperform `reduce()` in performance-critical scenarios because `reduce()` invokes a callback function on each iteration, introducing additional overhead.

When choosing between the two, here are some recommendations:

- Use a `for` loop when performance is critical or when fine-grained control is required
- Use `reduce()` when prioritizing readability, functional style, and expressiveness

Modern JavaScript engines are highly optimized, so for most real-world applications, the performance difference is negligible. The choice should often be guided by clarity and maintainability rather than micro-optimization.

## Key strategies for performance optimization

There are many proven ways to make TypeScript applications faster. The following strategies deliver the biggest wins for most projects. We will explore the exact implementation details with code examples, tool configurations, and setups in the upcoming section, *Performance-enhancing techniques*. For now, here's what you need to know at a high level:

- **Code splitting**: Instead of requiring users to download the entire application bundle just to load something simple, such as the home page, code splitting breaks the app into smaller, logical chunks. These chunks are loaded only when needed, such as when a user navigates to a specific route, interacts with a component, or triggers an on-demand feature. This approach dramatically reduces initial load time and improves the overall user experience.
- **Minification**: By removing unnecessary characters from your code (such as white spaces and comments), you can reduce file sizes, resulting in faster downloads.
- **Tree shaking**: This process involves removing unused code from your application during the build process. This helps in reducing the bundle size, making the application faster.
- **Caching**: Caching focuses on avoiding repeated work. Instead of recalculating values, re-fetching data, or rerunning expensive logic, applications can reuse previously computed results.

## Why these strategies matter

Performance issues often stem from a small set of common problems: oversized bundles, repeated computations, inefficient loops, excessive re-renders, and memory leaks. Applying the preceding strategies helps prevent these issues early and keeps applications fast and scalable as they grow. In the next section, we'll move from understanding the problems to actively finding and fixing them. You'll learn how to use powerful tools such as Chrome DevTools, Webpack Bundle Analyzer, and Node.js performance hooks to pinpoint bottlenecks, analyze slow functions, API calls, and memory usage, and apply targeted fixes so your application runs efficiently and scales smoothly.

# Identifying performance bottlenecks

Performance bottlenecks are areas in your application that slow down its overall performance; they take too long to execute, consume too much memory, or render more than necessary. Identifying these bottlenecks is crucial for optimizing your TypeScript applications effectively. In this section, we will explore how to pinpoint these issues using profiling tools, recognize common performance problems, and prioritize optimization efforts.

Bottlenecks can happen in many areas, including the following:

- Slow functions that take too much time to execute
- Unnecessary re-renders in frameworks such as React
- Memory leaks that cause the app to use more RAM over time
- Large JavaScript bundles that slow down downloading times
- Inefficient API calls that block or slow down other processes

To fix performance issues, we first need to measure performance, detect slow areas, and prioritize what to optimize.

## Using profiling tools to measure performance

Profiling tools help you analyze how well your application is running. They provide insights into how much time each function takes, how memory is being used, and which parts of the app are slowing things down. In this section, we will take a look at Chrome DevTools Performance Profiler and see how to use it to profile your application.

### Chrome DevTools Performance Profiler

If you are working on a web application, **Chrome DevTools Performance Profiler** is widely regarded as one of the best (and most accessible) tools for performance analysis. Here's why it stands out:

- It's built directly into Chrome, no extra installation required

- It offers a complete timeline of everything that happens in the browser: JavaScript execution, rendering, painting, layout, network requests, and even garbage collection
- The flame graph and call stack views make it easy to spot long tasks, poor-quality frames, and expensive functions with pinpoint accuracy
- It works seamlessly with modern frameworks (React, Angular, Vue, Svelte, etc.) and shows React/Vue re-renders when the respective DevTools extensions are installed
- Features such as the **Bottom-Up**, **Call Tree**, and **Event Log** views let both beginners and advanced developers drill down into performance bottlenecks quickly

Let's see an example of Chrome DevTools Performance Profiler in action.

## Simple DEMO of Chrome DevTools Performance Profiler

This tiny example proves why Chrome DevTools is so powerful: in seconds, with zero extra tools, you can see exactly which function is freezing the UI. Create a new file called `perf-demo.html` and open it in Chrome:

```
<!DOCTYPE html>
<html>
<head>
<title>DevTools Performance Demo</title>
<style>body { font-family: sans-serif; padding: 2rem; } button { padding: 1rem
2rem; font-size: 1.2rem; margin: 0.5rem; }</style>
</head>
<body>
<h1>Chrome DevTools Performance Demo</h1>
<button id="slow">Run Very Slow Code (~5 sec block)</button>
<button id="fast">Run Fast Code</button>

<script>
function wasteCpuTime() {
const start = performance.now();
while (performance.now() - start < 5000) { /* spin */ }
console.log("Done wasting 5 seconds");
}

document.getElementById("slow").onclick = wasteCpuTime;
document.getElementById("fast").onclick = () => console.log("Instant!");
</script>
</body>
</html>
```

Follow these steps precisely to generate the performance profile:

1. Press *F12* or right-click → **Inspect** to open DevTools.
2. Go to the **Performance** tab.
3. Click the **Record** button (●) at the top left of the **Performance** tab.
4. Now, immediately click the **Run Very Slow Code** button in your application window.

> **Note**
>
> The UI will freeze completely for about 5 seconds.

5. Once the freeze is over and the button is responsive again, click the **Stop** button, which replaced the **Record** button.

Your **Performance** tab should instantly populate with a colorful timeline, looking very similar to the following figure. This timeline is the visual proof of the long task you just created.

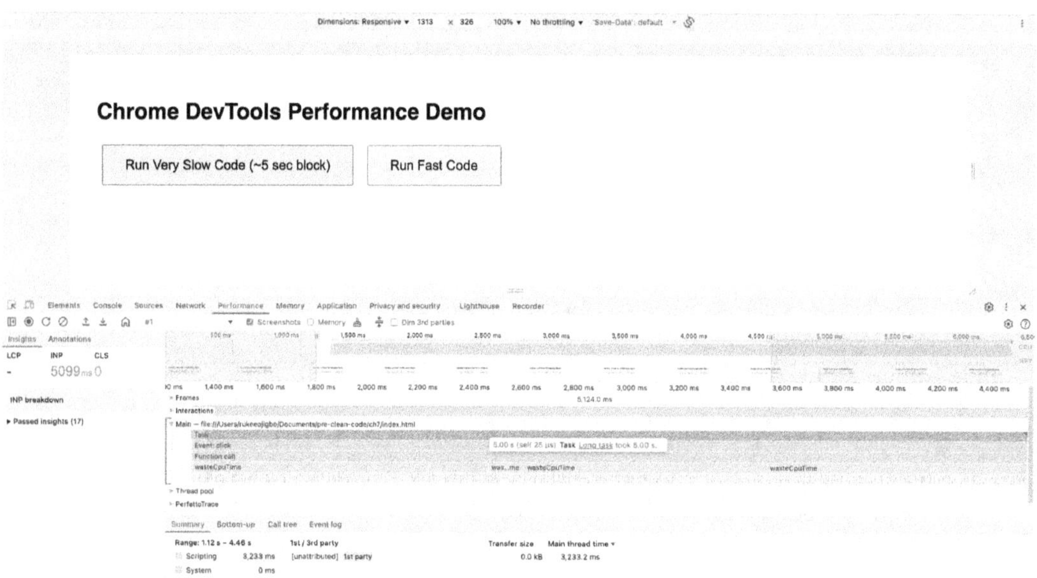


*Figure 7.1 – Chrome DevTools Performance recording showing a long main-thread task (~5 seconds) triggered by the slow implementation, illustrating how blocking code impacts responsiveness and interaction latency (INP)*

Let's go over the image to understand the **Performance** recording:

- **Key metrics (top left)**: The first thing to notice is the **Interaction to Next Paint** (**INP**) value: **5099 ms**. This is extremely poor. Anything above 200 ms is considered a bad user experience. INP measures how long the page takes to visually respond to user input, so a 5-second delay means the UI was completely unresponsive.
  **Largest contentful paint** (**LCP**) and **cummulative layout shift** (**CLS**) both show **0**, simply because those metrics weren't triggered during this recording (no major content loads or layout shifts occurred).
- **The timeline (main area)**: In the main timeline, the most obvious issue is the red bar spanning ~5,099 ms, which signals a long task. Directly beneath it is a yellow bar indicating continuous JavaScript execution on the main thread. This yellow span from 0–5,000 ms tells us the browser was blocked the entire time.
  Expanding the **Main** section reveals the full breakdown as we see in the preceding figure:
    - A red **Task** bar showing **Long task took 5.00 s**
    - A yellow **Event: click** frame
    - A yellow **Function call** frame
    - And finally, a long purple bar representing the offending function: **wasteCpuTime**

This view shows precisely where execution time went and which function caused the lock-up.

In the **Summary** section underneath, **Scripting** is roughly equal to 5,000 ms, confirming that the slowdown was entirely due to JavaScript, not rendering, not layout, and not painting. The browser simply couldn't do anything else because the main thread was monopolized by one long-running function.

This recording clearly pinpoints the problem: DevTools shows exactly which function (**wasteCpuTime**) blocked the main thread, how long the UI remained frozen, and where the stall occurred in the call stack. It also highlights that the delay was caused solely by JavaScript execution. When you see long purple bars stacked under red markers, DevTools is essentially telling you: *This code is blocking the main thread.*

Run the recording again using the fast code version, and you'll see the opposite behavior: no red bars, minimal scripting time, and a responsive main thread.

Now that we have an idea of how the Chrome DevTools Performance Profiler works, let's move on to the Webpack Bundle Analyzer in the next subsection.

## Webpack Bundle Analyzer

If your application is loading too slowly, it might be because your **JavaScript bundle** size is too large. The **Webpack Bundle Analyzer** helps you see what's taking up the most space.

Let's see how to use the Webpack Bundle Analyzer with the following demo. We will set up a simple React project with a huge bundle dominated by `moment` and `lodash`, then see how you would go about shrinking the bundle:

1. Create the project:

```
mkdir bundle-demo && cd bundle-demo
npm init -y
npm install react react-dom lodash moment dayjs
npm install --save-dev webpack webpack-cli webpack-bundle-analyzer
typescript ts-loader @types/react @types/react-dom @types/lodash
```

2. Create `tsconfig.json`:

```
{
  "compilerOptions": {
    "target": "es2020",
    "module": "esnext",
    "moduleResolution": "node",
    "jsx": "react-jsx",
    "strict": true,
    "esModuleInterop": true,
    "allowSyntheticDefaultImports": true,
    "skipLibCheck": true,
    "forceConsistentCasingInFileNames": true,
    "outDir": "./dist",
    "lib": ["dom", "dom.iterable", "es6"]
  },
  "include": ["src"]
}
```

3. Create `webpack.config.js`:

```
const { BundleAnalyzerPlugin } = require('webpack-bundle-analyzer');

module.exports = {
  mode: 'production',
```

```
  entry: './src/index.tsx',
  module: {
    rules: [{ test: /\.tsx?$/, use: 'ts-loader', exclude: /node_modules/ }]
  },
  resolve: { extensions: ['.tsx', '.ts', '.js'] },
  plugins: [
    new BundleAnalyzerPlugin()    // ← this line opens the visualizer
automatically
  ]
};
```

4. Create the source file:

```
mkdir -p src && touch src/index.tsx
```

5. Add the following code to `index.tsx`:

```
import React from 'react';
import ReactDOM from 'react-dom/client';
import moment from 'moment';    // ~280 KB of pain
import _ from 'lodash';         // ~70 KB more

console.log('moment&lodashareHUGE:',moment,_);

const root = document.createElement('div');
root.id = 'root';
document.body.appendChild(root);

ReactDOM.createRoot(root).render(
  <div style={{ padding: '3rem', fontFamily: 'system-ui', lineHeight:
1.6 }}>
    <h1>Webpack Bundle Analyzer Demo </h1>
    <p>Open <strong>http://127.0.0.1:8888</strong> to see the treemap!</p>
    <p>You'll see <code>moment</code> and <code>lodash</
code> eating almost the entire bundle.</p>
```

```
    </div>
  );
```

6. Build and see the magic:

```
npx webpack
```

Your browser automatically opens the interactive treemap at `http://127.0.0.1:8888`. See the following figure for reference:

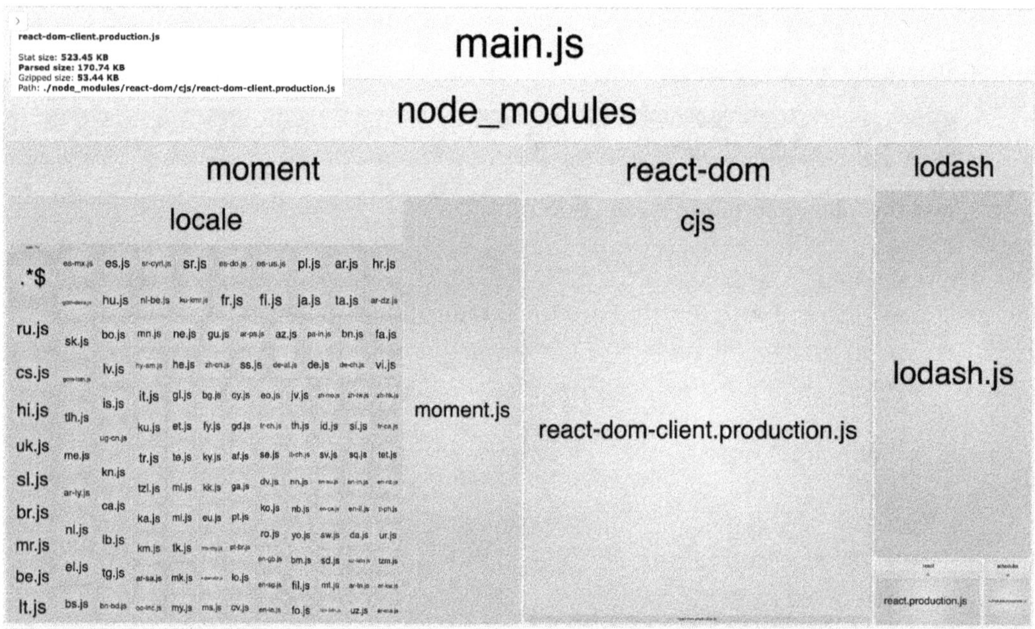


*Figure 7.2 – Webpack Bundle Analyzer – the before picture (real output from our demo)*

This is what the Webpack Bundle Analyzer treemap shows:

- The biggest green rectangle on the left is **moment**; it alone takes up roughly ⅓ of the entire bundle (~280–300 KB gzipped before tree-shaking).
  Under it, the sub-rectangle labeled **locale** is massive because the default **moment.js** build includes all 100+ locale files (most apps only need 1–2).
- **react-dom** is reasonably sized but still noticeable.
- Next to it, **lodash** is another huge block (~70 KB gzipped).
- Everything else (your own code, React itself, etc.) is tiny in comparison.

This visualization is the power of the analyzer: it uses a single screen to tell you precisely which libraries need replacement or optimization. While we dedicate the *Performance-enhancing techniques* section to the detailed solutions, such as replacing heavy libraries (e.g., swapping `moment` for `dayjs`), excluding unnecessary assets (e.g., removing `moment` locale files), and implementing tree-shaking (importing only necessary functions from libraries such as `lodash`), the treemap already confirms the fundamental cause: 100% of the bundle bloat is driven by external dependencies, not your own code.

## Node.js performance hooks (for backend performance)

If you're working on a **TypeScript backend**, you can use **Node.js performance hooks** to measure how long different functions take to execute.

Here is an example of measuring execution time in a TypeScript function:

```
import { performance } from "perf_hooks";

function slowFunction() {
  let total = 0;
  for (let i = 0; i < 1e7; i++) {
    total += i;
  }
  return total;
}

const start = performance.now();
slowFunction();
const end = performance.now();

console.log(`Execution time: ${end - start}ms`);
```

This script will show how many milliseconds the function takes to run. If it's too slow, you can look for ways to optimize it.

# Detecting slow functions, excessive re-renders, and memory leaks

Once you have identified slow areas in your application, you need to analyze the root cause. A slow function is one that takes too long to execute or performs unnecessary calculations.

This is how to detect slow functions:

- Use Chrome DevTools or Node.js performance hooks (as shown earlier)

- Check the CPU usage and execution time of your functions
- Avoid unnecessary loops or repetitive calculations inside critical functions

## Example: Optimizing a slow function by avoiding repeated work

A common cause of slow functions is performing expensive operations repeatedly inside performance-critical code paths. Sorting is a relatively expensive operation, and repeatedly sorting the same data can significantly impact performance.

Consider the following example:

```
function processData(data: number[]): number[] {

// Sorting happens every time the function is called

const sorted = data.sort((a, b) => a - b);

return sorted.map(value => value * 2);

}
```

In this implementation, the array is sorted on every invocation of `processData`. If this function is called frequently, such as during rendering, user interactions, or data updates, the repeated sorting becomes a performance bottleneck.

A more efficient approach is to sort the data once and reuse the result:

```
function processDataOptimized(sortedData: number[]): number[] {

return sortedData.map(value => value * 2);

}


const data = [5, 3, 1, 4, 2];

const sortedData = [...data].sort((a, b) => a - b);


// Reuse the sorted data instead of sorting repeatedly

processDataOptimized(sortedData);
```

By moving the sorting operation outside the hot path, this approach avoids unnecessary repeated work. The optimized version reduces CPU usage, improves execution time, and scales better as the size of the dataset or the number of function calls increases.

This example highlights an important performance principle: removing redundant computation often delivers far greater gains than micro-optimizing individual operations or APIs.

## Detecting excessive re-renders in React

If your React app is slow, unnecessary re-renders might be the cause. This is how to detect excessive re-renders:

1. Use React Developer Tools in Chrome.
2. Enable **Highlight updates when components render** in the React Profiler.
3. Check whether components re-render too frequently when they shouldn't.

Here is an example of preventing unnecessary re-renders. This is bad practice (causes re-renders on every state update):

```
function MyComponent({ count }: { count: number }) {
  return <div>Count: {count}</div>;
}
```

This is the optimized version using `React.memo()`:

```
import React from "react";

const MyComponent = React.memo(({ count }: { count: number }) => {
  return <div>Count: {count}</div>;
});
```

`React.memo()` prevents re-renders unless `count` changes.

## Detecting memory leaks

Memory leaks happen when an application keeps using memory without releasing it, eventually slowing everything down.

This is how to detect memory leaks:

- Use Chrome DevTools → **Memory** tab
- Look for increasing memory usage over time
- Check for unnecessary event listeners or variables that aren't garbage collected

Here is an example of fixing a memory leak in event listeners.

This is bad practice (does not remove event listener):

```
useEffect(() => {
  window.addEventListener("resize", () => console.log("Resized!"));
}, []);
```

Here is the optimized version (removes the listener when the component unmounts):

```
useEffect(() => {
  const handleResize = () => console.log("Resized!");
  window.addEventListener("resize", handleResize);

  return () => {
    window.removeEventListener("resize", handleResize);
  };
}, []);
```

By removing event listeners when they're no longer needed, we free up memory and prevent leaks. The following figure demonstrates how memory usage increases over time when cleanup is not properly handled.

```
+-----------------------+
|                       |
|   Parent Component    | <--- State Update Triggered
|                       |
+-----------------------+

      |      |      |
      v      v      v
+------+ +------+ +------+
|       | |       | |       |
| Child | | Child | | Child |
|  1    | |  2    | |  3    |
|       | |       | |       |
+-------+ +-------+ +-------+
      ^      ^      ^
      |      |      |
 Re-Render  Re-Render   Re-Render
 Triggered  (Unnecessary) (Unnecessary)

+-----------------------------------+
| CPU Usage                         |
|                                   |
| Useful Work          Wasted Work  |
| [----]               [----------]|
+-----------------------------------+
```

*Figure 7.3 – Parent state update triggering unnecessary child re-renders, resulting in wasted CPU work in component-based frameworks*

The preceding figure illustrates how state updates in component-based frameworks such as React can lead to wasted CPU work. When a state update occurs in a parent component, it triggers a re-render. By default, this re-render cascades down the component tree, forcing all child components to re-render as well. The problem is that many of these components, such as `Child 2` and `Child 3` in the example, may not have received any new data, yet they still go through the full re-render process.

This unnecessary work shows up as the `Wasted Work` portion of the CPU usage chart, representing time spent re-rendering components that produce no visible changes in the UI. The key takeaway is that optimization techniques such as `React.memo()` can break this automatic cascade. By preventing components from re-rendering when their inputs haven't changed, you can significantly reduce wasted CPU cycles and improve rendering efficiency.

In the next section, let's look at strategies we can use to optimize our applications.

## Strategies for prioritizing optimization efforts

Not all performance issues need to be fixed immediately. Here's how to prioritize:

- **Start with user experience**: Fix the slowest and most frustrating issues first
- **Look for quick wins**: Optimize things that require little effort but bring big improvements
- **Focus on high-impact areas**: Optimize functions that run frequently or affect multiple parts of the app
- **Reduce bundle size**: Use tree shaking and lazy loading to remove unnecessary code
- **Monitor and improve over time**: Regularly profile your app and make adjustments

In this section, you learned how to measure and analyze performance using tools such as Chrome DevTools, the Webpack Bundle Analyzer, and Node.js performance hooks. These tools help you detect issues such as slow functions, excessive re-renders, and memory leaks, giving you visibility into what's really happening under the hood.

You also learned how to apply practical code optimizations and prioritize performance improvements based on user impact and efficiency. With a clearer picture of where your application is slowing down, the next topic will focus on strategies for enhancing performance in a more structured and effective way.

# Performance-enhancing techniques

Optimizing the performance of your TypeScript applications involves various techniques that help improve loading times, responsiveness, and overall efficiency. In this section, we will explore several effective performance-enhancing techniques, including lazy loading, code splitting, tree shaking, caching mechanisms, and optimization of loops and asynchronous operations.

Some key methods include the following:

- **Lazy loading and code splitting**: Load only what's needed when it's needed
- **Tree shaking**: Remove unused code to reduce bundle size
- **Caching mechanisms**: Store data efficiently to reduce redundant operations
- **Optimizing loops, recursive functions, and asynchronous operations**: Write better-performing code

# Implementing lazy loading and code splitting

Lazy loading and code splitting are related techniques used to improve application performance by reducing the amount of JavaScript loaded during the initial render:

- Lazy loading delays loading specific components until they are needed
- Code splitting breaks large bundles into smaller chunks that can be loaded independently

Together, these techniques reduce initial bundle size and improve startup performance.

## How to implement lazy loading in React

Lazy loading is a technique that delays loading parts of the application until they are actually needed. Instead of loading everything at once, the app loads content as the user interacts with it. This improves page speed and reduces initial load time.

React provides a built-in `lazy()` function to dynamically import components only when they are needed.

This example shows the code before lazy loading (eager loading):

```
import Dashboard from "./Dashboard";
import Settings from "./Settings";

function App() {
  return (
    <div>
      <Dashboard />
      <Settings />
    </div>
  );
}
```

In this example, both `Dashboard` and `Settings` are bundled and loaded immediately, even if the user only interacts with one of them.

Now, let's see the code after lazy loading (deferred loading):

```
import React, { Suspense, lazy } from "react";

const Dashboard = lazy(() => import("./Dashboard"));
const Settings = lazy(() => import("./Settings"));
```

```
function App() {
  return (
    <div>
      <Suspense fallback={<div>Loading...</div>}>
        <Dashboard />
      </Suspense>
      <Suspense fallback={<div>Loading...</div>}>
        <Settings />
      </Suspense>
    </div>
  );
}
```

Here, `Dashboard` and `Settings` are loaded only when rendered. This reduces the initial JavaScript bundle size and improves startup performance.

Lazy loading works by leveraging dynamic `import()` statements, which signal the bundler to create separate chunks.

## Code splitting: breaking large bundles into smaller chunks

Code splitting allows an application to be divided into smaller JavaScript bundles (chunks) so that users download only the code required for the current view, instead of loading the entire application upfront.

Without code splitting, bundlers typically generate a single large bundle containing all features and dependencies. As applications grow, this increases the following:

- Download time
- Parse and execution time
- Main thread blocking during startup

  See the following examples:

- Before code splitting:

  ```
  main.bundle.js → 3.5 MB
  ```

  All code is downloaded and processed during initial load.

- After code splitting:

  ```
  main.bundle.js        → 800 KB
  dashboard.chunk.js    → 600 KB
  ```

```
settings.chunk.js     → 400 KB
reports.chunk.js      → 700 KB
```

Only the entry bundle loads initially. Additional chunks are fetched on demand (e.g., when navigating to a route).

This improves the following:

- Initial bundle size
- **First Contentful Paint** (**FCP**)
- **Time to Interactive** (**TTI**)
- Main thread blocking time

This is how to enable code splitting with Webpack:

```
module.exports = {
  optimization: {
    splitChunks: {
      chunks: "all",
    },
  },
};
```

This configuration enables automatic chunk splitting and shared dependency extraction.

> Note
>
> Key takeaway: Code splitting does not make individual functions faster. It improves startup performance by reducing upfront work and deferring non-critical code.

## Applying tree shaking to eliminate unused code

Tree shaking is a technique that removes unused JavaScript code from the final bundle. It ensures that only the required functions and modules are included.

For example, if a library contains 10 functions but you only use 2, tree shaking removes the unused 8 functions from the final bundle.

Let's see an example of unoptimized code without tree shaking:

```
// utils.ts
export function add(a: number, b: number) {
  return a + b;
```

```
}

export function multiply(a: number, b: number) {
  return a * b;
}

// main.ts
import { add } from "./utils";
console.log(add(2, 3));
```

Even though we only use `add()`, `multiply()` is still included in the final bundle.

## Optimized code with tree shaking

If you're using ES modules (`import` and `export`), Webpack and other bundlers automatically remove unused functions.

Here are the steps to enable tree shaking in Webpack:

1. Ensure you're using ES6 modules (`import`/`export`) instead of `require()`.
2. Set `"sideEffects": false` in `package.json`:

   ```
   {
     "sideEffects": false
   }
   ```

3. Use Webpack's `production` mode:

   ```
   webpack --mode production
   ```

This removes any **unused** functions, reducing your final file size.

# Leveraging caching mechanisms to improve speed

Caching is the process of storing data in memory so that it doesn't need to be recomputed or reloaded every time.

## Common ways to apply caching

Here are the types of caching:

- **Browser caching**: Store static files so they don't reload every time
- **API response caching**: Save API results to prevent unnecessary requests
- **Memoization**: Store function results to avoid repeated calculations

Here is an example of memoization in TypeScript. Memoization helps store function results, making repeated calls faster:

```
function memoize<T extends string | number>(fn: (arg: T) => number) {
  const cache: Record<string, number> = {};
  return (arg: T) => {
    const key = String(arg);

    if (key in cache) {
      return cache[key];
    }     const result = fn(arg);
    cache[key] = result;
    return result;
  };
}

const square = memoize((n: number) => n * n);
console.log(square(4)); // Calculates and stores result
console.log(square(4)); // Fetches from cache
```

This prevents redundant calculations, making the program faster.

## Optimizing loops, recursive functions, and asynchronous operations

Poorly written loops, unnecessary recursion, and unbounded asynchronous work can slow down an application. Performance optimization often comes from reducing repeated work, choosing appropriate algorithms, and selecting execution patterns that balance speed, memory usage, and predictability.

### Optimizing loops

A common misconception is that higher-level array methods, such as `reduce()`, are always faster than a manual loop. In practice, performance depends on factors such as the JavaScript engine, dataset size, and callback overhead.

In many performance-critical paths, a traditional loop offers predictable execution and minimal overhead, while methods such as `reduce()` trade a small amount of performance for cleaner and more expressive code.

This example uses a `for` loop (often fastest and most predictable):

```
const numbers = [1, 2, 3, 4, 5];
let sum = 0;

 for (let i = 0; i < numbers.length; i++) {
 sum += numbers[i];
}
```

This example uses `reduce()` (clean and expressive):

```
const numbers = [1, 2, 3, 4, 5];
const sum = numbers.reduce((acc, num) => acc + num, 0);
```

This is when to use which:

- Use a `for` loop when performance is critical, memory usage must be predictable, or the logic runs frequently in hot paths
- Use `reduce()` when readability, maintainability, and declarative style are more important than small performance differences

## Optimizing recursive functions

Recursive solutions can be elegant and expressive, but they may introduce performance and stability issues when inputs grow large. Each recursive call consumes stack memory, which can lead to stack overflows if the recursion depth becomes excessive:

```
Basic recursion (simple but unsafe for large inputs)function factorial(n:
number): number {
  if (n <= 1) return 1;
  return n * factorial(n - 1);
}
This implementation works well for small values but may fail when n is large due
to deep call stacks.
```

Let's look at an optimized version using **tail recursion**. A function is tail-recursive when the recursive call is the final operation performed, leaving no additional work after the call returns. This is typically achieved by carrying intermediate results forward using an accumulator:

```
function factorial(n: number, acc = 1): number {
  if (n <= 1) return acc;
```

```
  return factorial(n - 1, n * acc);
}
```

Note

Although tail recursion is a useful conceptual optimization, JavaScript and TypeScript do not consistently guarantee tail-call optimization across engines. As a result, tail-recursive functions may still consume stack frames and can overflow for large inputs.

Because of this, tail recursion should be viewed as a code clarity technique, not a reliable memory optimization in JavaScript.

For large inputs or performance-critical scenarios, an iterative approach is often the safest and most efficient option:

```
function factorialIterative(n: number): number {
let acc = 1;
for (let i = 2; i <= n; i++) {
  acc *= i;
}
return acc;
}
```

## Choosing between loops and recursion

When deciding between loops and recursion, it's important to consider memory usage and execution predictability, not just code elegance.

Recursive functions consume stack memory for each call, which can increase memory pressure and risk runtime failures under heavy load. Iterative loops use constant stack space, making them safer in environments where memory usage must remain predictable.

In time-sensitive systems—such as real-time monitoring, live data processing, or frequent UI updates—predictable execution paths matter more than abstraction style. Iterative approaches are generally easier to reason about in terms of worst-case execution time and memory behavior.

As a practical rule of thumb, follow these guidelines:

- Prefer loops when memory usage, stability, or predictable execution time is critical
- Use recursion when it improves clarity, and the recursion depth is small and well-bounded

## Optimizing asynchronous operations

Asynchronous code can become slow or unstable when too many tasks run in parallel or when work is repeated unnecessarily. While `async` operations prevent blocking the main thread, poor coordination can still degrade performance and increase resource usage.

Common optimization strategies include the following:

- Avoiding duplicate asynchronous calls by caching results when appropriate
- Limiting concurrency instead of launching large numbers of promises simultaneously
- Batching related operations to reduce coordination overhead
- Debouncing or throttling user-triggered events

Let's look at a practical example: debouncing API calls.

When users type into a search input, triggering an API request on every keystroke can generate excessive network traffic and unnecessary server load.

Instead of calling the API immediately on every change, we can debounce the function so that it executes only after the user stops typing for a short period. If your app fetches data multiple times, it can slow down performance.

Here is an example of debouncing API calls.

Instead of calling an API every time the user types, we can debounce it:

```
function debounce<T extends (...args: any[]) => void>(
  fn: T,
  delay: number
) {
  let timer: ReturnType<typeof setTimeout>;
  return (...args: Parameters<T>) => {
    clearTimeout(timer);
    timer = setTimeout(() => fn(...args), delay);
  };
}

const fetchResults = debounce((query: string) => {
  console.log("Fetching:", query);
}, 500);

fetchResults("Hello"); // Executes after 500ms if no further calls occur
```

By introducing a delay, we prevent repeated API calls during rapid user input. This reduces network overhead, improves perceived responsiveness, and lowers backend load.

### Beyond debouncing

Debouncing is just one example of asynchronous optimization. In larger applications, you may also need to do the following:

- Cache results to avoid repeated fetches of identical data
- Use concurrency limits (e.g., promise pools) to prevent overwhelming APIs
- Batch related requests into a single operation when possible
- Cancel stale requests to avoid race conditions

Optimizing asynchronous workflows improves stability, scalability, and user experience—especially in data-intensive applications.

## Summary

In this chapter, you learned various performance-enhancing techniques for your TypeScript applications. We covered lazy loading and code splitting to reduce initial load times, tree shaking to eliminate unused code, and caching mechanisms to speed up data retrieval. Finally, we discussed optimizing loops, recursive functions, and asynchronous operations to improve overall performance.

Throughout this chapter, you've gained a comprehensive understanding of how to enhance the performance of TypeScript applications. You started by recognizing the importance of performance optimization for user satisfaction, business success, and cost savings. Then, you learned how to identify performance bottlenecks using profiling tools and techniques. Finally, you explored and implemented performance-enhancing techniques such as lazy loading, code splitting, tree shaking, caching, and optimization of loops and asynchronous operations.

By applying these strategies, you can create TypeScript applications that are fast, responsive, and scalable, providing an optimal user experience and efficient resource utilization. Keep monitoring and profiling your application to address new performance challenges and sustain the effectiveness of your optimizations.

In the next chapter, we will look at mastering design patterns in TypeScript.

## Get this book's PDF copy, code bundle, and more

Scan the QR code (or go to `packtpub.com/unlock`). Search for this book by name, confirm the edition, and then follow the steps on the page.

UNLOCK NOW

*Note: Keep your invoice handy. Purchases made directly from the Packt website don't require an invoice.*

# 8

# Mastering Design Patterns in TypeScript

In this chapter, we will explore design patterns and how they can be effectively implemented using TypeScript. Design patterns are standard solutions to common problems in software design. They help developers create code that is more flexible, reusable, and easier to maintain. By mastering these patterns, you will improve your ability to solve design issues and enhance the quality of your code.

Understanding design patterns involves knowing their purpose, structure, and when to use them. This chapter will break down various design patterns into three main categories: creational, structural, and behavioral. Each category addresses different aspects of software design, making it easier for you to apply the right pattern for the right situation.

We will provide clear explanations of each pattern, practical examples in TypeScript, and discussions on the advantages and disadvantages of each approach. We will also cover essential best practices and tips to help you avoid common pitfalls. This way, you can make informed decisions when applying these patterns in your projects.

In this chapter, we will cover the following main topics:

- Introducing design patterns
- Creational patterns: Techniques for object creation
- Structural patterns: How to compose classes and objects
- Behavioral patterns: Patterns that define how objects interact
- Practical examples
- Advantages and disadvantages
- Best practices: Tips for implementing design patterns effectively

By the end of this chapter, you will have a solid understanding of how to use design patterns in TypeScript to create better software solutions.

# Technical requirements

You can download the example project and code for this book by following the instructions in the *Download the example code files* section in the *Preface* of this book.

This chapter's code files are included in the downloadable code bundle.

# Introducing design patterns

**Design patterns** are solutions to common problems that software developers face when designing applications. Think of a design pattern as a blueprint that helps you solve a recurring issue in your code. They are not specific pieces of code that you can copy and paste; instead, they provide a general approach to solving problems in software design.

The idea of design patterns started in other fields, such as architecture, where they were used to solve common building problems. In software development, the concept was popularized by a group of authors known as the **Gang of Four** (**GoF**). They wrote a famous book in 1994 called *Design Patterns: Elements of Reusable Object-Oriented Software*, which introduced 23 different design patterns.

Learning about design patterns is important because they give developers a common language. For example, if someone says, "*Use the Singleton pattern*," other developers know exactly what that means without needing an explanation. This shared understanding makes communication easier and more efficient among team members.

Beyond facilitating better communication, applying these patterns effectively improves your code in three key areas:

- **Flexibility**: By using design patterns, you can create code that is adaptable to change. If you need to modify how something works in your application, patterns allow you to do this without rewriting large parts of your code.
- **Reusability**: Design patterns encourage you to write code that can be reused in different projects. This means you don't have to start from scratch every time you encounter a similar problem.
- **Maintainability**: Code that follows design patterns is usually easier to read and understand. This makes it simpler for other developers (or even yourself) to maintain and update the code later.

In short, design patterns are powerful tools that help developers solve recurring problems efficiently, communicate ideas clearly, and write code that stands the test of time.

Next, we'll start with creational patterns, the first major category of design patterns, because object creation is one of the most common sources of rigidity and duplication in code. We'll explore patterns such as Factory, Abstract Factory, Builder, and Singleton, and see how they let you create objects flexibly, control instantiation, and keep your code clean and adaptable from the very beginning.

# Creational patterns: Techniques for object creation

When writing code, one of the most common tasks is creating objects. Sometimes, creating an object is simple, but in other cases, it can get complicated, especially if the object has many parts or needs to follow specific rules. Creational patterns are techniques that help you create objects in a smart, organized way. They make sure that your code stays clean, flexible, and easy to maintain, even as your project grows.

In this section, we'll discuss four popular creational patterns: Factory, Abstract Factory, Builder, and Singleton. Each pattern solves specific problems in object creation and can make your life as a developer much easier.

## Factory method: Simplifying object creation

The **Factory method** pattern allows you to create objects without specifying their exact class. Instead of using the `new` operator directly (e.g., `new PayPalProcessor()`), which tightly couples your code to a specific implementation, you delegate creation to a factory method.

This method decides which class to instantiate based on input logic. This abstraction allows you to swap or add new payment methods later (such as adding Apple Pay) without rewriting your application logic.

Let's see a real-world example using payment processors:

```
// 1. The Interface: Defines what a payment processor must do
interface PaymentProcessor {
  process(amount: number): void;
}

// 2. Concrete Classes: The specific implementations
class PayPal implements PaymentProcessor {
  process(amount: number) {
    console.log(`Processing $${amount} via PayPal.`);
  }
}

class Stripe implements PaymentProcessor {
```

```
  process(amount: number) {
    console.log(`Processing $${amount} via Stripe Credit Card.`);
  }
}

// 3. The Factory: Decides which object to create
class PaymentFactory {
  static getProcessor(method: "paypal" | "stripe"): PaymentProcessor {
    if (method === "paypal") {
      return new PayPal();
    } else if (method === "stripe") {
      return new Stripe();
    }
    throw new Error("Unknown payment method");
  }
}

// Usage: The client code asks for a processor, unaware of the specific class
logic
const processor = PaymentFactory.getProcessor("paypal");
processor.process(50); // Output: Processing $50 via PayPal.
```

In this example, the `PaymentProcessor` interface establishes a contract that both PayPal and Stripe follow, allowing them to be used interchangeably. The `PaymentFactory.getProcessor()` method acts as a central decision point, selecting and instantiating the correct implementation based on input.

This approach is commonly referred to as a **simple factory** (or **static factory**). It reduces coupling to concrete classes by centralizing object creation, though adding a new provider typically requires updating the factory's selection logic in one place.

In contrast, the GoF Factory method pattern delegates object creation to subclasses, and when applications need families of related objects, the Abstract Factory pattern becomes a natural extension.

So far, we've focused on choosing which single object to create. But what if your application needs coordinated objects that come as a matching set? That's where the Abstract Factory pattern comes in.

## Abstract Factory: Creating related objects

The **Abstract Factory** pattern lets you create entire families of related objects (e.g., all UI components for a light theme or all for a dark theme) while keeping your client code completely unaware of the concrete classes involved.

This is a step up from the Factory method: instead of producing just one type of object, Abstract Factory gives you a "factory of factories" that guarantees every created object belongs to the same consistent family.

Let's build a simple UI theming example in small, digestible chunks.

### Step 1: Define the product interfaces

First, we declare what every button and checkbox must be able to do. This establishes the "contract" that all specific themes must follow:

```
interface Button {
  render(): void;
}

interface Checkbox {
  toggle(): void;
}
```

### Step 2: Create the concrete products for each theme

Now we implement the **Light** and **Dark** variants. Notice that we are grouping them conceptually into two families, but they all adhere to the interfaces defined in *Step 1*:

```
// --- Family 1: Light Theme Components ---
class LightButton implements Button {
  render() {
    console.log("Rendering Light Button");
  }
}

class LightCheckbox implements Checkbox {
  toggle() {
    console.log("Toggling Light Checkbox");
  }
}

// --- Family 2: Dark Theme Components ---
```

```
class DarkButton implements Button {
  render() {
    console.log("Rendering Dark Button");
  }
}

class DarkCheckbox implements Checkbox {
  toggle() {
    console.log("Toggling Dark Checkbox");
  }
}
```

## Step 3: Define the Abstract Factory interface

This is the blueprint for our factories. It mandates that any factory we create (whether `Light` or `Dark`) must be capable of producing *both* a button and a checkbox:

```
interface ThemeFactory {
  createButton(): Button;
  createCheckbox(): Checkbox;
}
```

## Step 4: Implement the concrete factories

Each factory is responsible for producing a full set of components for one specific theme. This is where the guarantee happens: `LightThemeFactory` will *never* accidentally produce a **Dark** button:

```
class LightThemeFactory implements ThemeFactory {
  createButton(): Button {
    return new LightButton();
  }
  createCheckbox(): Checkbox {
    return new LightCheckbox();
  }
}

class DarkThemeFactory implements ThemeFactory {
  createButton(): Button {
    return new DarkButton();
  }
  createCheckbox(): Checkbox {
```

```
    return new DarkCheckbox();
  }
}
```

## Step 5: Use the factory (client code)

Now the magic happens—your application code never mentions `LightButton`, `DarkButton`, and so on. It relies entirely on the generic factory interface:

```
// Choose the theme once (could come from user settings, config, etc.)
const themeFactory: ThemeFactory = new DarkThemeFactory();

// Create a consistent family of components
const button = themeFactory.createButton();
const checkbox = themeFactory.createCheckbox();

button.render();   // Output: Rendering Dark Button
checkbox.toggle(); // Output: Toggling Dark Checkbox
```

Switching to `Light` mode tomorrow? Just change one line (`new LightThemeFactory()`) and every component automatically belongs to the new family—no other code changes required.

That's the power of Abstract Factory: it enforces consistency across related objects while keeping your main application logic clean and theme-agnostic.

In the next section, we'll explore the Builder pattern, perfect for creating complex objects step by step without bloated constructors.

# Builder: Constructing complex objects

The **Builder** pattern is ideal when you need to construct a complex object with many possible configurations.

Imagine trying to create a `Car` object using a standard constructor. If the car has 10 distinct options (engine, color, GPS, sunroof, etc.), your constructor becomes a messy list of arguments: `new Car("V8", 4, "Red", true, false, null...)`. This is hard to read and prone to errors.

The Builder pattern solves this by separating the construction of the object from its representation, allowing you to build it step by step.

## Step 1: Define the complex object (the product)

First, we define the class we want to build. In this case, it's `Car`. Notice that we aren't using a constructor with arguments here; the properties will be set later:

```
class Car {
  engine!: string;
  wheels!: number;
  color!: string;
  // Imagine many more properties here (sunroof, GPS, etc.)
}
```

## Step 2: Create the Builder class

Next, we create a separate class solely responsible for assembling the car. It holds a `private` instance of the object we are building (we start with the constructor):

```
class CarBuilder {
  private car: Car;

  constructor() {
    this.car = new Car();
  }

// We will add the methods below inside this class...
}
```

## Step 3: Implement fluent methods

Now, inside the `CarBuilder` class, we add methods to set each property. This is the unique feature of the Builder pattern. Each method sets one specific part of the car, but crucially, it returns `this` (the `builder` instance itself). Returning `this` allows us to "chain" methods together in a single, readable line (e.g., `.setEngine().setColor()`):

```
// ... continue inside CarBuilder
setEngine(engine: string): CarBuilder {
  his.car.engine = engine;
    return this; // Returning 'this' enables method chaining
  }

  setWheels(wheels: number): CarBuilder {
    this.car.wheels = wheels;
```

```
    return this;
  }
```

## Step 4: Use the build method

Finally, still inside the CarBuilder class, we need a method to finalize the process and release the finished object to the client:

```
// ... continue inside CarBuilder
build(): Car {
return this.car;
}
```

## Step 5: Use the builder (client code)

Now, creating a complex object becomes readable and expressive. Instead of passing a large configuration object or a long list of constructor arguments, you build the object step by step, explicitly stating what you want to configure and when. This makes the construction process easier to understand, validate, and evolve as new options are added:

```
const car = new CarBuilder()
  .setEngine("V8")
  .setWheels(4)
  .setColor("Red")
  .build(); // Finalizes the object

console.log(car);
// Output: { engine: 'V8', wheels: 4, color: 'Red' }
```

By using the Builder pattern, we transformed a potentially complex creation process into a clean, easy-to-read sentence.

# Builder pattern in modern TypeScript

While the Builder pattern is a classic and powerful technique for constructing complex objects, modern TypeScript provides several language features that reduce the need for traditional builders in many everyday scenarios.

TypeScript supports optional properties, partial types, object literals, and object spread syntax. Combined with strong type inference and editor autocomplete, these features often allow developers to construct complex objects clearly and concisely without introducing a dedicated builder class. This approach is especially common in modern frontend applications, such as those built with React, where data is frequently assembled incrementally.

For example, instead of using a builder, an object can often be composed like this:

```
const request = {
  ...defaultConfig,
  ...userInput,
  metadata: { orderId }
};
```

This style is flexible, readable, and fits naturally with how data flows through many TypeScript codebases.

That said, the Builder pattern remains valuable when object construction must follow a strict sequence, when validation is required at each step, or when the creation logic itself is complex and shared across multiple contexts. Builders are also commonly used in SDKs, configuration-heavy systems, and fluent APIs where readability and controlled construction are important.

Understanding the Builder pattern helps you recognize when it is the right tool—and when simpler TypeScript constructs are sufficient.

Next, we will look at the Singleton pattern, which handles the exact opposite problem: ensuring that an object is created only once.

## Singleton: One instance only

The **Singleton** pattern ensures that a class has only one instance throughout the entire lifecycle of your application and provides a single global point of access to it.

What does *global instance* mean? Imagine a printer in an office. You don't buy a new printer every time someone wants to print a document. Instead, everyone connects to the same existing printer. In software, this is useful for managing shared resources such as **database connections, logging services**, or **configuration settings**, where creating multiple copies would be wasteful or cause data conflicts.

Let's implement a **Database Connection Manager** to see how we enforce this "single instance" rule.

### Step 1: Use the private constructor

The core trick of a Singleton is preventing other code from creating new copies. We do this by making the constructor **private**:

```
class DatabaseConnection {
  // This static property holds the ONE unique instance
  private static instance: DatabaseConnection;
```

```
  // Private constructor prevents usage of 'new DatabaseConnection()'
  private constructor() {
    console.log("Initializing Database Connection...");
  }
  // We'll add the access logic next...
}
```

## Step 2: Use the static accessor method

Since we can't use new, we need a public method to get the instance. We call this `getInstance()`. The following method checks whether we already have an instance:

- If we don't, create it, save it, and return it
- If we do, return the existing one

```
// ... inside DatabaseConnection class

  public static getInstance(): DatabaseConnection {
    if (!DatabaseConnection.instance) {
      // If no instance exists, create one (Lazy Initialization)
      DatabaseConnection.instance = new DatabaseConnection();
    }
    // Return the existing instance
    return DatabaseConnection.instance;
  }

  // A generic method to simulate doing work
  public query(sql: string): void {
    console.log(`Executing query: ${sql}`);
  }
```

## Step 3: Verifying the Singleton (client code)

Let's try to access the database from two different parts of our application:

```
// Client A asks for the database
const db1 = DatabaseConnection.getInstance();
db1.query("SELECT * FROM users");

// Client B asks for the database
const db2 = DatabaseConnection.getInstance();
db2.query("SELECT * FROM products");
```

```
// Verify they are actually the exact same object
console.log(db1 === db2); // Output: true
```

How does it work? When `getInstance()` is called for `db1`, the internal instance property is undefined, triggering the code to execute a new `DatabaseConnection()` and printing the `"Initializing Database Connection..."` message. However, during the second call for `db2`, the method detects that an instance already exists, skips the creation step, and simply returns the original object. As a result, the initialization log prints only once, proving that the entire application is efficiently sharing a single resource without wasting memory on duplicate connections.

Now that we have explored how creational patterns (Factory, Abstract Factory, Builder, and Singleton) optimize object instantiation, we are ready to focus on how these objects fit together.

In the next section, we will examine **structural patterns**, which focus on organizing relationships between classes and objects. You will learn about the Adapter, Composite, Decorator, and Facade patterns, and discover how they help you assemble your objects into larger, more maintainable structures.

# Structural patterns: Techniques for class and object composition

Structural patterns focus on organizing the relationships between classes and objects. They help you build code that is easier to manage by simplifying the structure or making different parts of the code work better together. These patterns solve problems related to composition—how classes and objects are connected and interact with one another.

Here, we'll discuss four commonly used structural patterns: Adapter, Composite, Decorator, and Facade. Each of these patterns is designed to solve specific issues in software design by improving how code components work together.

## Adapter: Making incompatible interfaces compatible

The **Adapter** pattern allows two incompatible interfaces to work together. Think of it like a travel power adapter: you have a US plug (your code), but the wall socket is European (the external library). The adapter bridges the gap so electricity flows.

In coding, this is useful when you want to use a new class or library, but its methods don't match what your application currently expects.

Let's look at a migration scenario: moving from a legacy payment system to a modern one.

## Step 1: The old system (the expectation)

First, let's look at what our application currently uses. Our code expects a `makePayment(amount)` method:

```
// The interface our application expects
interface OldPaymentSystem {
  makePayment(amount: number): void;
}

// The existing implementation we want to replace
class LegacyPayment implements OldPaymentSystem {
  makePayment(amount: number) {
    console.log(`Payment of $${amount} made using legacy system`);
  }
}
```

## Step 2: The new system (the incompatible class)

Now, imagine we download a fancy new payment library. It works great, but there is a problem: its method is called `processPayment`, not `makePayment`. Our app doesn't know how to call it:

```
// The new interface (incompatible with the old one)
interface NewPaymentSystem {
  processPayment(amount: number): void;
}

class ModernPayment implements NewPaymentSystem {
  processPayment(amount: number) {
    console.log(`Payment of $${amount} processed using modern system`);
  }
}
```

## Step 3: The adapter (the bridge)

To fix this without rewriting our entire application, we create an adapter.

This class implements the old interface (so our app trusts it) but wraps an instance of the new system. Inside, it translates the call:

```
class PaymentAdapter implements OldPaymentSystem {
  private newPaymentSystem: NewPaymentSystem;
```

```
  constructor(newPaymentSystem: NewPaymentSystem) {
    this.newPaymentSystem = newPaymentSystem;
  }

  // The translation magic happens here
  makePayment(amount: number) {
    // We receive the call as 'makePayment'...
    // ...and forward it as 'processPayment'
    this.newPaymentSystem.processPayment(amount);
  }
}
```

### Step 4: Using the adapter

Now, we can use the `ModernPayment` system as if it were the old one. The client code calls `makePayment` just like it always has, completely unaware that the adapter is translating the request in the background:

```
// 1. Create the new service
const modernPayment = new ModernPayment();

// 2. Wrap it in the adapter
const adapter = new PaymentAdapter(modernPayment);

// 3. Use it! (The code thinks it's using the old system)
adapter.makePayment(100);
// Output: Payment of $100 processed using modern system
```

Having learned how to bridge incompatible interfaces with the Adapter pattern, let's now look at how to manage complex hierarchies of objects using the Composite pattern.

## Composite: Treating individual objects and compositions uniformly

The **Composite** pattern lets you treat a group of objects and individual objects the same way. It's like a folder on your computer: you can perform the same actions (such as copy or delete) on a single file or an entire folder containing files and subfolders.

For example, let's say you have graphic elements such as **circles** and **rectangles**, and you want to group them into a complex drawing. Using the Composite pattern, you can treat individual shapes and groups of shapes identically.

## Step 1: Define the common interface (the component)

First, we need a common interface that declares shared behavior. This ensures that both simple shapes and complex groups "look" the same to the rest of the application:

```
interface Shape {
  draw(): void;
}
```

## Step 2: Create the leaf nodes (individual objects)

Next, we create the basic building blocks. In the Composite pattern, these are called **leaf nodes**. They do the actual work (in this case, drawing to the console):

```
class Circle implements Shape {
  draw() {
    console.log("Drawing a Circle");
  }
}

class Rectangle implements Shape {
  draw() {
    console.log("Drawing a Rectangle");
  }
}
```

## Step 3: Create the Composite node (the container)

This is the core of the pattern. The Composite class (`ShapeGroup`) also implements the `Shape` interface, but instead of drawing itself, it holds a list of *other* shapes.

When you tell the group to draw, it iterates through its children and asks them to draw:

```
class ShapeGroup implements Shape {
  // This array can hold Circles, Rectangles, or even other ShapeGroups!
  private shapes: Shape[] = [];

  addShape(shape: Shape) {
    this.shapes.push(shape);
  }

  // The magic happens here: delegating the task to children
  draw() {
```

```
    console.log("--- Starting Group Draw ---");
    this.shapes.forEach((shape) => shape.draw());
    console.log("--- Finished Group Draw ---");
  }
}
```

## Step 4: Using the Composite structure

Finally, notice how the client code interacts with the objects. Whether it's adding a generic `Shape` or calling `draw()`, the code remains simple. It doesn't need to check whether the variable group is a single item or a list—it just calls the method:

```
const circle = new Circle();
const rectangle = new Rectangle();
const group = new ShapeGroup();

// Add individual shapes to the group
group.addShape(circle);
group.addShape(rectangle);

// Trigger the operation on the entire hierarchy at once
group.draw();

/* Output:
--- Starting Group Draw ---
Drawing a Circle
Drawing a Rectangle
--- Finished Group Draw ---
*/
```

The key takeaway is that the client code doesn't care whether it's dealing with a simple circle or a complex `ShapeGroup` containing a thousand shapes. It treats them exactly the same.

While the Composite pattern focuses on structuring hierarchies of objects, the Decorator pattern focuses on dynamically extending the functionality of individual objects.

# Decorator: Adding behavior without altering structure

The **Decorator** pattern allows you to add new behavior or functionality to an object without changing its underlying structure. Think of it like adding extra toppings to a pizza: you aren't baking a brand-new pizza from scratch; you are simply "decorating" the existing one with cheese or pepperoni.

In code, this is achieved by **wrapping** the original object inside a "decorator" class. Let's look at a coffee shop example where we dynamically add ingredients such as milk and sugar to a basic brew.

## Step 1: Define the base interface and component

First, we define a common interface that both the basic coffee and all decorators must follow. Then, we create the base concrete implementation (`BasicCoffee`):

```
// The common interface
interface Coffee {
  getCost(): number;
  getDescription(): string;
}

// The base component
class BasicCoffee implements Coffee {
  getCost(): number {
    return 5;
  }

  getDescription(): string {
    return "Basic Coffee";
  }
}
```

## Step 2: Create the decorators

Now we create the "wrappers." A decorator implements the `Coffee` interface (so it looks like a coffee) but also holds a reference to another `Coffee` object inside it.

When you call `getCost()` on the decorator, it calls `getCost()` on the inner coffee first, adds its own price, and returns the total:

```
class MilkDecorator implements Coffee {
  private coffee: Coffee;

  constructor(coffee: Coffee) {
    this.coffee = coffee;
  }

  getCost(): number {
    return this.coffee.getCost() + 2; // Add cost of milk
```

```
  }

  getDescription(): string {
    return this.coffee.getDescription() + ", Milk";
  }
}
```

## Step 3: Stack the decorators (usage):

The real power of this pattern is composition. We can wrap decorators around each other to create complex combinations without creating endless subclasses such as `MilkSugarCoffee` or `DoubleMilkCoffee`:

```
// 1. Start with a basic coffee
const coffee = new BasicCoffee();

// 2. Wrap it with Milk
const coffeeWithMilk = new MilkDecorator(coffee);

// 3. Wrap that result with Sugar
const fullCoffee = new SugarDecorator(coffeeWithMilk);

console.log(fullCoffee.getDescription());
// Output: Basic Coffee, Milk, Sugar

console.log(fullCoffee.getCost());
// Output: 8 (5 + 2 + 1)
```

Notice how `SugarDecorator` wraps `MilkDecorator`, which wraps `BasicCoffee`. This "Russian nesting doll" structure allows you to add infinite features dynamically at runtime.

While the Decorator pattern adds functionality by layering objects, the Facade pattern does the opposite: it hides complexity behind a simple interface.

# Facade: Simplifying complex subsystems

The **Facade** pattern provides a simplified interface to a complex subsystem. It's like a remote control for a TV: you press a single **Power** button to turn it on, without needing to know the technical details of how the power supply, screen, and receiver circuits inside the TV coordinate to wake up.

In software, this is used when you have a complex system with many moving parts, and you want to provide a clean, easy-to-use "front door" for the rest of your application.

Let's look at a **home theater** example. To watch a movie, you normally have to manually control the lights, the projector, and the amplifier.

## Step 1: The complex subsystems

First, we have individual components. These are the "moving parts" that do the actual work. In a real application, these might be complex API services or a database manager:

```
class Amplifier {
  on() { console.log("Amplifier is on"); }
}

class Projector {
  on() { console.log("Projector is on"); }
}

class Lights {
  dim() { console.log("Lights are dimmed"); }
}
```

## Step 2: The facade (the remote control)

Instead of forcing the user to talk to all three classes individually, we create a `HomeTheaterFacade` class. This class knows exactly which buttons to push and in what order.

It bundles the complexity of dimming lights, starting the projector, and turning on the amp into a single method called `watchMovie()`:

```
class HomeTheaterFacade {
  private amp: Amplifier;
  private projector: Projector;
  private lights: Lights;

  constructor(amp: Amplifier, projector: Projector, lights: Lights) {
    this.amp = amp;
    this.projector = projector;
    this.lights = lights;
  }

  // The simplified interface
  watchMovie() {
    console.log("--- Get Ready for the Movie ---");
    this.lights.dim();
```

```
    this.projector.on();
    this.amp.on();
    console.log("--- Ready to watch! ---");
  }
}
```

## Step 3: Using the facade (client code)

Finally, look at how clean the client code becomes. The user doesn't need to know that `Lights` or `Projector` classes even exist—they just interact with the facade:

```
// 1. Setup (usually done once in your app configuration)
const amp = new Amplifier();
const projector = new Projector();
const lights = new Lights();

// 2. Create the Facade
const homeTheater = new HomeTheaterFacade(amp, projector, lights);

// 3. One simple call triggers the complex sequence
homeTheater.watchMovie();

/* Output:
--- Get Ready for the Movie ---
Lights are dimmed
Projector is on
Amplifier is on
--- Ready to watch! ---
*/
```

The key takeaway is that the Facade doesn't reduce the complexity of the underlying system (the projector and amp are still there), but it reduces the complexity of using that system.

In this section, we learned how structural patterns allow us to assemble classes and objects into larger, more flexible structures—a crucial skill for maintaining clean code as applications grow. In the next section, we will shift our focus to behavioral patterns, where we will explore how to manage effective communication and responsibility assignment between these objects.

# Behavioral patterns: Defining object interaction and communication

**Behavioral patterns** focus on how objects interact with one another and share responsibilities. They are useful for managing communication, coordination, and relationships between objects, making your code more organized and adaptable.

Here, we'll discuss four key behavioral patterns: Observer, Strategy, Command, and Iterator. Each pattern solves a specific problem related to object behavior or interaction, allowing you to write flexible and maintainable code.

## Observer: Notifying dependent objects of changes in a subject

The **Observer** pattern lets one object (the subject) notify multiple other objects (the observers) when its state changes.

This is like subscribing to a YouTube channel: you don't check the channel every 5 minutes to see whether a video is up. Instead, when the channel uploads a new video, it "pushes" a notification to you and all other subscribers instantly.

For our example, imagine a **weather station**. When it detects a temperature change, it needs to automatically notify different devices, such as a simple display and a sophisticated alert system.

### Step 1: Define the observer interface

First, we need a common contract. Every object that wants to listen to the weather station *must* have an `update` method. This allows the station to treat all listeners exactly the same way:

```
interface Observer {
  update(temperature: number): void;
}
```

## Step 2: Implement the subject (the weather station)

We will build the `WeatherStation` class in two parts:

- **Part A: Managing subscriptions**: First, we set up the class to hold our data (`temperature`) and the list of subscribers. We also need methods to allow observers to sign up or leave:

```
class WeatherStation {
  // A list to hold everyone listening to this station
  private observers: Observer[] = [];
  private temperature: number = 0;

  // 1. Subscribe: Add someone to the list
  addObserver(observer: Observer) {
    this.observers.push(observer);
  }

  // 2. Unsubscribe: Remove someone from the list
  removeObserver(observer: Observer) {
    this.observers = this.observers.filter((obs) => obs !== observer);
  }
  // ... We will add the update logic next
}
```

- **Part B: Triggering notifications**: Now, inside the same class, we add the logic to change the temperature. Crucially, whenever the temperature changes, we immediately call `notifyObservers()` to loop through our list and alert everyone:

```
// ... continuing inside WeatherStation class

  // 3. The Trigger: Change data and tell everyone
  setTemperature(temp: number) {
    console.log(`\nNew Temperature measured: ${temp}°C`);
    this.temperature = temp;

    // The state changed, so we notify everyone immediately
    this.notifyObservers();
  }

  private notifyObservers() {
```

```
    // Loop through the list and update every single observer
    this.observers.forEach((observer) =>
  observer.update(this.temperature));
   }
```

## Step 3: Create concrete observers

Now, we create the listeners. Notice that they function differently: `TemperatureDisplay` simply shows the data, while `AlertSystem` runs logic to check for danger. Both implement `Observer`, so the `WeatherStation` accepts them both:

```
class TemperatureDisplay implements Observer {
  update(temperature: number) {
    console.log(`Display: Current temp is ${temperature}°C`);
  }
}

class AlertSystem implements Observer {
  update(temperature: number) {
    if (temperature > 30) {
      console.log("Alert: Temperature is too high! Evacuate!");
    }
  }
}
```

## Step 4: Seeing it in action

Finally, we wire everything together. We can add multiple observers, and a single change in the subject triggers all of them:

```
const weatherStation = new WeatherStation();
const tempDisplay = new TemperatureDisplay();
const alertSystem = new AlertSystem();

// Subscribe the devices
weatherStation.addObserver(tempDisplay);
weatherStation.addObserver(alertSystem);

// Simulate weather changes
weatherStation.setTemperature(25);
// Output: Display updates. (Alert stays silent)
```

```
weatherStation.setTemperature(35);
// Output: Display updates AND Alert triggers!
```

`WeatherStation` doesn't know what `AlertSystem` does. It just knows to call `.update()`. This allows you to add new types of listeners (such as `Logger` or `FanController`) without ever changing the `WeatherStation` code.

While Observer handles communication between objects, the Strategy pattern handles choosing the right behavior for a specific task.

## Strategy: Allowing interchangeable algorithms in a single interface

The **Strategy** pattern lets you define multiple algorithms and switch between them at runtime. It's like choosing a travel route: you might go by car, bus, or bike, depending on traffic or weather. The destination is the same, but the *strategy* for getting there changes.

For example, a payment system might need to support PayPal, credit cards, or bank transfers. Instead of writing one giant `if-else` block, we encapsulate each payment method as its own strategy.

### Step 1: Define the Strategy interface

First, we define a common interface. This ensures that our application knows how to pay, regardless of the specific method used:

```
interface PaymentStrategy {
  pay(amount: number): void;
}
```

### Step 2: Implement concrete strategies

Next, we create specific algorithms. Each class handles the payment logic differently, but they all adhere to the `PaymentStrategy` contract:

```
class PayPalPayment implements PaymentStrategy {
  pay(amount: number) {
    console.log(`Paid $${amount} using PayPal.`);
  }
}

class CreditCardPayment implements PaymentStrategy {
  pay(amount: number) {
```

```
    console.log(`Paid $${amount} using Credit Card.`);
  }
}

class BankTransferPayment implements PaymentStrategy {
  pay(amount: number) {
    console.log(`Paid $${amount} using Bank Transfer.`);
  }
}
```

## Step 3: Create the context

`Context` is the class that the user interacts with. It holds a reference to a strategy but doesn't know (or care) which specific one it is using. Crucially, it has a `setStrategy` method, allowing us to swap behavior dynamically:

```
class PaymentContext {
  // The context holds a reference to the INTERFACE, not a specific class
  private strategy!: PaymentStrategy; // Using '!' to assert it will be set

  setStrategy(strategy: PaymentStrategy) {
    this.strategy = strategy;
  }

  executePayment(amount: number) {
    if (!this.strategy) {
      console.log("No payment method selected!");
      return;
    }
    this.strategy.pay(amount);
  }
}
```

## Step 4: Switch strategies at runtime

Finally, look at how flexible the client code becomes. We can process a payment with PayPal, change our mind, and process the next one with a credit card using the exact same `Context` object:

```
const paymentContext = new PaymentContext();

// 1. User selects PayPal
```

```
paymentContext.setStrategy(new PayPalPayment());
paymentContext.executePayment(100);
// Output: Paid $100 using PayPal.

// 2. User switches to Credit Card
paymentContext.setStrategy(new CreditCardPayment());
paymentContext.executePayment(200);
// Output: Paid $200 using Credit Card.
```

The Strategy pattern eliminates complex `if/else` or `switch` statements. If you need to add Bitcoin payments later, you simply create a new `BitcoinStrategy` class without touching the `PaymentContext` code. Now, let's take a look at the Command pattern.

## Command: Encapsulating requests as objects to enable Undo and logging

The **Command** pattern turns a request (such as `Play Song` or `Turn Up Volume`) into a standalone object. This allows you to parameterize objects with operations, queue requests, or log them. It is the secret sauce behind features such as **Undo/Redo** because you can store the command history and reverse it later.

Let's build a music player control system. We want to separate the buttons (the invoker) from the actual music hardware (the receiver).

### Step 1: The receiver (the hardware)

First, we create a class that actually knows how to perform the work. This `MusicPlayer` class knows nothing about commands or buttons; it just plays audio:

```
class MusicPlayer {
  play(track: string) {
    console.log(`Now playing: ${track}`);
  }

  stop() {
    console.log("Music stopped.");
  }
}
```

## Step 2: The Command interface

Next, we define the contract. Any command we create, whether it's for playing music, stopping it, or shuffling, must implement this interface:

```
interface Command {
  execute(): void;
}
```

## Step 3: Concrete commands (the cartridges)

Now, we wrap the specific actions into objects. `PlayMusicCommand` binds the receiver (`MusicPlayer`) to a specific action (`.play()`). Notice that we can even pass data (such as the track name) into the command's constructor:

```
class PlayMusicCommand implements Command {
  private player: MusicPlayer;
  private track: string;

  constructor(player: MusicPlayer, track: string) {
    this.player = player;
    this.track = track;
  }

  execute() {
    this.player.play(this.track);
  }
}

class StopMusicCommand implements Command {
  private player: MusicPlayer;

  constructor(player: MusicPlayer) {
    this.player = player;
  }

  execute() {
    this.player.stop();
  }
}
```

## Step 4: The invoker (the controller)

This is our *remote* or *smart app*. It holds a command and executes it when triggered. Crucially, it doesn't know it's playing music. It just knows it has a command to execute:

```
class SmartController {
  private command!: Command;

  setCommand(command: Command) {
    this.command = command;
  }

  pressButton() {
    console.log("Button pressed...");
    this.command.execute();
  }
}
```

## Step 5: Wiring it together (client code)

Finally, we assemble the system. We can queue up different songs or actions dynamically:

```
// 1. Set up the hardware
const player = new MusicPlayer();

// 2. Create commands
const playJazz = new PlayMusicCommand(player, "Smooth Jazz");
const stopMusic = new StopMusicCommand(player);

// 3. Set up the controller
const controller = new SmartController();

// 4. Load 'Play' and press
controller.setCommand(playJazz);
controller.pressButton();
// Output: Button pressed... Now playing: Smooth Jazz

// 5. Load 'Stop' and press
controller.setCommand(stopMusic);
controller.pressButton();
// Output: Button pressed... Music stopped.
```

## Iterator: Accessing elements in a collection without exposing its structure

The **Iterator** pattern provides a standard way to access elements of a collection (such as an array, list, or tree) one by one, without exposing the **collection's** underlying memory structure.

Think of it like reading a book. You read one page at a time and flip to the next. You don't need to know how the binding glue works or how the pages were stitched together; you just need a standard way to move forward.

### Step 1: Define the Iterator interface

First, we define the contract. Any iterator in our system must provide two methods: one to get the next item and one to check whether there are any items left. We use a generic `<T>` type so this interface can work for numbers, strings, or complex objects:

```
interface Iterator<T> {
  next(): T | null;
  hasNext(): boolean;
}
```

### Step 2: Create the iterator logic

This class does the heavy lifting. It keeps track of the current position in the collection. Notice that this logic is separated from the collection itself:

```
class NumberIterator implements Iterator<number> {
  private collection: number[];
  private position: number = 0;

  constructor(collection: number[]) {
    this.collection = collection;
  }

  // Returns the current item and moves the pointer forward
  next(): number | null {
    if (this.hasNext()) {
      return this.collection[this.position++];
    }
    return null;
  }

  // Checks if we have reached the end of the list
```

```
  hasNext(): boolean {
    return this.position < this.collection.length;
  }
}
```

## Step 3: Create the collection (the aggregate)

Now, we define our storage. This class holds the actual data. Crucially, it has a method called `createIterator()`. This allows the collection to pass its data to the iterator without forcing the user to access the private `numbers` array directly:

```
class NumberCollection {
  private numbers: number[] = [];

  addNumber(num: number) {
    this.numbers.push(num);
  }

  // Returns a fresh iterator starting at index 0
  createIterator(): NumberIterator {
    return new NumberIterator(this.numbers);
  }
}
```

## Step 4: Traversing the collection (client code)

Finally, look at the client code. We don't write a `for (let i=0; i < collection.length; i++)` loop. We rely entirely on the iterator's `hasNext()` and `next()` methods:

```
// 1. Populate the collection
const numbers = new NumberCollection();
numbers.addNumber(1);
numbers.addNumber(2);
numbers.addNumber(3);

// 2. Ask the collection for an iterator
const iterator = numbers.createIterator();

// 3. Loop through using the standard interface
while (iterator.hasNext()) {
  console.log(iterator.next());
}
```

```
// Output:
// 1
// 2
// 3
```

In this section, we explored behavioral patterns, which are essential for managing effective communication between objects. In the next section, we will shift our focus to practical examples, where we will apply these patterns to real-world scenarios, such as notification services and API integrations, to cement your understanding.

# Practical examples: Applying design patterns in real-world scenarios

Now that we have covered the major design patterns, it's time to see how they function in real-world TypeScript applications. Understanding *when* and *where* to apply a pattern is key to writing better, more efficient code.

In this section, we'll walk through practical examples that show how each pattern solves common architectural challenges. We begin with the **creational patterns**, using clear scenarios to illustrate the problem, followed by an explanation of why a particular pattern is the right solution.

## Creational patterns

Creational patterns focus on flexible and scalable object creation. Let's start with a practical example using a notification system.

### Example: Factory method in a notification system

**Scenario**: A marketing dashboard needs to send alerts to users. Some users prefer email, while others prefer SMS. We need a way to send messages without hardcoding the logic for every single type.

**Why use the Factory method?** To decouple the *message creation* from the *message sending*. The main application just asks for a notification, and the Factory handles the details.

Here are the steps:

1. **Define the product**: First, we define the common behavior that all notifications must share:

   ```
   abstract class Notification {
     abstract send(message: string): void;
   ```

```
}

class EmailNotification extends Notification {
  send(message: string) {
    console.log(`Sending Email: ${message}`);
  }
}

class SMSNotification extends Notification {
  send(message: string) {
    console.log(`Sending SMS: ${message}`);
  }
}
```

2. **Create the factory**: This class contains the logic to decide which notification type to create based on a runtime parameter:

```
class NotificationFactory {
  static getNotification(type: "email" | "sms"): Notification {
    if (type === "email") return new EmailNotification();
    if (type === "sms") return new SMSNotification();
    throw new Error("Unsupported notification type.");
  }
}
```

3. **Usage**: The client code is clean and flexible:

```
const alert = NotificationFactory.getNotification("email");
alert.send("Your report is ready!");
// Output: Sending Email: Your report is ready!
```

This example shows how the Factory method simplifies object creation and centralizes decision-making, keeping your main code clean and extensible.

It's worth noting that this scenario could also be modeled using the Strategy pattern, depending on what varies in your system. If the primary variation is which object to create, Factory is a natural fit. If instead the main variation is how behavior changes at runtime (for example, dynamically switching notification methods), Strategy may be more appropriate. Understanding whether creation or behavior is the true point of change helps you select the right pattern. Now, we move on to a structural pattern that helps unify incompatible APIs.

## Structural patterns: Adapter for third-party APIs

Structural patterns help you compose objects into larger, more flexible structures. A common challenge is integrating external systems that don't match your application's expected interfaces.

**Scenario**: Your application needs to display weather data, but the two providers you integrate with (`WeatherAPI1` and `WeatherAPI2`) return results in different formats.

**Why use Adapter?** To create a unified interface. This allows your app to treat both APIs exactly the same way, preventing the need for complex `if/else` logic in your UI code.

Here are the steps:

1. **The problem (incompatible APIs)**: Here are the two services. Notice the method names don't match (`fetchTemp` vs. `getTemp`):

```
interface WeatherService {
  getTemperature(): number;
}

class WeatherAPI1 {
  fetchTemp(): number { return 28; }
}

class WeatherAPI2 {
  getTemp(): number { return 30; }
}
```

2. **The adapters**: We build wrappers that translate the external API calls into the format our app expects:

```
class WeatherAdapter1 implements WeatherService {
  constructor(private api: WeatherAPI1) {}

  getTemperature(): number {
    return this.api.fetchTemp();
  }
}

class WeatherAdapter2 implements WeatherService {
  constructor(private api: WeatherAPI2) {}
```

```
  getTemperature(): number {
    return this.api.getTemp();
  }
}
```

3. **Unified usage**: Now, the client code treats both services as generic `WeatherService`:

```
const serviceA: WeatherService = new WeatherAdapter1(new WeatherAPI1());
console.log(`Temperature: ${serviceA.getTemperature()}°C`);
```

By using the Adapter pattern, your application can work with any provider through a consistent interface, reducing code duplication and improving maintainability. Next, we will look at a behavioral pattern that handles real-time updates across multiple components.

# Behavioral patterns

Behavioral patterns focus on how objects interact and communicate with each other. They are particularly useful when changes in one part of the system should automatically trigger updates elsewhere.

## Example: Observer in a real-time chat room

**Scenario**: A chat application needs to instantly update all users whenever a new message is sent.

**Why use Observer?** It implements a push-based mechanism where the subject (`ChatRoom`) notifies all observers (users) automatically, avoiding tight coupling between components

Here are the steps:

1. **Define the subject (`ChatRoom`)**:

```
class ChatRoom {
  private users: User[] = [];

  addUser(user: User) {
    this.users.push(user);
  }

  sendMessage(message: string) {
    // Notify every user in the list
    this.users.forEach((user) => user.notify(message));
```

```
  }
}
```

2. **Define the observer (**`User`**):**

```
interface User {
  notify(message: string): void;
}

class ChatUser implements User {
  constructor(private name: string) {}

  notify(message: string) {
    console.log(`${this.name} received: ${message}`);
  }
}
```

3. **Usage**: When `room.sendMessage` is called, everyone gets the message:

```
const room = new ChatRoom();
const user1 = new ChatUser("Alice");
const user2 = new ChatUser("Bob");

room.addUser(user1);
room.addUser(user2);

room.sendMessage("Hello, everyone!");
// Output:
// Alice received: Hello, everyone!
// Bob received: Hello, everyone!
```

This example demonstrates how the Observer pattern allows multiple components to react automatically to changes in a single object, keeping your system responsive and decoupled. Next, we will explore another behavioral pattern that enables undo functionality in applications.

## Example: Command for undo functionality in a text editor

**Scenario**: A text editor needs to allow users to undo their last action (such as writing text).

**Why use Command?** To encapsulate the action of "writing" into an object. Because the object exists, we can call an `undo()` method on it to reverse the action.

Here are the steps:

1. **The receiver (the document)**: This is the file we are editing:

```
class TextDocument {
  private text: string = "";

  write(text: string) {
    this.text += text;
  }

  getText() {
    return this.text;
  }

  erase() {
    this.text = ""; // Simplified undo logic
  }
}
```

2. **The Command object**: We create `WriteCommand` that knows how to execute the write and how to reverse it:

```
interface Command {
  execute(): void;
  undo(): void;
}

class WriteCommand implements Command {
  constructor(private doc: TextDocument, private text: string) {}

  execute() {
    this.doc.write(this.text);
  }

  undo() {
    this.doc.erase();
```

```
    }
  }
```

3. **Usage (undo in action)**:

```
const doc = new TextDocument();
const command = new WriteCommand(doc, "Hello, World!");

// 1. Execute Command
command.execute();
console.log(doc.getText()); // Output: Hello, World!

// 2. Undo Command
command.undo();
console.log(doc.getText()); // Output: (empty string)
```

The Command pattern makes it easy to implement undo/redo functionality and maintain a clean separation between the user interface and action logic. This pattern can also be applied to queues, transactions, or any operation that may need to be undone or replayed.

## When and where each pattern is most useful

Choosing the right design pattern depends on the problem you're trying to solve. Each pattern shines in specific situations, whether you need flexible object creation, a cleaner way to structure complex systems, or better control over how components communicate. The following guidelines summarize when each category is most effective:

- **Creational patterns**:
  - Use Factory or Abstract Factory when you want flexibility in creating objects without knowing their exact classes
  - Builder is great for creating objects with many optional fields
  - Singleton works best for managing global instances such as configuration or logging
- **Structural patterns**:
  - Use Adapter to integrate incompatible systems
  - Composite helps manage tree structures, such as filesystems or menus

    - Decorator is perfect for adding features dynamically without modifying the base object
    - Facade simplifies complex subsystems for easier use
- **Behavioral patterns**:
    - Observer works for real-time updates, such as notifications or event systems.
    - Strategy is ideal for swapping algorithms easily
    - Command is useful for encapsulating tasks such as undo or logging
    - Iterator shines when iterating over custom collections

In this section, you learned the following:

- How to apply design patterns such as Factory, Adapter, Observer, and Command to real-world problems
- Which patterns work best for specific scenarios, such as simplifying object creation, managing interactions, and making systems compatible

In this section, we explored when each design pattern is most useful, which helps you choose the right solution for the right problem. Understanding this context is essential for avoiding misuse and keeping your architecture clean. In the next section, we'll look at the advantages and disadvantages of design patterns to help you decide when they add value and when they might introduce unnecessary complexity.

# Advantages and disadvantages of design patterns

While design patterns offer valuable guidance for structuring and organizing code, they also come with trade-offs. Understanding both sides helps you decide when a pattern truly adds value and when it may introduce unnecessary complexity.

## Advantages of using design patterns

Here are the adavantages of using design patterns:

- **Standard solutions to common problems**: Design patterns provide tried-and-true solutions that are widely understood by developers. This saves time and effort since you don't need to invent a new approach every time.
- **Improved code organization**: Patterns encourage better organization of code by separating concerns and defining clear roles for different parts of your application. For example, the Facade pattern hides complexity, making systems easier to manage.
- **Reusability**: Many design patterns, such as Factory and Builder, promote code reusability by creating flexible structures that can adapt to future changes.

- **Better communication**: Using design patterns improves communication among developers. Saying *Let's use a Singleton here* quickly conveys the intent without needing a lengthy explanation.
- **Ease of maintenance**: Patterns such as Observer and Strategy make it easier to update or modify parts of a system without affecting others. This reduces the risk of bugs when making changes.

## Disadvantages of using design patterns

Although design patterns offer many benefits, they aren't always the right choice. In some cases, they can introduce drawbacks that make your code harder to maintain or understand. Being aware of these limitations helps you avoid using patterns where they do more harm than good. Let's look at some of the most common disadvantages:

- **Unnecessary complexity**: Some patterns can make code more complicated than it needs to be. For example, using the Abstract Factory pattern for a small application with just one type of object might be overkill.
- **Steep learning curve**: For beginners, design patterns can be hard to understand at first. Concepts such as Decorator or Command might feel abstract and difficult to apply.
- **Overengineering**: Sometimes developers use patterns where simple code would suffice, leading to overly engineered solutions. This is known as **pattern obsession**.
- **Reduced performance**: Some patterns, such as Decorator, may add extra layers of abstraction that can slow down performance in resource-intensive applications.
- **Not always flexible**: While patterns such as Singleton provide global access to a single instance, they can make your application rigid and harder to test, especially in larger systems.

## When patterns might add complexity

Even when design patterns are used correctly, there are situations where they can introduce more complexity than they solve. Understanding these scenarios helps you choose patterns thoughtfully and avoid unnecessary overhead. Here are some cases where patterns might complicate your project instead of improving it:

- **Small projects**: For a small app or prototype, the overhead of applying patterns might not be worth it. A simpler approach can work just as well.

- **Misuse of patterns**: Using the wrong pattern for a problem can make your code harder to understand and maintain. For instance, applying the Composite pattern to a simple list structure might be unnecessary.
- **Too many patterns at once**: Mixing too many patterns in one system can make the codebase confusing and difficult to navigate.

## Striking the right balance

To get the most out of design patterns, consider the following:

- **Start simple**: Only introduce a pattern if it clearly solves a problem in your project
- **Understand the problem**: Choose a pattern based on the specific issue you're solving, not just because it's popular
- **Document usage**: Explain why a pattern is used so that other developers understand its purpose

In this section, we examined both the advantages and disadvantages of using design patterns, helping you understand not only where patterns add value but also where they can create unnecessary complexity. This balanced view is important because effective use of design patterns requires knowing when *not* to apply them. In the next topic, best practices, we'll explore how to choose and implement patterns wisely so you can avoid common pitfalls and build cleaner, more maintainable code.

# Best practices for implementing design patterns in TypeScript

Design patterns are powerful tools, but to use them well, you need to apply them thoughtfully. The following best practices will help you implement design patterns effectively in TypeScript without introducing unnecessary complexity:

- **Understand the problem before choosing a pattern**:
  - Avoid forcing a design pattern into your code. Instead, analyze the problem you are solving.
  - Ask yourself, *Does this pattern make my solution simpler, clearer, or more flexible?*

  For example, use the Observer pattern when multiple objects need updates based on changes in a central object, such as in event-driven systems.

- **Keep it simple**:
  - Use patterns only when they add real value. Don't over-engineer your code.
  - If a simple function or class solves the problem, it's okay to skip a pattern.

  For instance, if your app has a single global configuration, a simple object might suffice instead of using the Singleton pattern.
- **Combine patterns when necessary**:
  - Sometimes, combining patterns provides better solutions. For example, use Factory to create objects and combine it with Decorator to add extra functionality dynamically.
  - Always document why the patterns are combined to help others understand the reasoning.
- **Make your patterns flexible**:
  - Write your patterns in a way that allows changes in the future. For example, use interfaces in TypeScript to define reusable types.
  - With Strategy, define different algorithms through interfaces so you can easily add new ones later.
- **Test thoroughly**:
  - Patterns such as Command and Observer involve complex interactions. Ensure you have proper tests to verify behavior, especially when changes are made.
  - Use unit tests to confirm that each component works as expected.
- **Document your code**:
  Explain why you chose a specific pattern. This helps others understand your design and makes your code base easier to maintain. Here is an example:

```
// Using the Observer pattern to notify subscribers of stock price updates
class StockTicker { ... }
```

The comment clarifies the purpose of the class, signaling that it implements the Observer pattern to manage updates to multiple subscribers efficiently.

- **Stick to TypeScript strengths**:
  Use TypeScript's features such as interfaces, abstract classes, and generics to enhance your design patterns. For example, in the Builder pattern, use interfaces to ensure consistency in object construction:

```
interface ICarBuilder {
  setEngine(engine: string): this;
  setWheels(wheels: number): this;
  build(): Car;
}
```

  This interface enforces a strict contract, ensuring that any class implementing `ICarBuilder` provides the necessary methods. Crucially, using `this` as the return type tells TypeScript that these methods return the builder instance itself, which enables "fluent" method chaining (e.g., `.setEngine(...).setWheels(...)`) while keeping type safety intact.

- **Avoid misusing patterns**:
  - Don't apply a pattern just because it's popular. Patterns such as Abstract Factory may be unnecessary for simple systems.
  - Always weigh the complexity that a pattern introduces against the benefits it offers.
- **Learn from examples**:
  - Study real-world applications of patterns to understand their practical use.
  - Practice implementing patterns in small projects to build confidence.
- **Refactor when needed**:
  Patterns aren't set in stone. If your system evolves and a pattern no longer fits, refactor your code to simplify it or switch to a more suitable pattern.

In this section, you learned practical strategies for implementing design patterns effectively in TypeScript. By focusing on understanding the problem before selecting a solution, you can ensure that your implementation remains simple and flexible. We also highlighted the value of combining patterns wisely and leveraging TypeScript's specific strengths, such as interfaces and generics, to build robust architectures. Finally, by prioritizing thorough testing and documentation, you can avoid common pitfalls and ensure that your code remains clear, maintainable, and efficient.

# Summary

In this chapter, you learned how design patterns provide proven solutions to common software design challenges and how to implement them effectively using TypeScript. We explored what design patterns are and why they matter, followed by a deep dive into creational, structural, and behavioral patterns—each showing different ways to create objects, organize code, and manage communication between components. You also walked through practical, real-world examples that demonstrated when and where each pattern is most useful, and examined their advantages and disadvantages to help you avoid unnecessary complexity or misuse.

Finally, we looked at best practices for applying patterns wisely and making the most of TypeScript features such as interfaces and generics. With this understanding, you are now prepared to use design patterns confidently to build clean, scalable, and maintainable applications. In the next chapter, we'll move into advanced TypeScript features that will further strengthen your ability to design robust and flexible systems.

## Get this book's PDF copy, code bundle, and more

Scan the QR code (or go to `packtpub.com/unlock`). Search for this book by name, confirm the edition, and then follow the steps on the page.

UNLOCK NOW

*Note: Keep your invoice handy. Purchases made directly from the Packt website don't require an invoice.*

# 9

# Understanding Advanced TypeScript Features

In this chapter, we will explore some of the more complex features of TypeScript. These features help you write better code that is easier to maintain, debug, and understand. We will break down these concepts into simple terms with practical examples to ensure clarity.

TypeScript offers many tools and options that allow you to create flexible and powerful applications. By mastering these advanced features, you will gain the skills to confidently handle larger and more challenging projects while improving your overall coding expertise.

In this chapter, we will cover the following main topics:

- Exploring generics
- Introducing advanced types
- Understanding decorators
- Creating mapped types
- Using conditional types
- Working with utility types

By the end of this chapter, you will have a strong understanding of these advanced TypeScript features and how to apply them effectively in real-world projects. These skills will prepare you to build scalable, robust, and high-quality applications with ease.

## Technical requirements

You can download the example project and code for this book by following the instructions in the ***Download the example code files*** section in the *Preface* of this book.

This chapter's code files are included in the downloadable code bundle.

# Exploring generics

**Generics** are a powerful feature in TypeScript that lets you create flexible and reusable components. They allow you to write functions, classes, and interfaces that can work with different data types while keeping your code type-safe. In other words, you don't have to write the same code multiple times for different types.

Generics are especially useful when you don't know the exact type of data your function or class will handle, but still want to enforce type safety. With generics, you can write code that adapts to different data types while avoiding common errors.

But why should we use generics?

- **Reusability**: Generics let you write code once and use it for any type
- **Type Safety**: They ensure the correct types are used, reducing runtime errors
- **Flexibility**: They adapt to different types without sacrificing code clarity

Now that we understand the benefits, let's look at how to implement generics in practice.

## Generics at work

Generics are defined using angle brackets (`<>`) and a placeholder type, such as `T`. The `T` represents **type parameter**, which will be replaced with a specific type when the code is used.

Here's a simple example of a generic function:

```
function wrapInArray<T>(value: T): T[] {
  return [value];
}

// Using the generic function
const numberArray = wrapInArray(42); // T is inferred as number
const stringArray = wrapInArray("Hello"); // T is inferred as string
```

In this example, the `wrapInArray` function can work with any type (number, string, etc.), and TypeScript infers the type of `T` based on the argument passed. Let's look at generic classes now.

## Generic classes

Generics can also be used in classes to make them work with different types. This is particularly useful when you need to create a container that holds a group of items. Without generics, you would have to write a separate class for every type of item you want to store, which creates a lot of extra work.

Let's look at how to implement a generic `Storage` class to solve this:

```
class Storage<T> {
  private items: T[] = [];

  addItem(item: T): void {
    this.items.push(item);
  }

  getItems(): T[] {
    return this.items;
  }
}

// Using the generic class
const stringStorage = new Storage<string>();
stringStorage.addItem("Item 1");
stringStorage.addItem("Item 2");

const numberStorage = new Storage<number>();
numberStorage.addItem(100);
numberStorage.addItem(200);
```

In this example, the `Storage` class can store any type (string, number, etc.), and the `T` type parameter ensures type safety for the stored items. Next, let's understand interfaces in generics.

## Generic interfaces

Just like with classes, we can apply generics to interfaces to make them more flexible. This is helpful when you want to define a standard structure for an object, but the types of data inside it might change depending on the situation. For example, imagine you want to link two values together. Instead of creating one interface for numbers and another for strings, you can create a single `Pair` interface that handles any combination.

Here is how you can define that using generics:

```
interface Pair<T, U> {
  first: T;
  second: U;
}
```

```
const coordinate: Pair<number, number> = { first: 10, second: 20 };
const nameAndAge: Pair<string, number> = { first: "Alice", second: 30 };
```

Here, the `Pair` interface works with two different types (`T` and `U`), and this makes it easy to define pairs of different data types. Finally, let us take a look at constraints and generics.

## Generic constraints

You can restrict the types that a generic can accept using constraints. This is necessary when your code needs to access specific properties on the generic type. For example, if you want to write a function that logs the length of an item, you need to guarantee that the item actually *has* a `.length` property. Without a constraint, TypeScript would stop you because `T` could be a number (which doesn't have a length).

Here is how you use the `extends` keyword to enforce that rule:

```
function logLength<T extends { length: number }>(item: T): void {
  console.log(item.length);
}

// Valid usage
logLength("Hello"); // T is string
logLength([1, 2, 3]); // T is array

// Invalid usage
// logLength(42); // Error: number does not have a length property
```

In this example, the `T` type must have a `length` property, ensuring only compatible types are used.

## Advantages of generics

Now that we've seen how generics work in practice, it's important to understand what generics specifically enable, beyond what TypeScript's type system already provides.

Generics allow types to be parameterized, meaning they can adapt to different data types while preserving relationships between inputs and outputs. This makes generics especially powerful when writing reusable utilities, data structures, and abstractions.

One of the key advantages of generics is that they help avoid code duplication without sacrificing type safety. Instead of writing the same function or class multiple times for different types, generics allow a single implementation to work across many types while still enforcing correct usage at compile time.

Generics also enable strong type relationships. For example, a generic function can ensure that the type of its return value is directly tied to the type of its input, something that is not possible with any or loosely typed abstractions. This prevents entire classes of bugs that would otherwise only appear at runtime.

Finally, generics provide flexibility with precision. They allow code to remain adaptable while still benefiting from TypeScript's static checking, autocomplete, and refactoring support. This balance makes generics a foundational tool for building type-safe libraries, reusable components, and scalable application architectures.

In this section, you learned how generics allow you to write reusable and adaptable code without losing type information. By parameterizing types, generics enable flexible abstractions that remain safe, expressive, and easy to maintain as applications grow.

In the next section, we will explore advanced types, including how to combine types, create more specific types with unions and intersections, and handle optional or nullable values. These features will help you handle complex type scenarios in your TypeScript projects.

# Introducing advanced types

**Advanced types** in TypeScript allow you to create more complex and flexible data structures. They help you define types in ways that go beyond basic types. This means you can combine and manipulate types to better fit your needs in a program. By mastering advanced types, you can handle challenging scenarios in your applications while keeping your code clean and type-safe.

In this section, we'll break down the most important advanced types and explain how they work with practical examples.

- **Union types**: These let you define a variable that can hold multiple types. You use the pipe (|) symbol to create a union.
  Here is an example of a union type:

  ```
  function formatValue(value: string | number): string {
    return `Value: ${value}`;
  }

  // Usage
  console.log(formatValue("Hello")); // Works with string
  console.log(formatValue(42)); // Works with number
  ```

In this example, the `value` parameter can be either `string` or `number`. Union types are great for handling different types in a single function.

- **Intersection types**: These combine multiple types into one. You use the ampersand (&) symbol to create an intersection.
  An example of an intersection type is shown here:

```
interface Person {
  name: string;
}

interface Employee {
  id: number;
}

type EmployeeDetails = Person&Employee

const employee: EmployeeDetails = {
  name: "Alice",
  id: 101,
};
```

  Here, the `EmployeeDetails` type combines `Person` and `Employee`, and the `employee` object must have all the properties of both interfaces.

- **Type aliases**: Type aliases let you give a custom name to a type. This is useful for simplifying long or complex types.
  Let's look at an example here:

```
type Coordinate = { x: number; y: number };

const point: Coordinate = { x: 10, y: 20 };
```

  In this example, the `Coordinate` alias makes the object type more readable and reusable.

- **Literal types**: Literal types allow you to specify an exact value that a variable can have.
  Here's an example:

```
type Direction = "up" | "down" | "left" | "right";
```

```
function move(direction: Direction): void {
  console.log(`Moving ${direction}`);
}

// Usage
move("up"); // Valid
// move("forward"); // Error: "forward" is not assignable to type
"Direction"
```

In this code, the `Direction` type restricts the function to only accept specific string values.

- **Nullable types**: Nullable types let you handle values that could be null or undefined. Let's see an example of a nullable type:

```
function greet(name: string | null): string {
  return name ? `Hello, ${name}` : "Hello, stranger";
}

// Usage
console.log(greet("Alice")); // Hello, Alice
console.log(greet(null)); // Hello, stranger
```

In this example, the function can accept either `string` or `null` and handles both cases safely.

- **Mapped types**: Mapped types allow you to transform existing types into new ones by applying operations to their properties.
An example of a mapped type is shown here:

```
type ReadonlyType<T> = {
  readonly [K in keyof T]: T[K];
};

interface Person {
  name: string;
  age: number;
}

const person: ReadonlyType<Person> = {
  name: "John",
```

```
  age: 30,
};

// person.name = "Doe"; // Error: Cannot assign to 'name' because it is a
read-only property
```

Here, the `ReadonlyType` mapped type makes all properties of a type read-only.

- **Index signatures**: Index signatures define the shape of objects with dynamic keys. Here's an example:

```
interface StringDictionary {
  [key: string]: string;
}

const dictionary: StringDictionary = {
  hello: "world",
  goodbye: "everyone",
};
```

In this example, the `StringDictionary` interface can have any number of string keys with string values.

- **Conditional types**: Conditional types allow you to create types based on conditions. Finally, let's look at an example of a conditional type:

```
type IsString<T> = T extends string ? true : false;

type Test1 = IsString<string>; // true
type Test2 = IsString<number>; // false
```

Here, the `IsString` type checks if a type is a string and returns `true` or `false`.

In this section, you learned about advanced types in TypeScript, including union types, intersection types, type aliases, and literal types. These features allow you to create more complex and flexible types, making your code easier to manage and understand.

Next, we will explore decorators, a powerful feature in TypeScript that allows you to modify or enhance the behavior of classes, methods, and properties. Decorators are especially useful when implementing metadata-driven programming and creating reusable patterns in your applications.

# Understanding decorators

**Decorators** in TypeScript are special functions that let you change or extend the behavior of classes, methods, properties, or parameters. They are used as annotations in your code and allow you to add reusable functionality without modifying the original implementation. Decorators are commonly used in frameworks such as Angular and NestJS for tasks such as dependency injection, metadata, and routing. Therefore, decorators are a powerful way to write clean and reusable code.

## How do decorators work?

Decorators are functions that run at runtime and take arguments, such as the target they are applied to. TypeScript uses the @ symbol to apply decorators. To enable decorators in your TypeScript project, you must turn on the `experimentalDecorators` flag in your `tsconfig.json` file:

```
{
  "compilerOptions": {
    "experimentalDecorators": true
  }
}
```

Now that we have enabled the necessary configuration, let's dive into the four specific types of decorators TypeScript supports—class, method, property, and parameter—and see how to implement each one.

## Types of decorators

TypeScript provides several kinds of decorators, each targeting a different element of your class. Decorators use the `@DecoratorName` syntax and are placed directly above the class, method, property, or parameter they modify. Under the hood, a decorator is simply a function that receives metadata about the decorated element (such as the constructor, method descriptor, or parameter index) and can observe, modify, or extend its behavior. In the following examples, we'll explore how each decorator type works and what arguments it receives. Let's walk through the most common ones and see how they're used.

- **Class decorators**: A class decorator modifies or adds functionality to an entire class. It is applied to the class itself.
  Here's an example of a class decorator:

  ```
  function LogClass(constructor: Function) {
    console.log(`Class ${constructor.name} has been created.`);
  ```

```
}

@LogClass
class User {
  constructor(public name: string) {}
}

// Output: Class User has been created.
```

- **Method decorators**: A method decorator is applied to a specific method of a class. It allows you to modify the method's behavior or add metadata.
  Let's look at an example of a method decorator:

```
function LogMethod(target: Object, propertyKey: string, descriptor:
PropertyDescriptor) {
  const originalMethod = descriptor.value;
  descriptor.value = function (...args: any[]) {
    console.log(`Method ${propertyKey} called with args: ${args}`);
    return originalMethod.apply(this, args);
  };
}

class Calculator {
  @LogMethod
  add(a: number, b: number): number {
    return a + b;
  }
}

const calc = new Calculator();
console.log(calc.add(2, 3));
// Output: Method add called with args: 2,3
//        5
```

- **Property decorators**: A property decorator is used to add functionality or metadata to a specific property of a class.
  Here's an example:

```
function LogProperty(target: Object, propertyKey: string) {
  console.log(`Property ${propertyKey} was accessed.`);
}
```

```
class User {
  @LogProperty
  name: string = "John Doe";
}

// Output: Property name was accessed.
```

- **Parameter decorators**: A parameter decorator is applied to a method's parameter to add metadata about it.

  Finally, let's look at an example of a parameter decorator:

```
function LogParameter(target: Object, propertyKey: string, parameterIndex:
number) {
  console.log(`Parameter in ${propertyKey} at index ${parameterIndex} was
accessed.`);
}

class Greeter {
  greet(@LogParameter message: string) {
    console.log(message);
  }
}

const greeter = new Greeter();
greeter.greet("Hello!");
// Output: Parameter in greet at index 0 was accessed.
//         Hello!
```

Now that we have explored the implementation details of the four main decorator types, let's consolidate this knowledge by examining the core advantages they bring to your code base.

# Benefits of decorators

Here are the benefits of decorators:

- **Code reusability**: Common functionality can be abstracted into reusable decorators
- **Separation of concerns**: Helps keep core logic separate from auxiliary features such as logging or validation
- **Readability**: Decorators provide a clean and concise way to annotate behavior in the code

In this section, you learned about decorators in TypeScript and how they can enhance your classes, methods, and properties. You saw examples of class decorators, method decorators, and property decorators, each showing how you can add additional functionality without changing the core logic of your code.

Next, we will explore mapped types, where you will learn how to create new types based on existing ones, helping you manage and transform your data structures effectively.

# Creating mapped types

**Mapped types** in TypeScript let you create new types by transforming existing ones. This feature is helpful when you want to work with object types, especially when you need to apply the same transformation to all properties of a type. Mapped types are great for creating flexible, reusable type definitions in your projects.

## How mapped types work

A mapped type iterates over the keys of a given type and applies a transformation to each key. The syntax uses the `keyof` operator and a template literal to define how properties should be modified.

Here is the basic structure:

```
type MappedType<T> = {
  [Key in keyof T]: Transformation;
};
```

Let's break down this code:

- `T` is the input type
- `keyof T` gets all the keys of the type `T`
- `Key in keyof T` means "for each key in `T`"
- `Transformation` is the new definition or modification for each property

## Examples of mapped types

To truly understand the power of mapped types, it helps to see them in action. Let's explore several common patterns, ranging from simple modifiers such as making fields optional to complex type transformations, that demonstrate how to manipulate object structures efficiently.

- **Making all properties optional**: The built-in `Partial<T>` type makes all properties of a type optional. Let's recreate it using a custom-mapped type:

```
type MakeOptional<T> = {
  [Key in keyof T]?: T[Key];
};

// Example
type User = {
  name: string;
  age: number;
};

type OptionalUser = MakeOptional<User>;
/*
OptionalUser is:
{
  name?: string;
  age?: number;
}
*/
```

- **Making all properties read-only**: You can use a mapped type to make all properties of an object read-only, just like TypeScript's built-in `Readonly<T>` type.

```
type MakeReadOnly<T> = {
  readonly [Key in keyof T]: T[Key];
};

// Example
type User = {
  name: string;
  age: number;
};
```

```
type ReadOnlyUser = MakeReadOnly<User>;
/*
ReadOnlyUser is:
{
  readonly name: string;
  readonly age: number;
}
*/
```

- **Changing property types**: You can modify the type of each property in an object. For example, you can turn all properties into strings:

```
type ConvertToString<T> = {
  [Key in keyof T]: string;
};

// Example
type User = {
  name: string;
  age: number;
};

type StringifiedUser = ConvertToString<User>;
/*
StringifiedUser is:
{
  name: string;
  age: string;
}
*/
```

- **Mapping with conditional types**: Mapped types become even more powerful when combined with conditional types. You can transform properties based on their original type.
  In the following example, we'll transform only the properties that match a specific condition – in this case, converting numbers to strings.

```
type TransformNumbersToStrings<T> = {
  [Key in keyof T]: T[Key] extends number ? string : T[Key];
```

```
};

// Example
type User = {
  name: string;
  age: number;
  isActive: boolean;
};

type TransformedUser = TransformNumbersToStrings<User>;
/*
TransformedUser is:
{
  name: string;
  age: string; // Transformed because it's a number
  isActive: boolean;
}
*/
```

In this example, you saw how conditional types let you selectively transform only certain properties of a type – in this case, converting number fields into strings while leaving everything else unchanged. This pattern is especially useful when you need fine-grained control over type transformations.

Now that you've seen how to build your own mapped types, let's look at the built-in mapped types TypeScript provides and how they can simplify everyday type operations.

## Built-in mapped types

TypeScript provides several built-in mapped types that you can use immediately without writing custom logic. These are available globally in your project:

- `Partial<T>`: Makes all properties optional
- `Required<T>`: Makes all properties required
- `Readonly<T>`: Makes all properties read-only
- `Record<K, T>`: Creates a type with keys of type `K` and values of type `T`
- `Pick<T, K>`: Creates a type by picking specific properties from `T`
- `Omit<T, K>`: Creates a type by omitting specific properties from `T`

## Advantages of mapped types

Mapped types offer several benefits that make them a powerful tool when designing flexible and maintainable type systems. By abstracting repetitive type transformations, they help you write cleaner and more expressive code. Some of the key advantages include the following:

- **Reusability**: You can define reusable transformations that work with any type
- **Flexibility**: Mapped types adapt to changes in the original type automatically
- **Clarity**: They help you define and enforce consistent rules for object types

## Best practices

To make the most of mapped types in real projects, it's important to use them thoughtfully. The following guidelines will help you apply mapped types effectively, avoid common pitfalls, and ensure your type transformations remain predictable as your code base grows:

- Use mapped types to simplify complex type transformations
- Combine them with utility types and conditional types for maximum flexibility

Always test custom-mapped types to ensure they behave as expected.

In this section, you learned about mapped types in TypeScript and how they allow you to create new types based on existing ones. You saw examples of making properties optional, readonly, and even changing their types. Mapped types help you keep your code maintainable and adhere to the **Don't Repeat Yourself** (**DRY**) principle.

Next, we will explore conditional types, where you will learn how to create types that depend on certain conditions, allowing for even more flexible type definitions.

# Using conditional types

**Conditional types** in TypeScript allow you to create types that adapt based on certain conditions. They are like `if-else` statements for types, helping you define dynamic and flexible type logic.

The basic structure of a conditional type is as follows:

```
T extends U ? X : Y;
```

This means if type `T` can be assigned to type `U`, then the result is type `X`. Otherwise, the result is type `Y`. Conditional types are powerful for creating dynamic type transformations and making your TypeScript code more type-safe and adaptable.

Now that we have defined the syntax, let's look under the hood to see how TypeScript evaluates these conditions and how you can use them to build intelligent type definitions.

# How conditional types work

At its core, a conditional type acts as a gatekeeper. It checks if a specific type relationship exists and returns one result if true, and another if false. We will start with a basic type check to see this syntax in action, and then explore how to use the advanced `infer` keyword to extract specific details from inside a type.

- **A basic example**: Here's a simple example to check if a type is `string` or something else:

```
type IsString<T> = T extends string ? "Yes, it's a string" : "No, it's not
a string";

// Example usage
type Test1 = IsString<string>; // "Yes, it's a string"
type Test2 = IsString<number>; // "No, it's not a string"
```

- **Inferring types**: Conditional types can extract or *infer* parts of a type using the `infer` keyword. This is helpful for working with complex types.
  Let's take a look at an example of extracting the return type of a function:

```
type ReturnType<T> = T extends (...args: any[]) => infer R ? R : never;

// Example usage
type MyFunction = () => number;
type Result = ReturnType<MyFunction>; // number
```

  Here, `infer R` captures the return type of the function.

Now that we have established the syntax and the power of the `infer` keyword, let's bridge the gap between theory and practice. Next, we will examine specific, real-world patterns where conditional types are essential for creating robust and clean type definitions.

# Common use cases for conditional types

Conditional types are rarely used in isolation. They are most effective when used to filter, clean, or transform complex unions. Let's explore three specific scenarios:

- **Filtering types**: You can create types that exclude or include certain types from a union.

Let's see an example where we exclude a type:

```
type ExcludeType<T, U> = T extends U ? never : T;
// If T is assignable to U, remove it (never); otherwise keep T

// Example usage
type AllTypes = string | number | boolean;
type Result = ExcludeType<AllTypes, boolean>; // string | number
```

- **Handling nullable types**: One of the most practical uses of conditional types is cleaning up data structures. You can use them to automatically remove null and undefined values from a union type, ensuring you are working with valid data.
  **Example: Creating a NonNullable utility**: To achieve this, we define a utility called `NonNullable`. It checks if the type is `null` or `undefined`; if so, it discards it (by returning `never`). If not, it keeps the type.

```
type NonNullable<T> = T extends null | undefined ? never : T;

// Example usage
type MaybeNullable = string | null | undefined;
type Result = NonNullable<MaybeNullable>; // string
```

- **Creating flexible utility types**: Conditional types allow you to define utility types for various scenarios.
  Let's use this example to check if a type is an array:

```
type IsArray<T> = T extends any[] ? true : false;

// Example usage
type Test1 = IsArray<number[]>; // true
type Test2 = IsArray<string>; // false
```

We have seen how conditional types work in isolation to filter or check types. But their real power shines when they team up with other TypeScript features.

## Combining conditional types with other features

TypeScript features are designed to be composable. By weaving conditional logic into mapped types or template literals, you can create highly sophisticated type definitions that react dynamically to your data's structure. Let's look at how these combinations work in practice.

- **Conditional types with mapped types**: You can use conditional types inside mapped types to create more dynamic transformations.
  As an example, let's mark properties as optional based on their type:

```
type OptionalIfString<T> = {
  [K in keyof T]: T[K] extends string ? T[K] | undefined : T[K];
};

// Example usage
type User = {
  name: string;
  age: number;
};

type ModifiedUser = OptionalIfString<User>;
/*
ModifiedUser is:
{
  name?: string; // because it's a string
  age: number;   // unchanged
}
*/
```

- **Conditional types with template literals**:
  Template literal types allow you to build string types using the same backtick syntax (`) found in JavaScript. When combined with conditional types, they become incredibly powerful, allowing you to dynamically construct specific string patterns based on input types.

  **Example: Generating dynamic status messages**: In this example, we use a template literal to construct a full sentence. The specific word inside the sentence (`"Success"` or `"Error"`) is chosen dynamically based on the status code provided.

```
type Status<T extends number> = T extends 200 ? "Success" : "Error";
```

```
// Example usage
type Result1 = Status<200>; // "Success"
type Result2 = Status<404>; // "Error"
```

You now have the tools to write complex custom logic, but you don't always need to reinvent the wheel. For many standard type transformations, TypeScript has already done the heavy lifting for you.

## Built-in conditional types

TypeScript ships with several global utility types that are built directly on top of the conditional logic we just discussed. These utilities allow you to perform common set operations—such as filtering unions or extracting return values—without having to write the verbose `extends` ? syntax from scratch.

TypeScript provides several utility types built using conditional types:

- `Exclude<T, U>`: Removes types from `T` that are assignable to `U`
- `Extract<T, U>`: Extracts types from `T` that are assignable to `U`
- `NonNullable<T>`: Removes `null` and `undefined` from `T`
- `ReturnType<T>`: Extracts the return type of a function
- `InstanceType<T>`: Extracts the instance type of a class

While these built-in utilities cover many common scenarios, you will inevitably need to write your own custom conditional logic. To ensure your types remain maintainable and don't become a debugging nightmare, let's establish some ground rules.

## Best practices

Conditional types are among the most powerful features in TypeScript, but with great power comes the potential for great complexity. Deeply nested conditions and overuse of `infer` can quickly make your code unreadable to other developers. Here are some guidelines to keep your type definitions clean:

- **Start simple**: Begin with straightforward conditional types before combining them with other features
- **Use for reusability**: Create reusable utility types for common patterns
- **Test for clarity**: Always test your conditional types to ensure they behave as expected

In this section, you learned what conditional types are and how they work. You saw how to use conditional types for type transformations. You also looked at practical examples, such as filtering types, inferring return types, and creating utility types, and how to combine conditional types with mapped types and other features.

Next, we will explore utility types, where you will learn about the built-in types that TypeScript provides to help you manipulate and transform data types easily.

# Working with utility types

**Utility types** are built-in tools provided by TypeScript to make working with types easier. They are designed to simplify common type transformations and help you write more concise, reusable, and maintainable code. Instead of writing custom types for every scenario, utility types save you time and reduce complexity by offering ready-made solutions.

## Key utility types in TypeScript

TypeScript provides over 20 utility types, but the following selection represents the most fundamental tools for transforming object types and manipulating property statuses (optionality, mutability, and selection). Let's examine how each one works with a simple example.

- `Partial`: The `Partial` utility type makes all the properties of a type optional. This is useful when you want to work with objects that might not have all their properties defined.

  Before we move on, let's look at the syntax:

  ```
  type Partial<T> = {
    [P in keyof T]?: T[P];
  };
  ```

  Let's demonstrate how applying `Partial<T>` makes the originally required properties optional:

  ```
  interface User {
    name: string;
    age: number;
  }

  type PartialUser = Partial<User>;

  // Now this is valid:
  const user: PartialUser = {
    name: "Alice",
  };
  ```

- `Required`: The `Required` utility type does the opposite of `Partial`. It makes all the properties of a type mandatory.
  Here's the syntax:

```
type Required<T> = {
  [P in keyof T]-?: T[P];
};
```

Let's look at an example demonstrating how `Required<T>` enforces all properties to be present:

```
interface User {
  name?: string;
  age?: number;
}

type FullUser = Required<User>;

// This will throw an error if `name` or `age` is missing:
const user: FullUser = {
  name: "Alice",
  age: 25,
};
```

- `Readonly`: The `Readonly` utility type makes all the properties of a type read-only, meaning they cannot be reassigned after initialization. This is useful for defining immutable configuration objects.
  The syntax for `Readonly` is shown here:

```
type Readonly<T> = {
  readonly [P in keyof T]: T[P];
};
```

The following example demonstrates that any attempt to modify a property after the object has been created will result in a compilation error:

```
interface User {
  name: string;
  age: number;
}
```

```
type ReadonlyUser = Readonly<User>;

const user: ReadonlyUser = {
  name: "Alice",
  age: 25,
};

// This will throw an error:
user.name = "Bob";
```

- `Pick`: The `Pick` utility type allows you to create a new type by selecting specific properties (`K`) from an existing type (`T`). This is valuable when you want to create a type that includes only a subset of properties from a larger type.
  The `Pick` utility uses a combination of generics and mapped types. Here is the **canonical TypeScript definition**, which illustrates how it constructs the new type by iterating only over the provided keys (`K`):

  ```
  type Pick<T, K extends keyof T> = {
    [P in K]: T[P];
  };
  ```

  Let's look at an example demonstrating how `Pick` extracts only the necessary properties to define a new type:

  ```
  interface User {
    name: string;
    age: number;
    email: string;
  }

  type UserSummary = Pick<User, "name" | "email">;

  const summary: UserSummary = {
    name: "Alice",
    email: "alice@example.com",
  };
  ```

- `Omit`: The `Omit` utility type creates a new type by removing specific properties (`K`) from an existing type (`T`). This is often used to pass a type to a function that doesn't need all the data (e.g., omitting the `id` property when creating a new database record).
  Let's look at its syntax here:

```
type Omit<T, K extends keyof T> = Pick<T, Exclude<keyof T, K>>;
```

  Let's demonstrate how `Omit` creates a new type by explicitly excluding one or more properties from the original interface:

```
interface User {
  name: string;
  age: number;
  email: string;
}

type UserWithoutEmail = Omit<User, "email">;

const user: UserWithoutEmail = {
  name: "Alice",
  age: 25,
};
```

- `Record`: The `Record` utility type creates an object type with specified keys (`K`) and uniform values (`T`). This is useful when you want to enforce a map structure based on a set of known keys (such as a union type or enum).
  Here is its syntax:

```
type Record<K extends keyof any, T> = {
  [P in K]: T;
};
```

  Let's see how `Record` forces an object to adhere to a specific set of predefined keys, ensuring every defined key has the same value type:

```
type Roles = "admin" | "user" | "guest";

type Permissions = Record<Roles, boolean>;

const permissions: Permissions = {
```

```
  admin: true,
  user: false,
  guest: false,
};
```

- `Exclude`: The `Exclude` utility type lets you start with a union type (`T`) and subtract certain types (`U`) from it, leaving only the ones you want to keep. This is helpful when you want to narrow down a union by removing members you no longer need.
  Its syntax is shown here:

  ```
  type Exclude<T, U> = T extends U ? never : T;
  ```

  Let's see how `Exclude` performs this subtraction and keeps only the remaining members:

  ```
  type AllRoles = "admin" | "user" | "guest";
  type NonAdminRoles = Exclude<AllRoles, "admin">;

  // NonAdminRoles = "user" | "guest"
  ```

- `Extract`: The `Extract` utility type lets you start with a union type (`T`) and keep only the members that match (`U`). It's essentially the opposite of `Exclude`: instead of subtracting types, it filters a union down to the ones you want.
  Here's the syntax:

  ```
  type Extract<T, U> = T extends U ? T : never;
  ```

  Let's see how `Extract` selects only the matching members:

  ```
  type AllRoles = "admin" | "user" | "guest";
  type AdminRole = Extract<AllRoles, "admin">;

  // AdminRole = "admin"
  ```

- `NonNullable`: The `NonNullable` utility type starts with a type (`T`) and removes `null` and `undefined` from it. This is useful when you want to ensure a value is always present and cannot be nullish.

Let's look at its syntax here:

```
type ReturnType<T extends (...args: any) => any> = T extends (...args: any) => infer R ? R : any;
```

Let's see how `NonNullable` cleans up a type by removing nullish values:

```
function getUser() {
  return {
    name: "Alice",
    age: 25,
  };
}

type UserType = ReturnType<typeof getUser>;

// UserType = { name: string; age: number; }
```

Now that we've explored the core utility types—tools for making properties optional or required, selecting or omitting keys, working with unions, and removing nullish values—let's shift our attention to some best practices for using these utilities effectively in real-world TypeScript projects.

## Best practices

To get the most out of utility types, it's important to use them with intention. Here are key practices that will help you apply them effectively and keep your code clean.

- **Use utility types for reusability**: Avoid rewriting common patterns by using utility types where possible
- **Combine utility types**: Combine multiple utility types to create more complex but reusable types
- **Test your types**: Test the utility types you use to ensure they behave as expected

In this section, you learned what utility types are and how they simplify working with types, and about the key utility types such as `Partial`, `Pick`, `Omit`, `Record`, and more.

You also looked at how to use these types to create reusable, maintainable code and practical examples of each utility type.

## Summary

In this chapter, we explored advanced TypeScript concepts such as generics, advanced types, decorators, mapped types, conditional types, and utility types. These tools enable developers to write more flexible, reusable, and type-safe code. By mastering these features, you can confidently handle complex TypeScript projects and improve the quality of their code.

In the next chapter, you will learn how to apply TypeScript in real-world web development scenarios. We'll cover topics such as integrating TypeScript with React, working with Node.js and Express, building full stack applications, and using TypeScript with modern tools such as webpack. The chapter will focus on practical applications, making TypeScript a core part of your development workflow.

## Get this book's PDF copy, code bundle, and more

Scan the QR code (or go to `packtpub.com/unlock`). Search for this book by name, confirm the edition, and then follow the steps on the page.

UNLOCK NOW

*Note: Have your invoice handy. Purchases made directly from the Packt website don't require an invoice.*

# 10

# Setting Up Scalable TypeScript Projects

You've learned TypeScript's syntax and advanced patterns—now it's time to apply that knowledge to real-world projects. This chapter bridges the gap between theory and practice by guiding you through the setup of a production-ready TypeScript environment that's scalable, maintainable, and optimized for team collaboration.

You'll go beyond writing code to making architectural decisions that real teams face daily: choosing between monorepo and polyrepo strategies, selecting the right tools for package management, and enforcing code quality standards automatically. These are the foundational practices that empower professional teams to build and scale full stack applications confidently.

In this chapter, you'll create a complete development workspace using Nx, configure it with pnpm for efficient dependency management, and automate quality enforcement using Git hooks. You'll also learn how to set team standards, manage environment configurations, and optimize your development workflow for long-term productivity.

By the end of this chapter, you'll have a production-grade project foundation built on smart defaults and battle-tested tools. More importantly, you'll understand the reasoning behind each choice—skills critical for leading technical decisions on any team or project.

In this chapter, we're going to cover the following main topics:

- From product spec to technical architecture
- Repository strategy—monorepo versus polyrepo
- Setting up your Nx workspace

- Package management with pnpm
- Code quality automation with Git hooks

# Technical requirements

In this chapter, you'll need the following tools and technologies installed on your system:

- Node.js (v18 or later)
- pnpm (v8 or later)
- Nx CLI (`npx create-nx-workspace@latest`)
- Git
- VSCode (recommended)
- Basic knowledge of TypeScript and terminal commands

You can download the example project and code for this book by following the instructions in the *Download the example code files* section in the *Preface* of this book. This chapter's code files are included in the downloadable code bundle.

# From product spec to technical architecture

It's tempting to think that building software is just about writing code. I used to think this way in my early days, but I quickly learned, as I moved from a fast-paced start-up environment in Lagos, Nigeria (my home country) to large, structured organizations, that there's a crucial gap between what we're building, why we're building it, and how we're building it. The decisions made in this space often determine whether a project succeeds or fails.

Software development is similar to building any other product, such as a car or phone. Knowing the technical details is important, but who are we building this for? What problems should it solve? What are the timeline expectations? Is this a flagship model or an upgrade to an existing one? These questions shape every technical decision you make.

This section walks you through the collaborative decision-making process that transforms product requirements into technical architecture. We'll explore the strategic planning phase: what kind of project are we building, how will it grow, who will work on it, and how often will it ship? The answers to these questions directly influence your choices around tooling, architecture, and team collaboration.

Let's start off by understanding what a product specification is.

## Understanding product specifications

Before diving into technical decisions, it's important to understand what drives them. A product specification (or "product spec") is a concise document that outlines what you're building and why. It's not code; it's a shared source of truth between technical and non-technical stakeholders.

A good product spec defines the following:

- The core features of the product
- The users it serves
- The problems it solves (for both users and the business)
- Any relevant constraints (timelines, technologies, budget)

Why does this matter to you as a developer? Technical decisions shouldn't be made in isolation. A clear product spec helps teams prioritize features, choose the right tools, and estimate effort more accurately. Without it, code bases often evolve without direction, resulting in rework and technical debt.

To keep this practical, let's work with a concrete example. Imagine you've been handed this fictional specification by a product manager or start-up founder:

- **DevJobs Platform Specification**:
  Build a modern job board specifically for developers. Users should be able to browse and filter job listings by technology, experience level, and location. Companies can post jobs with clear technical requirements and salary transparency. Developers can create basic profiles showing their skills and GitHub username.

  The platform must support user authentication and allow companies to manage their own job postings. Initial scope focuses on web-only (desktop-first), with no immediate need for real-time updates or external API integrations. Target launch is 3 months with a team of 3-5 engineers.

  From this specification, several critical technical decisions emerge:

  - Do we need multiple applications or a monolithic structure?
  - How should we organize code for shared types and validation?
  - What tooling will help our team collaborate effectively?
  - How do we structure the code base for future growth?

In addition to these core code-related decisions, teams often consider other factors such as whether to use serverless architectures or traditional servers, which database technology to adopt, or how to structure deployment pipelines. While these topics are crucial, this book focuses primarily on writing clean, maintainable TypeScript code and designing robust application architecture. We will therefore keep the discussion centered on the code base itself and the collaboration around it.

Team size and skill levels also influence decisions. Smaller or less experienced teams may prefer simpler architectures and fewer moving parts to reduce complexity, while larger teams might benefit from modular designs and clear separation of concerns to enable parallel development.

Once we have a product spec in place, we've done more than just capture an idea; we've defined the foundation every technical choice will rest on. At this stage, the question shifts from *What are we building?* to *How are we going to build it?*.

# From product spec to technical architecture

In the previous section, we looked at product specifications, which tell us *what* to build and *why*. But knowing that isn't enough to start coding. Before writing a single line, we need a **technical plan**: a high-level architecture that's concrete enough to guide decisions, but not so detailed that we get stuck in theory.

Think of it like a building project. The product spec is the client's wish list: *We want a three-story office with a rooftop terrace.* The technical plan is the architect's drawing measurements, layouts, and structural notes that engineers can actually build from.

In software, this means translating the product specification into clear requirements, constraints, and guiding choices that developers will reference throughout the project. In larger organizations, this role often falls to a dedicated software architect; in smaller teams, it's typically handled by one or more senior engineers. Either way, there needs to be a technical plan, or more specifically, a system design. While full system design is beyond the scope of this book, we'll take a quick walk through the process so you can see how it works, and how it influences the way we structure the project and, eventually, our code.

Let's look at the thought process behind creating this technical plan—step by step—and see how we go from a product specification to the high-level architecture decisions that will guide the rest of the development.

## Breaking down the specification into a technical plan

Creating a technical plan starts with a careful review of the product specification. The aim isn't to re-describe the project, but to translate the "what" into actionable technical requirements and constraints that shape how the system will be built.

Let's go over the following steps to build one:

## Step 1—Review and break down the specification

Our DevJobs platform specification says the following:

- Two categories of users: job seekers and companies
- Both can create accounts
- Companies can post jobs
- Job seekers can view and filter jobs by technology, experience level, and location
- The platform supports authentication and authorization
- Out of scope: no real-time updates, no mobile app, no external API integrations

From this, we separate **functional requirements** (what the system must do) from **non-functional requirements** (how it must behave).

### Functional requirements (DevJobs):

- Account creation for both user types
- Developer profile creation with skills and GitHub username
- Job posting and management for companies
- Job browsing and filtering for seekers
- Authentication and role-based authorization

### Non-functional requirements (DevJobs):

- Fast search results (efficient filtering and querying)
- Scalable enough to handle large volumes of job listings and peak search traffic
- Secure authentication and role-based access control
- Responsive user experience, even when displaying many job results

Once we have our functional and non-functional requirements in place, in the next steps, we will look into some constraints that would act as guardrails.

## Step 2—Add contextual constraints

The specification defines features, but context shapes the architecture. To design a system effectively, we must account for two broad categories of constraints: technical and non-technical.

- **Technical constraints**: These capture the system's operational demands and limitations. They typically include factors such as the expected number of daily active users, the peak number of concurrent sessions, the type and size of data that needs to be stored, and the frequency of incoming requests. Each of these elements directly influences how the system is designed, scaled, and maintained. To make informed decisions, we often rely on rough estimates—sometimes referred to as back-of-the-envelope calculations. While the details of performing such estimates are outside the scope of this discussion, there are plenty of resources available online that can guide you through the process. Here are some that we personally find useful:

    - `https://bytebytego.com/courses/system-design-interview/back-of-the-envelope-estimation`
    - `https://gist.github.com/mwakaba2/8ad25dda8c71fe529855994c70743733`

- **Non-technical constraints**: These reflect organizational and team realities that shape architectural choices. They may include the size of the development team, delivery deadlines, and the specific skills and experience the team brings. For instance, if the team consists of three to five developers working toward a three-month deadline, that scope will naturally favor simpler solutions. Similarly, if the team has strong React expertise, React Native may be a more practical choice for mobile development than Flutter. On the other hand, if the team has limited experience with Kubernetes or complex DevOps setups, opting for a serverless architecture can help reduce operational overhead and risk.

How constraints shape architecture

With both technical and non-technical constraints in mind, architectural decisions become clearer. Here are some examples:

- For storing **company logos and CVs**, you may need **object storage** (e.g., Amazon S3) alongside a **relational database** for job and user data
- Given a tight timeline and limited DevOps expertise, a **serverless deployment** may be more practical than setting up Kubernetes clusters or dedicated servers

Once we've settled on our decisions and identified the core components of our system, this information has to be captured. Let's see how to do this in the next step.

## Step 3—Capture decisions before coding

Once we've clarified requirements, constraints, and high-level choices, the next step is to record them. These records—often called **Architecture Decision Records** (**ADRs**)—ensure everyone knows why a decision was made and what trade-offs were considered. Without them, decisions live only in conversations and are easily lost.

# Documenting architecture decisions with ADRs

Before we set up the code base, we need to document the key architectural choices we've made. This prevents decisions from being lost in chat threads or meetings, and it gives the team a single reference point as they work. The simplest and most effective way to do this is through ADRs.

ADRs are short, version-controlled documents that capture the following:

- **Context**: why a decision was needed
- **Decision**: what option was chosen
- **Consequences**: trade-offs or follow-up actions

Unlike long design documents, ADRs stay close to the code base and remain lightweight. This means they're practical enough for small teams while still valuable for larger organizations.

## Writing a simple ADR

Let's create a sample ADR for our DevJobs project. This one covers the choice of database technology. We'll save it in a dedicated folder inside our repository, such as `/docs/adr/`.

Create a new file in your project here:

```
/docs/adr/0001-database-choice.md
```

Add the following content:

```
# ADR 0001: Database Choice
## Context
The DevJobs platform requires storing job postings, company accounts, and
developer profiles. The data is relational and includes filters such as
technology, experience, and location. We also need support for queries that must
remain performant as the dataset grows.
## Decision
We will use PostgreSQL as the primary database. It supports relational data,
indexing for fast queries, and has strong community and hosting support.
## Consequences
Pros: Strong querying support, well-known by most developers, easy to host on
cloud providers.
Cons: Less flexible than NoSQL databases for unstructured data.
We will review this decision if traffic or data patterns change significantly
(e.g., very large-scale filtering, analytics-heavy use cases).
```

### Why this matters

This ADR shows how we can turn abstract technical planning into concrete, actionable records. Every developer on the team can understand the context in which PostgreSQL was chosen, including the constraints, requirements, and trade-offs that shaped the decision. Later, if the team considers switching technologies, they won't have to start from scratch—they can review the original reasoning, assumptions, and conditions that influenced the choice.

As we continue, you can repeat this process for other key choices, such as the following:

- Monolith versus microservices
- Deployment strategy (serverless versus managed servers)
- Authentication and authorization approach

These don't need to be long documents—just enough to capture the reasoning.

## Choosing a repository strategy for your project

In this section, we'll explore how to organize your project's code base using either a monorepo or polyrepo approach. Making the right decision early on can do the following:

- Simplify collaboration across teams
- Streamline CI/CD pipelines
- Improve scalability and maintainability

By understanding the benefits and trade-offs of each strategy, you'll be better equipped to structure your DevJobs code base for long-term productivity.

We'll begin by defining both approaches:

- **Monorepo:** A monorepo (short for **monolithic repository**) is a single repository that contains all the code for multiple projects or services. This can include frontend apps, backend services, shared libraries, and utilities—all living together in one place.
- **Polyrepo**: A polyrepo (or multiple repositories) approach keeps each project, service, or library in its own separate repository. Each team or service can evolve independently, and changes are isolated to that repository.

Now that we know what they are, let's look at why you might choose one over the other and how each affects your team's workflow.

## Comparing monorepo and polyrepo approaches

In this sub-section, we are going to compare the benefits of monorepo versus polyrepo. Here are the benefits of monorepo:

- **Shared tooling**: One set of scripts, build tools, and configurations for all projects
- **Atomic changes**: Refactor across multiple projects in a single commit
- **Simplified dependency management**: Easier to share and update libraries

Here are the benefits of polyrepo:

- **Independent deployments**: Teams can release services without coordinating changes elsewhere
- **Team autonomy**: Teams own their repositories and can adopt different workflows or technologies
- **Technology diversity**: Easier to mix stacks, frameworks, or languages

Sometimes, the best option is a hybrid. For example, you may keep shared libraries in a monorepo while hosting independent services in separate repos. This allows centralized control where it is most valuable, without losing the autonomy of independent services.

Now that we know what they are, let's look at why you might choose one over the other and how each affects your team's workflow.

## Deciding between monorepo and polyrepo strategies

Now that we've compared the basic benefits of monorepos and polyrepos, the next step is to evaluate which approach best fits your project. Choosing a repository strategy is not just about technical preference. It is shaped by how your team works, how you deploy software, and how much code needs to be shared across projects.

Here are the main factors to consider when making the decision for DevJobs (or similar projects):

**Team Structure**

- A **monorepo** can help when your team is small and working across multiple parts of the project, since everyone can see and contribute to the same code base
- A **polyrepo** may fit better if you have multiple independent teams, each owning a service or product with minimal overlap

**Deployment requirements**

- If your services need to be deployed independently, polyrepos make it easier to release updates on their own schedule
- If you prefer coordinated releases (for example, frontend and backend always ship together), a monorepo simplifies the process

**Code sharing needs**

- A **monorepo** makes it easier to share common libraries, types, or utilities, since they live in the same repository
- A **polyrepo** can make code sharing more complex, as it often requires publishing shared code as packages and managing versions across repos

Now that you know about the factors that influence our choice between monorepo and polyrepo, let's see what our strategy would be for our DevJobs application.

## Choosing for DevJobs

Now that we've looked at the decision factors, it's important to decide what makes the most sense for our project. For DevJobs, we'll use the monorepo approach. This gives us a single place to manage frontend, backend, and shared libraries, while keeping our workflows simple and consistent as a small team.

To do this effectively, we'll need a tool that helps us manage complexity as the monorepo grows. There are several options available, but in the next section, we'll look at Nx, a popular choice for TypeScript projects that provides advanced tooling, intelligent builds, and enterprise-ready features.

# Nx—the professional choice

Now that we've chosen a monorepo approach for DevJobs, the next question is how to manage it effectively. As projects grow, a monorepo can become complex: builds slow down, teams need clear boundaries, and shared libraries must stay consistent. Without the right tooling, these challenges can quickly outweigh the benefits.

This is where Nx comes in. Nx is a build system and monorepo manager designed with TypeScript projects in mind. It provides intelligent tooling, advanced configuration, and enterprise-ready features that make working with a monorepo not just feasible but highly productive.

## Why Nx works well for TypeScript projects

Before diving into the setup, let's look at why Nx is such a strong choice for TypeScript developers:

- **Advanced tooling**: Nx comes with generators for creating applications, libraries, and configurations. This ensures consistency and reduces repetitive setup.
- **Intelligent builds**: Instead of rebuilding everything, Nx analyzes the project graph to rebuild or retest only what's affected by a change. This keeps builds and tests fast, even as your project grows.
- **Extensibility**: Nx provides plugins for popular frameworks such as React, Next.js, Express, and NestJS, allowing you to scale your stack without reinventing the wheel.

Together, these features help you maintain a professional-grade project structure that stays manageable over time.

### Comparing Nx with alternatives

There are several tools available for managing monorepos. Let's briefly compare Nx with the most common options:

- **Turborepo**: A modern build system from Vercel that focuses heavily on caching and parallel execution. It's fast, simple to adopt, and integrates well with most CI environments.
  **Why Nx still**: Nx offers similar caching capabilities but goes further with built-in code generators, project graph visualization, and deep TypeScript integration, making it easier to manage large, structured code bases over time.
- **Lerna**: Once the go-to monorepo management tool, primarily focused on versioning and publishing packages. It pairs well with Yarn or npm workspaces but lacks intelligent builds or native TypeScript support.
  **Why Nx still**: Nx provides dependency-aware builds, incremental testing, and automated scaffolding, supporting modern TypeScript workflows that extend beyond Lerna's scope.
- **Rush**: A Microsoft-backed monorepo manager built for very large organizations with hundreds of packages. It's powerful but requires more setup and can feel heavyweight for smaller teams.

**Why Nx still**: Nx delivers similar scalability while remaining lightweight. Its plugin ecosystem and affected-command system make it flexible for growing teams yet robust enough for enterprise projects.

- **Yarn Workspaces:** Useful for managing dependencies across multiple packages and simplifying internal linking. However, it lacks advanced build orchestration and CI optimization features on its own.

**Why Nx still**: Nx builds on top of workspaces, adding caching, dependency graph analysis, and task orchestration—turning basic package management into a full development platform. Nx versus Turborepo in particular is a common decision point: both are modern, fast, and support caching. But Nx distinguishes itself by offering the following:

- First-class TypeScript support and plugins for React, Next.js, NestJS, and more
- Built-in code generators and scaffolding for consistent project structures
- Dependency graph visualization and affected-command analysis for CI/CD optimization

For DevJobs, these TypeScript-focused features and project graph insights make NX a better choice.

# Setting up your Nx workspace

In this section, we will work through setting up an Nx workspace for the DevJobs monorepo. You'll create the workspace, explore its structure, and configure it to support both frontend and backend applications. By the end, you'll have a solid foundation that makes development, code sharing, and scalable architecture much easier.

## Workspace creation and configuration

To get started, we run the following command in your terminal to create a new Nx workspace for DevJobs using pnpm as the package manager:

```
npx create-nx-workspace@latest devjobs --preset=ts --package-manager=pnpm
```

This command will launch an interactive series of prompts. Here's a quick overview of what you'll see and the choices we recommend for our project:

- Prettier for code formatting
    - Prompt: Would you like to use Prettier for code formatting?
    - Choice: Yes
    - Reason: Ensures consistent code style across your project and makes collaboration easier

- CI provider
    - Prompt: Which CI provider would you like to use?
    - Choice: Skip
    - Reason: We'll cover CI/CD configuration in a dedicated chapter, so we can defer this step
- Remote caching
    - Prompt: Would you like remote caching to make your build faster?
    - Choice: Skip
    - Reason: Optional for now; we can configure caching later for performance optimization

Nx will then create the workspace, install dependencies with **pnpm**, and set up the initial project structure.

With the workspace in place, the next step is to **understand the generated folder structure and configuration files** before creating applications and libraries.

## Workspace structure and configuration

Once your Nx workspace is created, you'll notice a set of files and folders that form the foundation of your project. Understanding these early on will help you navigate and configure your monorepo efficiently.

### Top-level folders

- `.vscode`: Contains workspace-specific VS Code settings. This helps maintain consistent editor behavior for all developers on the project.
- `node_modules`: Standard folder where dependencies are installed. Since we're using pnpm, packages are symlinked for faster installs and smaller disk usage.
- `packages`: This is where your applications and libraries will live. Nx encourages organizing code into reusable libraries and independent apps here.

### Important configuration files

- `.gitignore` and `.gitkeep`: Standard Git files for ignoring unwanted files and ensuring empty folders are tracked.
- `.npmrc`: Configures npm/pnpm behavior for this workspace.
- `nx.json`: Nx-specific configuration, including workspace-wide settings, tags, and default project behaviors.
- `package.json`: Contains dependencies, scripts, and metadata for the workspace.

- `pnpm-lock.yaml` and `pnpm-workspace.yaml`: pnpm's lockfile and workspace definition. These ensure consistent installations and allow multiple projects to share dependencies efficiently.
- `README.md` and `LICENSE`: Basic documentation and licensing for your project.

How this structure helps:

- Keeps apps and libraries **organized** and separated, making scaling easier.
- Provides a **central place for configuration**, reducing duplication across projects.
- Works seamlessly with Nx tooling to support **intelligent builds**, **testing**, and **dependency graphs**.

With this foundation in place, we can now move on to **creating applications and shared libraries** in our workspace. This is where Nx really starts to show its power by helping you structure your code professionally.

## Generating and organizing your projects

Now that we have our Nx workspace, the next step is to generate the projects that will live inside it. For DevJobs, we'll structure the workspace around three main parts: a frontend application, a backend application, and shared packages.

- **Frontend application**: The user-facing React/Next.js app where job seekers can browse postings, search by filters, and view company details
- **Backend application**: An Express or NestJS service that powers the API, handling job listings, authentication, and business rules
- **Shared packages**: TypeScript libraries for code that needs to be reused across frontend and backend, such as data models, utility functions, or domain-specific logic

Before we proceed, let's examine a convention we would use.

### Establishing the apps/ and libs/ convention

The latest versions of Nx might default to a `packages/` directory, but a very common and well-documented convention uses `apps/` for applications and `libs/` for libraries. To ensure clarity and consistency with many existing projects, we'll adopt this structure.

To follow this convention, let's first remove the default `packages/` directory:

```
rm -rf packages
```

Now, let's create the directories that will house our applications and libraries by running the following.

```
mkdir apps libs
```

Your workspace now has clean, dedicated folders where applications (`apps/`) and libraries (`libs/`) will live. Next, we'll continue with installing the relevant plugins.

## Installing required Nx plugins

Before generating applications, we need to install the relevant Nx plugins.

Nx organizes functionality into **plugins**, which are like toolkits for specific frameworks and technologies (e.g., Next.js, Express, Angular). Each plugin comes with the following:

- **Generators**: These are scripts that automatically create or modify files in your workspace. Think of them as templates or "blueprints" that scaffold projects, components, or configurations for you.
  Here's an example:

  ```
  nx g @nx/next:app my-app
  ```

  This command runs a generator that creates a new Next.js application. Behind the scenes, it copies template files, sets up configuration such as `next.config.js`, updates workspace configuration files, and installs any required dependencies. In other words, generators automatically build the structure of your app or library so you don't have to set everything up manually.

- **Executors:** These are like specialized scripts that know how to build, serve, or test the projects created by the generators.

Let's use the following analogy: if you think of Nx as a big workshop, the **plugins** are toolboxes for different crafts (a Next.js toolbox, an Express toolbox, etc.). Inside each toolbox, the **generators** are the ready-made stencils or templates to get you started, and the **executors** are the power tools that actually run tasks such as building or serving your app.

For DevJobs, we'll need two specific toolboxes:

- The **Next.js plugin** for creating and running our frontend app
- The **Express plugin** for creating and running our backend API

Install them by running the following:

```
pnpm nx add @nx/next
pnpm nx add @nx/express
```

Now that the required plugins are installed, we'll generate our applications inside the apps/ directory to establish the core of the DevJobs workspace.

# Generating the frontend and backend applications

With the necessary plugins installed, we can now proceed to generate our applications. Following the convention we established earlier, we'll place each project under apps/ so the structure matches common Nx monorepos. Nx will also create a matching E2E project for each app automatically; we'll note their locations but defer the testing details for a later chapter.

## Generate the frontend (Next.js) application

We'll scaffold a Next.js app named `devjobs-frontend`. Note that, by default, Nx would place a new app at the repository root; to keep our `apps/` convention, we prefix the path:

```
pnpm nx g @nx/next:app apps/devjobs-frontend --style=css --tailwind
```

Let's see what the preceding command does:

- `apps/devjobs-frontend` ensures the app is created under `apps/`
- `--style=css --tailwind` sets up standard CSS plus TailwindCSS out of the box

Running the preceding command launches a few interactive prompts. Here are the choices we made and why they work well for this project.

- **Which linter would you like to use? → ESLint**: ESLint is the de facto standard in the TypeScript/React ecosystem. It ensures consistent code quality and integrates seamlessly with Nx.
- **What unit test runner should be used? → Jest**: Jest is battle-tested, fast, and widely used in the React/Next.js community. Nx also has excellent built-in support for Jest.
- **Which E2E test runner would you like to use? → Playwright**: Playwright provides modern cross-browser testing with auto-waiting and great debugging tools. It's an excellent fit for our frontend application.

- **Would you like to use the App Router (recommended)? → Yes**: We're opting for Next.js's modern App Router since it simplifies routing, enables server components, and aligns with current best practices.
- **Would you like to use the src/ directory? → Yes**: Placing code under `src/` keeps the project structure clean and avoids mixing configuration files with source code.

Once the setup finishes, Nx will generate the app along with a matching E2E project (`apps/devjobs-frontend-e2e/`). We'll keep the E2E project in place but defer its implementation details until later. See the following screenshot for more details:

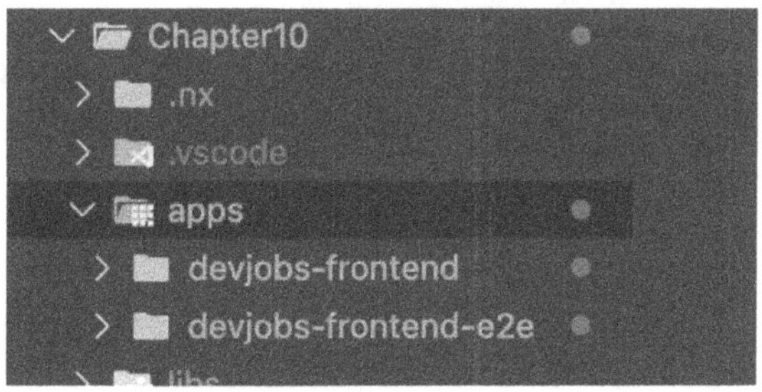


*Figure 10.1 – The generated frontend and e2e directories*

We can now try to start the application by running the following command:

```
pnpm nx serve devjobs-frontend
```

This should start the application. Mine is on port `http://localhost:3000`. That's the default, but you should see the localhost address on your terminal. If you navigate to that URL in your browser, you should see our web app as shown in the following screenshot:

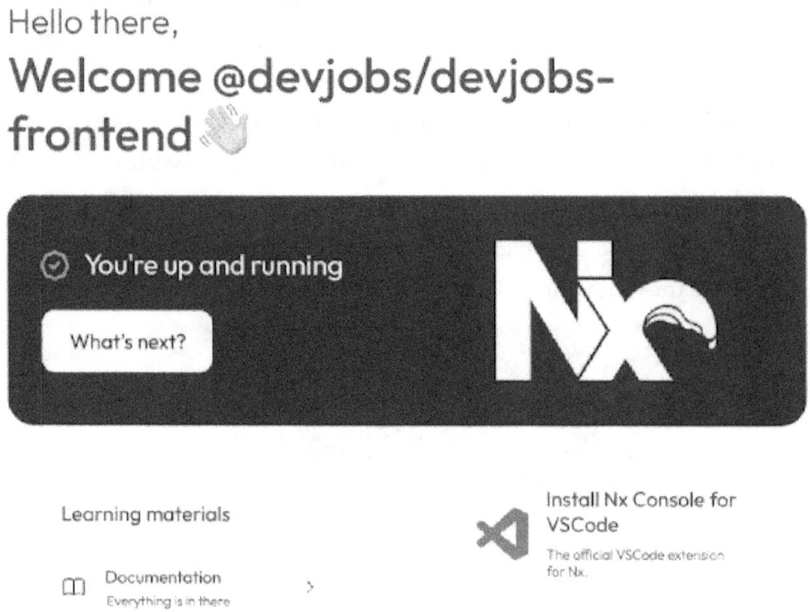


*Figure 10.2 – The devjobs frontend application in the browser*

Great, now that we have our frontend application in place, let's generate the backend Express application.

## Generate the backend (Express) application

To generate the scaffold for the API service with Express, we run the following command:

```
pnpm nx g @nx/express:app apps/devjobs-backend
```

Nx will ask a couple of setup questions. Here are the answers we chose and why:

- **Which linter would you like to use? → ESLint**: As with the frontend, ESLint ensures code quality and consistency across the workspace. Keeping the same linter across apps reduces context switching.
- **Which unit test runner would you like to use? → Jest**: Jest integrates smoothly with Nx and provides fast, reliable unit testing. Using the same test runner for both the frontend and backend makes our tooling consistent.

Once complete, Nx generates the `apps/devjobs-backend/` application along with a matching E2E testing project, (`apps/devjobs-backend-e2e/`). As with the frontend, we'll leave the E2E setup in place but won't dive into its details just yet.

Your project should look like what we have in the following screenshot:

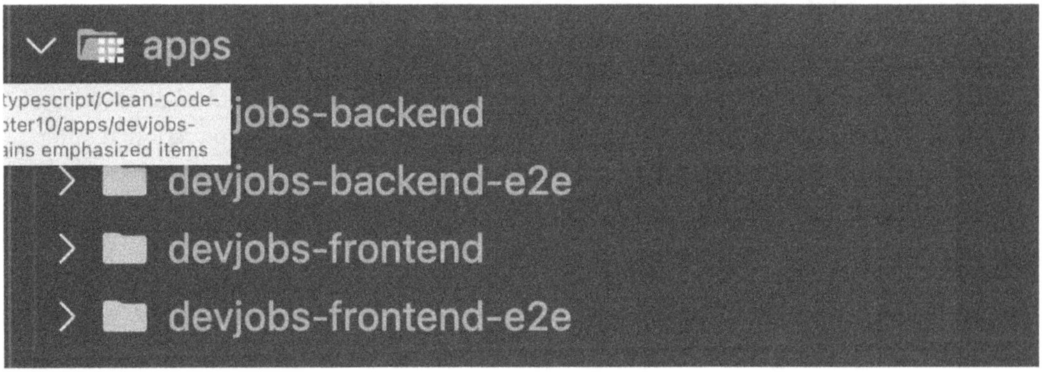


*Figure 10.3 – The newly created devjobs-backend application*

## Running the backend

To start the backend server in development mode, we use the following command:

```
pnpm nx serve devjobs-backend
```

Once the application is started, you should see the backend URL (`http://localhost:3333/api`) displayed in the terminal. If you navigate to that address in your browser, you should see the message **"Welcome to devjobs-backend!"**, as shown in the following screenshot.

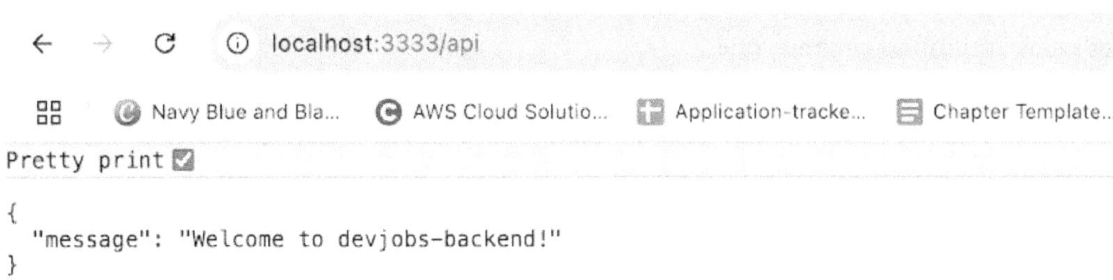


*Figure 10.4 – Welcome message for dev-jobs backend*

With our workspace scaffolded and the core projects in place, the next step is learning how to work effectively within Nx. While Nx sets up a lot for us automatically, most of our day-to-day development boils down to a handful of powerful commands. By understanding these commands early, you'll be able to run applications, test changes, and visualize dependencies with confidence.

# Essential Nx commands and workflows

Now that our DevJobs workspace has both frontend and backend applications in place, let's look at how to actually work with them. Nx provides a small set of commands that cover most of what you'll do day-to-day: running apps in development, building for production, testing, and analyzing how projects depend on each other.

Before diving into the commands themselves, it's important to understand one key concept: **targets**.

A **target** is simply a named task that you can run for a project—for example, `dev`, `serve`, `build`, or `test`. Every Nx project comes with its own set of targets, and you run them with a consistent command pattern:

```
nx <target> <project-name>
```

For example, to start our frontend in development mode, you'd run the following:

```
nx dev devjobs-frontend
```

You can think of **targets** as **buttons on a control panel** for each project. Sometimes the wiring (configuration) for these buttons could live in `nx.json`, `project.json`, or `package.json`, depending on the plugin, but pressing the button looks exactly the same to you as a developer.

Let's look at the most common ones:

- `nx serve <project>`: Runs a project in development mode. This is the standard way to start backend apps (e.g., Express, NestJS) and can also be used by frontend apps depending on the plugin.
- `nx dev <project>`: Used by some frontend frameworks such as Next.js to run the app in development mode with hot reloading.
- `nx build <project>`: Compiles the project into a production-ready output.
- `nx test <project>`: Runs the unit tests for the project using the chosen test runner.

So, in our case, here's a list of the commands we would need:

```
pnpm nx serve devjobs-backend
pnpm nx dev devjobs-frontend
pnpm nx build devjobs-frontend
pnpm nx test devjobs-backend
```

With our DevJobs workspace set up, the frontend and backend applications generated, and the key Nx commands understood, we now have a solid foundation for development. Before writing more code, it's a good practice to put **automated quality checks** in place so that every commit meets your team's standards.

While `pnpm` manages dependencies efficiently behind the scenes, our focus now shifts from project setup and task execution to **enforcing code quality**. This is where **Git hooks** come in—lightweight scripts that run at specific points in your workflow, such as before a commit or push, helping prevent errors and maintain consistency.

In the next section, we'll explore how to configure Git hooks using tools such as **Husky** and **lint-staged**, so checks run automatically on staged files and ensure your code meets agreed-upon standards before reaching the repository.

In this section, we'll start by exploring the core development commands (`nx serve`, `nx dev`, `nx build`, `nx test`), then learn how to use the dependency graph to visualize project relationships, and finally look at affected commands, which make CI/CD pipelines smarter by running tasks only where changes are detected.

# Code quality automation with Git hooks

Now that our workspace and projects are set up, it's important to ensure that the code we commit and push adheres to consistent standards. Manual checks can be error-prone and time-consuming, so we turn to **Git hooks** to automate this process.

Git hooks are scripts that run at specific points in your Git workflow—for example, before a commit or a push. They allow us to enforce code quality rules, run tests, and prevent problematic code from entering the repository. By integrating tools such as **Husky** and **lint-staged**, we can run checks only on files that have changed, keeping the workflow fast and developer-friendly.

In this section, we'll cover the following:

- **Git hooks strategy**: Deciding where and how to enforce checks
- **Husky + lint-staged setup**: Installing and configuring the tools
- **Advanced quality gates**: Commit message standards, branch protection, and handling hook failures

By the end, your DevJobs monorepo will automatically enforce key quality practices, helping maintain a healthy, consistent code base across the team.

## Git hooks strategy

Git hooks give us convenient points in the development workflow where we can run automated checks. Choosing the right hook for the right purpose is crucial—we want to enforce standards without slowing developers down unnecessarily.

The two most common hooks for code quality automation are as follows:

- **Pre-commit**: runs before a commit is created.
  - Best for fast checks such as linting, formatting, or running tests on staged files only
  - Ensures low-level issues are caught early, right on the developer's machine
- **Pre-push**: runs before pushing commits to a remote repository.
  - Better suited for heavier checks, such as full test suites or integration checks
  - Ensures that broken or untested code never reaches the shared repository

To balance thoroughness with a smooth developer experience, employ pre-commit hooks for quick, lightweight checks that complete in just a few seconds, ensuring rapid feedback without disrupting workflow. For more comprehensive and potentially time-consuming checks, utilize pre-push hooks, which allow for deeper validation while keeping the commit process efficient. By combining the two wisely, you get a workflow that enforces consistency without frustrating developers with long feedback loops.

Before setting up Git hooks, make sure you commit all your current changes. This ensures a clean slate and prevents hooks from interfering with ongoing work. You can commit everything with the following:

```
git add .
git commit -m "chore: setup Nx workspace with frontend and backend apps"
```

With a clean repository state, we're now ready to automate quality checks using Husky and lint-staged.

## Husky and lint-staged setup

Git hooks are small scripts that Git can run automatically at key points in your workflow—for example, before a commit (pre-commit) or before pushing (pre-push). Instead of writing these scripts manually, we use **Husky** to manage Git hooks, and **lint-staged** to run commands only on the files you're about to commit.

## Step 1—Install dependencies

We'll add `husky` and `lint-staged` as dev dependencies:

```
pnpm add -D husky lint-staged -w
```

The `-w` flag tells `pnpm` to install these dependencies at the workspace root, since Git hooks apply to the whole repo rather than a single project.

## Step 2—Initialize Git

Husky requires a Git repository to work, so if you haven't already initialized one, do so now:

```
git init
git add .
git commit -m "chore: initial commit"
```

## Step 3—Initialize Husky

Next, initialize Husky. This creates a `.husky/` directory and a `prepare` script in `package.json`, so Husky will be ready whenever someone installs dependencies:

```
pnpm exec husky init
```

At this point, your workspace root should have a `.husky/` folder with an example hook inside. See the following screenshot for more details:

*Figure 10.5 — Screenshot of the .husky/ folder with a pre-commit hook*

## Step 4—Add a pre-commit hook

We'll use Husky to create a pre-commit hook that runs `lint-staged`. `lint-staged` is a package that ensures only the files you've staged for commit get linted and formatted, which keeps checks fast and makes sure that only clean code gets into your Git history.

With Husky v9, we create the `pre-commit` hook manually:

```
echo "pnpm exec lint-staged" > .husky/pre-commit
chmod +x .husky/pre-commit
```

This generates a `.husky/pre-commit` file and makes it executable. Inside, it runs `pnpm exec lint-staged` whenever you attempt a commit.

The final `.husky/pre-commit` file should look like this:

```
#!/bin/sh
. "$(dirname "$0")/_/husky.sh"

pnpm exec lint-staged
```

With our `husky` file in place, the next step is to configure `lint-staged` so it knows what to do with staged files. Without a config, running `pnpm exec lint-staged` won't actually run any checks.

You can define the `lint-staged` configuration in either `package.json` or a dedicated config file. To keep things clean and easier to manage, we'll use the `.lintstagedrc.json` option.

Create a new file named `.lintstagedrc.json` in the root of your repository and add the following:

```
{
  "*.{js,ts,tsx}": [
    "eslint --fix",
    "prettier --write"
  ],
  "*.json": "prettier --write",
  "*.md": "prettier --write"
}
```

This tells `lint-staged` to run ESLint and Prettier on staged JavaScript/TypeScript files, and Prettier on JSON and Markdown files.

### Example commit flow

With this setup in place, here's what happens during a typical commit:

```
git add .
git commit -m "chore: update code"
```

Here's what happens when you run the preceding command in your terminal:

Husky triggers the `pre-commit` hook.

- `lint-staged` runs ESLint and Prettier only on the files you staged
- If the linters fix issues, they'll update the staged files before the commit goes through
- If errors remain (such as linting rules that can't be auto-fixed), the commit is blocked until you resolve them

This way, you and your team can be confident that only properly formatted, linted code makes it into the repository.

Let's do a quick test to confirm that everything works.

## Testing the Git hook with a sample file

To see Husky + `lint-staged` in action, we'll create a test file with deliberately **poor formatting**. This will allow us to observe how the `pre-commit` hook automatically fixes staged files before committing.

### Step 1—Create a test file

Let's create a new file in the frontend application:

```
touch apps/devjobs-frontend/src/somefile.ts
```

Open `somefile.ts` and add the following unformatted code:

```
export function greet(name:string){console.log("Hello,"+name+"!")}
```

See the following screenshot for more information:

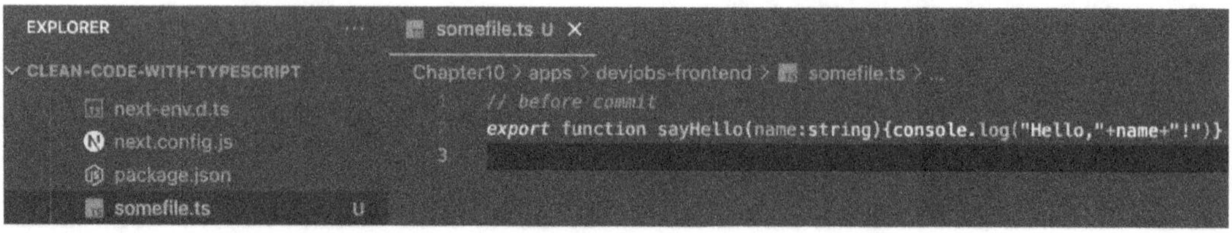


Figure 10.6 – somefile.ts is a random unformatted file to test our Git hooks

## Step 2—Stage the file

Add the file to Git:

```
git add apps/devjobs-frontend/src/somefile.ts
```

## Step 3—Commit the file

Run the `commit` command:

```
git commit -m "chore(frontend): add somefile to test Git hooks"
```

When you run that command, you should see something like what's shown in the following screenshot:

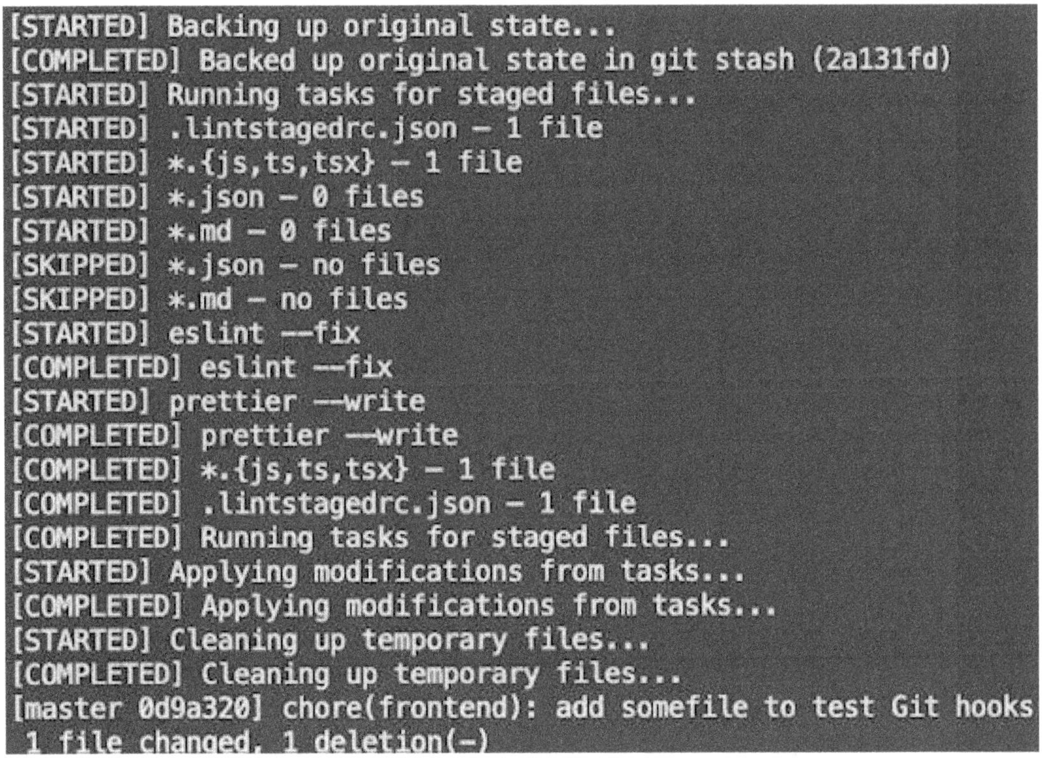


*Figure 10.7 – Terminal showing Git hooks at work, after a commit is made*

Here's a quick overview of what is happening:

- Husky triggers the pre-commit hook
- `lint-staged` runs ESLint + Prettier only on the staged file
- The staged file is automatically fixed according to your rules
- If any errors remain that cannot be auto-fixed, the commit is blocked until you resolve them

## Step 4—Verify the changes

Open `somefile.ts` again — you should see the file **automatically formatted**:

```
export function greet(name: string) {
  console.log(`Hello, ${name}!`);
}
```

See the following screenshot for more details:

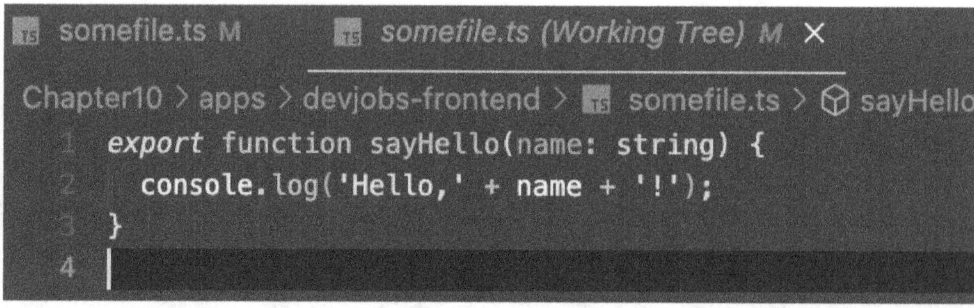


*Figure 10.8 – somefile.ts is now properly formatted after Husky + lint-staged have run.*

This simple example demonstrates how Husky and `lint-staged` work together to enforce code quality automatically before code enters your repository. While here we focused on linting and formatting TypeScript files, Git hooks can be extended to enforce many other standards and workflows.

Here are some examples:

- Run unit or integration tests on staged files before committing
- Check commit messages to ensure they follow a conventional format using tools such as commitlint
- Enforce security or dependency checks on changed files before pushing
- Verify documentation or Markdown formatting automatically

Using these hooks effectively helps maintain a clean, consistent, and reliable code base across both frontend and backend projects, all without slowing down developers.

# Summary

In this chapter, we focused on building a solid foundation for scalable TypeScript projects. We started by structuring a full-stack Nx workspace, clearly separating the frontend, backend, and shared libraries. You learned how to manage dependencies and tooling efficiently using pnpm workspaces, ensuring that your code base remains consistent and maintainable. We then introduced automated code quality measures using Husky and `lint-staged`, so that linting and formatting happen automatically before commits, helping maintain a clean Git history. This setup prepares your workspace for collaboration, enforces standards, and lays the groundwork for team productivity.

At the end of this chapter, your workspace includes a Next.js frontend application (`devjobs-frontend`), an Express backend application (`devjobs-backend`), a shared `libs/` directory for reusable utilities and types, and pre-commit Git hooks that automatically enforce linting and formatting rules. While this chapter focused primarily on workspace setup and automation, the next chapter will shift toward building real features. You will begin applying TypeScript across the stack, developing type-safe React components for the frontend and building server logic with Express for the backend. A key goal will be sharing types between the frontend and backend to improve maintainability and reduce bugs.

## Get this book's PDF copy, code bundle, and more

Scan the QR code (or go to `packtpub.com/unlock`). Search for this book by name, confirm the edition, and then follow the steps on the page.

UNLOCK NOW

*Note: Keep your invoice handy. Purchases made directly from the Packt website don't require an invoice.*

# 11

# TypeScript in Action: Building Full Stack Applications

In the previous chapter, we established the groundwork for scalable TypeScript projects. We moved from defining a product specification all the way to setting up the monorepo for our devjobs portal using Nx. We also saw how to set up automated checks and enforce coding standards with Git hooks.

With both the backend and frontend scaffolding in place, this chapter focuses on bringing the project to life. We'll begin with a NestJS backend, defining type-safe APIs with validation, and then move on to the React frontend, where we consume those APIs using shared **Data Transfer Objects** (**DTOs**). Along the way, we'll explore how TypeScript strengthens collaboration by reducing runtime errors and ensuring consistency between the client and server.

By the end of this chapter, you'll have a production-ready, type-safe full stack application that demonstrates the real power of TypeScript in modern web development.

We will cover the following main topics:

- Server-side TypeScript with Node.js
- Client-side TypeScript with React

## Technical requirements

To follow along with this chapter, you will need to have completed the project setup in *Chapter 10*. You can download the example project and code for this book by following the instructions in the *Download the example code files* section in the *Preface* of this book.

This chapter's code files are included in the downloadable code bundle.

# Server-side TypeScript with Node.js

One of the most significant contributions of Node.js was giving developers the ability to run JavaScript outside the browser. This opened the door to full stack development, where teams could build both frontend and backend applications using the same language. With TypeScript, this story gets even stronger: we gain type safety, better tooling, and a more reliable foundation for collaboration across the stack.

In this section, we'll focus on developing the backend for our devjobs application using TypeScript and NestJS. Our goal is to see how professional teams approach building type-safe APIs that improve collaboration with frontend developers and reduce runtime errors. Since we've already set up the project structure, we'll dive straight into the implementation, starting with the contract-first approach, where we define shared schemas and DTOs, lightweight data structures that standardize how information is exchanged between the client and server, serving as the single source of truth for both.

## Implementing the contract-first approach

The **contract-first approach** is less about tools and more about mindset. Instead of diving straight into backend implementation details, we will begin by defining the *expected schemas* for our API—that is, the request and response data types, along with the available methods. These definitions are usually created in close collaboration with frontend developers or any other teams that will consume the API.

Once both sides agree on what the API should provide, this agreement becomes the **contract**. In practice, this is often captured using **OpenAPI documentation** (formerly known as Swagger), which serves as a formal, machine-readable specification of the API.

So, why take this approach before writing code? Let's look at the main benefits:

- **Shared source of truth**: Both backend developers and consumers work from the same agreed-upon schema, removing ambiguity.
- **Parallel development**: Frontend developers don't have to wait for backend implementation. Since they already know the expected responses, they can mock data and continue building their features in parallel. This saves significant development time.

- **Backward compatibility**: Because the contract specifies the shape of data, any refactoring or internal changes on the backend must still honor the same output. This keeps clients stable, even as the backend evolves.
- **Type safety across the stack**: Teams don't need to redefine or duplicate types. Instead, they can generate typings directly from the OpenAPI documentation, ensuring consistency between the backend and frontend.

Now that we understand the what and why of the contract-first approach, let's start building by going through the following steps.

## Step 1: Creating the openapi.yml file

In the directory of your `devjobs-backend` project, create an `openapi.yml` file (leave this empty for now).

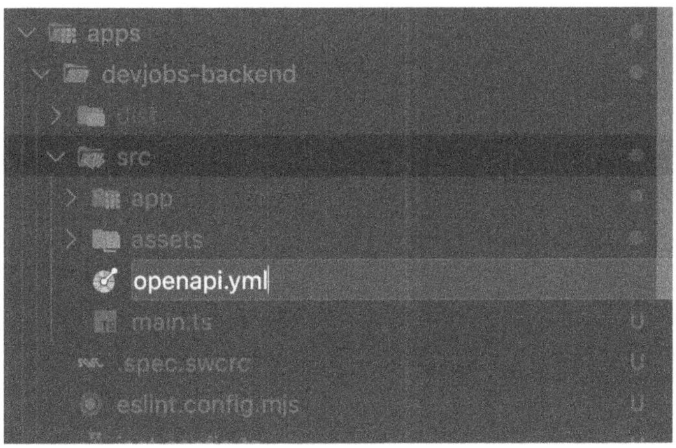


*Figure 11.1 – Creating the openapi.yml file*

With the file in place, we can now start defining our schemas and what the API would look like.

## Step 2: Defining the API specification

In this step, we add the API definition to the project. The specification contains schemas, request paths, and other relevant details. The full specification is already defined in the repository under `devjobs-backend/openapi.yml`.

Here's a sneak peek of what the file looks like (truncated for brevity):

```
openapi: 3.0.3
info:
  title: DevJobs API
  version: 1.0.0
```

```yaml
  description: API for the DevJobs platform

servers:
  - url: http://localhost:3000
    description: Local development server

paths:
  /users:
    get:
      summary: List all users
      responses:
        '200':
          description: Array of users
          content:
            application/json:
              schema:
                type: array
                items:
                  $ref: '#/components/schemas/User'

    post:
      summary: Register a new user
      requestBody:
        required: true
        content:
          application/json:
            schema:
              $ref: '#/components/schemas/CreateUser'
      responses:
        '201':
          description: Created user
          content:
            application/json:
              schema:
                $ref: '#/components/schemas/User'
```

The full Swagger/OpenAPI document defines the following main endpoints:

- `/users`
    - `GET`: List all users
    - `POST`: Register a new user
- `/companies`
    - `GET`: List all companies
    - `POST`: Create a new company
- `/jobs`
    - `GET`: List all jobs
    - `POST`: Create a new job posting

Each of these endpoints references schemas defined under components, including the following:

- `User/CreateUser`
- `Company/CreateCompany`
- `Job/CreateJob`

These schemas describe request/response structures and required fields (e.g., `id`, `name`, `email`, `title`, etc.).

For the **full API specification**, refer to the `openapi.yml` file in the project repository.

Now that we have our OpenAPI spec in place, the next step would be to generate types for our project. These types are going to be generated directly from the OpenAPI spec allowing for consistency between the frontend and the backend. To generate the types directly from the OpenAPI spec, we would use some packages in the next step.

## Step 3: Installing Orval and adding Orval config

Orval is a Node.js package that allows us to generate type signatures from any valid OpenAPI v3 or v2 documentation. To install Orval, we use the following command:

```
npm install --save-dev orval
```

The preceding command installs Orval as a dev dependency. Once we have that in place, we need to create the `orval.config.ts` file in the root of our project directory and add the following:

```
export default {
  devjobs: {
    input: './apps/devjobs-backend/src/openapi.yml',
    output: {
      schemas: './libs/api-types/model',
      target: './libs/api-types',
    },
  },
};
```

This snippet is a **configuration object for Orval**. Let's break it down piece by piece:

- `export default { ... }`: This exports the configuration object so Orval can read it when you run the generator.
- `devjobs: { ... }`: `devjobs`: This is just a key to identify this configuration. You can have multiple configurations in the same file if your project has multiple APIs.
- `input: './apps/devjobs-backend/src/openapi.yml'`: This points to the **OpenAPI spec file** you want Orval to use. Orval reads this file to understand your API endpoints, request bodies, response schemas, and so on.
  Here, the file is located in the `apps/devjobs-backend/src/` folder.
- `output: { ... }`: This section tells Orval where to generate TypeScript code.
  - `schemas: './libs/api-types/model'`: All **data models** (such as `User`, `Job`, and `Company`) will be generated here. Think of this as a folder for your types and interfaces.
  - `target: './libs/api-types/devJobsAPI.ts'`: This is the main **API client file** that Orval will generate. It contains functions or hooks to call your backend API directly from TypeScript.

  We won't be focusing much on this file. For the purposes of this book, we are just going to use the generated types.

## Step 4: Generating the types

With our Orval config in place, we run the following command in our terminal to generate the typings for our project:

```
npx orval
```

That should generate the relevant types in the corresponding directory as shown in the image below:

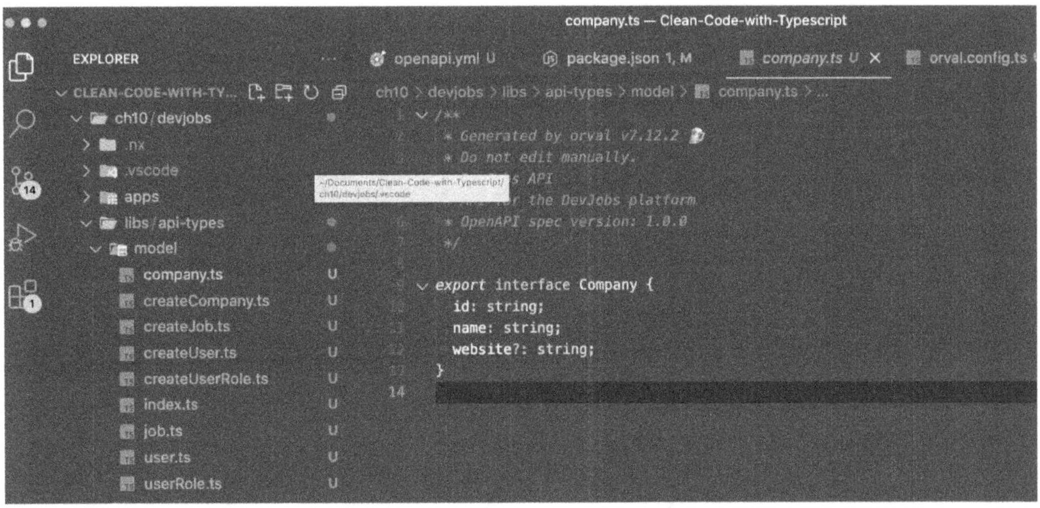


*Figure 11.2 – Types generated by Orval*

The files under the `model` directory should contain the types for each entity. For example, in the preceding TypeScript file, we define the interface for `Company`.

With our shared API contract in place, we can now move on to building the backend. Let's start with a quick overview of what our NestJS project looks like.

If you peek into the `src` directory in our `devjobs-backend`, the first file you'll notice is `main.ts`. This is the entry point for our NestJS application. Inside, you'll find a function that bootstraps the app. Bootstrap here simply means starting up the application with everything it needs to run and spinning up the server.

Moving on from `main.ts`, you'll see an `app` directory (still inside `src`). This is where most of our code will live. Inside, we already have a few files generated by Nest:

- `app.module.ts`

- `app.controller.ts`
- `app.service.ts`

Let's go over what each of these does:

- `app.module.ts`: This is the *root module* of our application. In NestJS, modules are containers that group together related code. The `AppModule` wires up our controllers, services, and any imported feature modules. As our project grows, we'll add new modules (e.g., `UsersModule`, `CompaniesModule`) and import them here.
- `app.controller.ts`: Controllers define the routes of our application. If you've used Express, think of them as route handlers (`app.get('/jobs', ...)`). Controllers receive incoming requests and return responses, but they don't hold the actual logic—they delegate that to services.
- `app.service.ts`: Services hold the *business logic*. Instead of writing all logic in the controller, we push it down into a service. That way, controllers remain thin (just handling requests/responses), while services handle the heavy lifting (fetching from the database, enforcing rules, etc.).

So, in short, we have the following:

- **Modules**: Organize features
- **Controllers**: Define routes (such as Express)
- **Services**: Business logic layer

Now that we understand the defaults, let's see how this grows in practice.

## Adding feature modules

Suppose we want to handle **users** as a feature; for example, instead of cluttering the root app files, we generate a new `Users` module. Our structure would be as follows:

```
src/
├── app.controller.ts
├── app.module.ts
├── app.service.ts
├── main.ts
└── users/
      ├── users.module.ts
      ├── users.controller.ts
      └── users.service.ts
```

Let's understand its components:

- `users.module.ts` groups everything user-related
- `users.controller.ts` defines the routes/endpoints for users (e.g., `GET /users`, `POST /users`)
- `users.service.ts` holds the business logic (e.g., fetching users from a database)

Each module is self-contained; it has its own controller (routes) and service (logic). Finally, to make Nest aware of this new feature, we'd import `UsersModule` into `AppModule`. This way, our application grows in a clean, modular way: each feature gets its own space, making things easy to organize, scale, and maintain. Your `AppModule` should now look like this:

```
// app.module.ts

import { Module } from '@nestjs/common';
import { AppController } from './app.controller';
import { AppService } from './app.service';
import { UsersModule } from './users/users.module';

@Module({
  imports: [UsersModule],   // registering feature module
  controllers: [AppController],
  providers: [AppService],
})
export class AppModule {}
```

This modular approach is one of Nest's biggest strengths: instead of dumping everything into one place, we organize features into separate modules.

Now that we have a basic understanding of how Nest handles things, let's go back to our product spec and build out the relevant features.

# Tying it back to our product spec

Back in the product requirements, we saw that our system needs four major domains:

- `User`: Job seekers and companies (register, login)
- `Companies`: Company profiles, related to jobs
- `Jobs`: Postings tied to companies, browsable by seekers
- `Auth`: Authentication (JWT) and authorization (role-based guards)

Each of these naturally maps to a **NestJS module**:

- `users/`: `UsersModule` with `UsersController` + `UsersService`
- `companies/`: `CompaniesModule` with `CompaniesController` + `CompaniesService`
- `jobs/`: `JobsModule` with `JobsController` + `JobsService`
- `auth/`: `AuthModule` with `AuthController` + `AuthService`

All of them get registered in `AppModule`, so the application can serve their routes. If you've worked with Express, here's a comparison.

In Express, you'd write the following:

```
app.get('/jobs', (req, res) => { ... });
```

In Nest, you'd instead write the following:

```
@Controller('jobs')
export class JobsController {
  constructor(private readonly jobsService: JobsService) {}

  @Get()
  findAll() {
    return this.jobsService.findAll();
  }
}
```

Controllers in Nest are like your Express route handlers.

Services in Nest are like the functions you would normally inline in your Express routes (but here they live in their own class for cleaner organization).

With this understanding in mind, let's continue with building the relevant modules for our devjobs applications. We will start with the `Users` and `Auth` modules, since these power the registration and login.

## Users module

Our API contract defines a `User` schema, along with `RegisterUser` for creating accounts. That means we need `UsersModule` to handle basic user operations.

Run these commands to generate it with NestJS schematics:

```
npx nx g @nx/nest:module --path=apps/devjobs-backend/src/app/users/users
npx nx g @nx/nest:controller --path=apps/devjobs-backend/src/app/users/users
npx nx g @nx/nest:service --path=apps/devjobs-backend/src/app/users/users
```

Running the preceding command creates a new users feature directory inside our backend app directory. You should now have a structure like this:

```
apps/
└── devjobs-backend/
    └── src/
        └── app/
            └── users/
                ├── users.controller.spec.ts
                ├── users.controller.ts
                ├── users.module.ts
                ├── users.service.spec.ts
                └── users.service.ts
```

At this point, `UserService`, for example, is just an empty class:

```
import { Injectable } from '@nestjs/common';

@Injectable()
export class UsersService {}
```

That's fine; we'll flesh this out soon. The important thing is that we now have the scaffolding in place: a module, a controller, and a service, all wired together the "NestJS way."

As stated previously, remember to import `UsersModule` into `AppModule`, so NestJS knows about it. With that in place, we are going to connect our first endpoint, `POST /users`, to the API contract, and then we can start writing some business logic in `UserService`.

## Creating the first endpoint

Let's wire up the `POST /users/register` endpoint we defined in our OpenAPI contract.

Open `users.controller.ts` and update it:

```
import { Body, Controller, Post } from '@nestjs/common';
import { UsersService } from './users.service';
```

```
@Controller('users')
export class UsersController {
  constructor(private readonly usersService: UsersService) {}

  @Post()
  register(@Body() body: any) {
    return this.usersService.register(body);
  }}
```

Here's a quick explanation of what's happening in the preceding code:

- `@Controller('users')`: All routes here will start with `/users`
- `@Post()`: Defines `POST /users`
- `@Body()`: Tells NestJS to parse the request body into `body`

We forward the request to our service: `this.usersService.register(body)`.

- The register method doesn't exist yet on the `UserService` class. Let's add it in the next subsection.

## Adding business logic to UserService

In this section, we are going to update `users.service.ts` to actually handle registration. We'll start with a simple in-memory implementation: we'll store users in an array within the service (no database yet), generate a unique ID for each user, and return the created user. This keeps things lightweight for now.

Before saving a new user to the store (an in-memory array for now), we should use a package known as **bcrypt** to *hash* passwords. Storing plaintext passwords is a big no-no in production. Hashing prevents storing the actual passwords and protects users. We will go through this step by step and show the code updates so you can follow along easily.

## Step 1: Installing bcrypt for hashing passwords

In this step, we just run the following command to install bcrypt:

```
pnpm install bcrypt -w
pnpm install --save-dev @types/bcrypt -w
```

The preceding command installs bcrypt and its types in the root of your workspace.

With this installed, we can now focus on the actual register method in `UserService`.

## Step 2: Basic in-memory registration with Orval types

In this step, we'll extend `UsersService` so it can register new users **in memory**. We'll break this down into smaller, actionable substeps so you can follow along easily. Each substep includes a code snippet that you can copy-paste or adapt into your file:

1. Define an in-memory users store. We keep registered users in a simple array:

```
@Injectable()
export class UsersService {
  private users: User[] = []; // Temporary in-memory storage
}
```

2. Create a register method. This method will take a `CreateUser` object (coming from your API contract types that we generated previously) and return a `UserResponse`:

```
async register(user: CreateUser): Promise<UserResponse> {
  // Logic goes here
}
```

3. Hash the password. We never want to store plaintext passwords. Use bcrypt to hash the password before saving:

```
const hashedPassword = await bcrypt.hash(user.password, 10);
```

4. Build the new user object:

```
Generate a unique ID and combine all user data.const newUser = {
  id: randomUUID(),
  name: user.name,
  email: user.email,
  role: user.role,
  companyId: user.companyId,
  password: hashedPassword,
};
```

5. Save the user in memory. Push the new user into the `users` array:

```
this.users.push(newUser);
```

6. Return the user (without the password). We don't want to leak the password back in the response. Strip it out before returning:

```
const { password, ...userWithoutPassword } = newUser;
return userWithoutPassword;
```

With everything in place, your register method on `UserService` should look like this:

```
async register(user: CreateUser): Promise<UserResponse> {
const hashedPassword = await bcrypt.hash(user.password, 10);

const newUser = {
id: randomUUID(),
name: user.name,
email: user.email,
role: user.role,
companyId: user.companyId,
password: hashedPassword,
};

this.users.push(newUser);

const { password, ...userWithoutPassword } = newUser;

return userWithoutPassword;
}
```

Now that we have a basic registration flow in place, let's add a method to retrieve users by their email address. This is essential for authentication, as we'll need to look up users during login. Now, with our service logic in place, we can make a request to our user endpoint to register a user.

## Making a request to our newly created endpoint

With our logic and controller in place, we can now make a request to register a new user.

We make a `POST` request to the following URL: `http://localhost:3000/api/users`.

Your request body should look like this:

```
{
    "name": "John Doe",
    "email": "john@example.com",
    "password": "securePassword123",
    "role": "user",
    "companyId": "company-uuid-123"
  }
```

You should get a response like this:

```
{
  "id": "e9e330ae-31bb-4d1c-b202-f7afca956772",
  "name": "John Doe",
  "email": "john@example.com",
  "role": "user",
  "companyId": "company-uuid-123"
}
```

Congratulations! You've successfully completed your first user registration flow. Your controller is now correctly handling requests to the `/users` route and delegating them to the service layer. As you saw, a user was created with a generated ID, confirming that everything is wired up properly.

Before we move on, let's add a small but important enhancement to `UsersService`: a method to retrieve users by their email address. This will be crucial when we implement authentication in `AuthModule`.

## Adding the findByEmail method to UsersService

We'll extend `UsersService` with a `findByEmail` method. This method will search the in-memory users array for a user with a matching email address and return the full user object (including the hashed password, which is needed for comparison during login).

Here's how to implement it:

```
findByEmail(email: string): User | undefined {
  return this.users.find((user) => user.email === email);
}
```

This method is simple and efficient for our current in-memory setup. Later, the logic can be updated for when working with a database. With this in place, we can now move on to our `Auth` module, which will handle the authentication process.

# Adding authentication to our backend

Authentication is the process of validating the identity of the entity making a request to our service. It's different from authorization, which is like checking what permissions the entity has; for example, a person with the role of company can create a job, whereas a regular user can't.

In this section, we are going to generate the `Auth` module. We will create an auth controller and a route to handle login requests (`POST /auth/login`). We will also validate user credentials using bcrypt, and issue JWT tokens to prove the identity and role. Once that is in place, we will add guards so that only authenticated users can hit protected routes.

## Step 1: Installing packages to help with authentication

Let's start by installing some dependencies:

```
pnpm install @nestjs/jwt @nestjs/passport passport passport-jwt bcrypt
pnpm install -D @types/passport-jwt
```

Let's briefly go over what each dependency does:

- `@nestjs/jwt`: Adds support for the JWT, used to securely transmit user identity
- `@nestjs/passport`: Integrates Passport.js with NestJS for modular authentication strategies
- `passport` and `passport-jwt`: Core Passport libraries for handling JWT-based authentication
- `bcrypt`: Used to securely hash and compare passwords
- `@types/passport-jwt`: Type definitions for Passport JWT, needed for TypeScript support

These packages form the foundation of our `Auth` module, enabling secure user login and token-based access control.

## Step 2: Scaffolding the Auth module, controller, and service

We run the following commands to create the Auth module, controller, and service:

```
npx nx g @nx/nest:module --path=apps/devjobs-backend/src/app/auth/auth
npx nx g @nx/nest:controller --path=apps/devjobs-backend/src/app/auth/auth
npx nx g @nx/nest:service --path=apps/devjobs-backend/src/app/auth/auth
```

Running the preceding commands should create the relevant files, just like when we worked on the Users module. In the next step, we will start configuring the Auth module.

## Step 3: Importing the relevant packages

We start by importing the relevant packages that we will need:

```
import { Module } from '@nestjs/common';
import {JwtModule} from '@nestjs/jwt'
import { PassportModule } from '@nestjs/passport';
import { UsersModule } from '../users/users.module';
import { AuthController } from './auth.controller';
import { AuthService } from './auth.service';
```

With our imports in place, we can move on to configuring the Auth module.

## Step 4: Configuring the Auth module

The following is the code to configure the Auth module:

```
@Module({
  imports: [
    UsersModule,
    PassportModule,
    JwtModule.register({
      secret: 'super-secret-key', // replace with env var in production
      signOptions: { expiresIn: '1h' },
    }),
  ],
  controllers: [AuthController],
  providers: [AuthService, JwtStrategy],
  exports: [AuthService],
})
```

Here is a quick overview of what each piece of code does:

- `UsersModule` gives access to user lookups to validate credentials
- `PassportModule` integrates Passport strategies and guards
- `JwtModule.register` configures how tokens are signed and their lifetime
- `AuthController` exposes endpoints such as `POST /auth/login`
- `AuthService` handles login and token signing
- `JwtStrategy` parses and validates incoming JWTs
- `exports: [AuthService]` lets other modules reuse auth methods if needed

## Production note: Symmetric versus asymmetric JWT signing

In the preceding example, we used a shared secret (HS256 signing) for simplicity. This works well for small applications or single-service deployments. However, in production or distributed systems, it's common to use asymmetric signing (such as RS256).

With asymmetric signing, note the following:

- The private key signs tokens
- The public key verifies tokens

This is especially useful when multiple services need to verify tokens without having access to the signing key. Here is an example configuration:

```
JwtModule.register({
  privateKey: process.env.JWT_PRIVATE_KEY,
  publicKey: process.env.JWT_PUBLIC_KEY,
  signOptions: {
    algorithm: 'RS256',
    expiresIn: '1h',
  },
});
```

When you see RS256 or similar algorithms, it usually indicates an asymmetric key setup designed for higher security and better scalability across services.

With the `Auth` module configured, the next steps will involve creating the authentication logic within `AuthService`, setting up `AuthController` to handle requests, and implementing strategies for user validation and token generation.

## Step 5: Adding the authentication logic to the AuthService class

Now that we've scaffolded the module, the next step is to add the authentication logic inside `AuthService`. We begin by importing the dependencies we need—`JwtService` for signing tokens, `bcrypt` for password comparison, and `UsersService` for looking up user details:

```
import { Injectable, UnauthorizedException } from '@nestjs/common';
import { JwtService } from '@nestjs/jwt';
import * as bcrypt from 'bcrypt';
import { UsersService } from '../users/users.service';
```

With these in place, we inject `UsersService` and `JwtService` into the constructor so they're available throughout the class:

```
@Injectable()
export class AuthService {
  constructor(      private usersService: UsersService,
    private jwtService: JwtService,
  ) {}
//......
}
```

Next, we create a `validateUser` method. This checks whether the user exists and verifies the password using bcrypt. If the credentials are correct, we return the user object without the password; otherwise, we return `null`:

```
async validateUser(email: string, pass: string) {
const user = await this.usersService.findByEmail(email);
if (user && (await bcrypt.compare(pass, user.password))) {
const { password, ...result } = user;
return result;
}
return null;
}
```

Finally, we implement the login method. It calls `validateUser` and, if the credentials are valid, creates a payload and signs it with `JwtService`. If validation fails, it throws `UnauthorizedException`:

```
async login(email: string, password: string) {
const user = await this.validateUser(email, password);
if (!user) {
throw new UnauthorizedException('Invalid credentials');
}
const payload = { sub: user.id, role: user.role };
return {
access_token: this.jwtService.sign(payload),
};
}
```

This flow ensures that only valid users receive a signed JWT, which they can use for subsequent authenticated requests.

This method starts by calling `validateUser`, which checks the user's credentials and returns `null` if the credentials don't match. If `null` is returned, the login method throws an error; else, it signs the payload with `jwtService` and returns a token that can be used for subsequent requests.

With the login logic in place for our service class, we can now expose it via the controller.

## Step 6: AuthController – exposing /auth/login

We update the `AuthController` service with a login method to handle requests to the `auth/login` route. Your code should now look like this:

```
import { Body, Controller, Post } from '@nestjs/common';
import { AuthService } from './auth.service';

@Controller('auth')
export class AuthController {
constructor(private readonly authService: AuthService) {}

@Post('login')
async login(@Body() body: { email: string; password: string }) {
return this.authService.login(body.email, body.password);
}
}
```

## Step 7: Testing the authentication flow

Now that `AuthModule`, `AuthService`, and `AuthController` are in place, let's test the login functionality.

Before testing, confirm that `UsersService` is exported from `UsersModule`. This allows `AuthModule` to inject it properly:

```
@Module({
  providers: [UsersService],
  exports: [UsersService], // Add this line
})
export class UsersModule {}
```

Since we store users in memory, we must create a new user each time the app restarts.

To register a user, you can make a request via Postman or Bruno, as shown previously, or you can just make a `curl` request by copying and pasting the following in your terminal:

```
curl -X POST http://localhost:3000/users \
  -H "Content-Type: application/json" \
  -d '{
    "name": "Test User",
    "email": "test@example.com",
    "password": "password123",
    "role": "user",
    "companyId": "demo-company"
  }'
```

Now log in with the same credentials (email and password). You make a request through your `AuthController` at `POST /auth/login`:

```
curl -X POST http://localhost:3000/auth/login \
  -H "Content-Type: application/json" \
  -d '{
    "email": "test@example.com",
    "password": "password123"
  }'
```

You can also do the same via Postman/Bruno if you want, as shown before. You should get a successful response with the generated token:

```
{
  "access_token": "eyJhbGciOiJIUzI1NiIsInR5cCI6IkpXVCJ9..."
}
```

You can copy the generated token and decode it at: `https://www.jwt.io/`. You should see something like:

```
{
  "sub": "c6762198-c77d-4aab-a0b2-009ae1df94a7",
  "role": "user",
  "iat": 1759521269,
  "exp": 1759524869
}
```

The JWT payload includes four key fields: `sub` is the unique identifier for the user, typically their ID; `role` specifies the user's role, which is useful for access control; `iat` marks when the token was issued; and exp defines when it will expire, ensuring tokens are short-lived for security. These claims allow the server to authenticate requests and enforce permissions effectively.

> **Note**
>
> In production, never hardcode the secret in your code. Instead, store it in an environment variable (e.g., `.env`) and load it using `@nestjs/config`.

Here is an example:

```
JwtModule.registerAsync({
  inject: [ConfigService],
  useFactory: (config: ConfigService) => ({
    secret: config.get<string>('JWT_SECRET'),
    signOptions: { expiresIn: '1h' },
  }),
})
```

You can create a `.env` file in your `devjobs-backend`, and it should include the following:

```
JWT_SECRET=super-secret-key
```

This approach keeps sensitive data out of your source code and makes it easier to rotate keys when needed. We are able to generate a token, `create`, but at this point, we aren't using it for anything yet. In the next section, we are going to look at how to protect routes.

# Adding JWT guards to protect routes

Now that we have authentication in place and users can log in successfully, it's time to make use of the JWT tokens we're issuing.

So far, our backend doesn't actually prevent unauthenticated users from accessing routes; anyone could hit our endpoints and modify data. To fix that, we'll use **guards**.

In NestJS, guards determine whether a given request should be processed or not. The most common one is `AuthGuard`, which integrates directly with Passport (the authentication library we installed earlier).

Since we already configured JWTs in our `AuthModule`, enabling route protection is straightforward. All we need to do is use the `@UseGuards(AuthGuard('jwt'))` decorator.

Let's see a quick example:

```
import { Controller, Get, UseGuards, Request } from '@nestjs/common';
import { AuthGuard } from '@nestjs/passport';

@Controller('profile')
export class ProfileController {
  @UseGuards(AuthGuard('jwt'))
  @Get()
  getProfile(@Request() req) {
    return req.user; // The decoded JWT payload
  }
}
```

When a request includes a valid token (for example, `Authorization: Bearer <token>`), NestJS verifies it using the configured JWT strategy. If the token is valid, the user payload (decoded from the token) becomes available under `req.user`. If it's missing or invalid, NestJS automatically rejects the request with a `401 Unauthorized` error.

We'll apply this same approach to protect routes in our `Companies` and `Jobs` modules. But for now, let's extend our in-memory store. Instead of using a simple array, we'll transition to writing data to a JSON file, which ensures that we don't lose information every time the application restarts.

## Adding file-based persistence

So far, we've been storing users in memory. That's fine for quick testing, but there's a problem whenever we restart the server: our data disappears. To fix this without introducing a full database, we'll store our data in simple JSON files using Node.js's built-in `fs` module.

### Step 1: Creating a file storage utility

We'll begin by creating a small helper class that can read and write JSON files. Inside your backend app, create a new folder named common and add a file called `file-storage.ts`:

```
import { existsSync, readFileSync, writeFileSync } from 'fs';
import { join } from 'path';

export class FileStorage<T> {
  private filePath: string;

  constructor(filename: string) {
    this.filePath = join(process.cwd(), 'data', filename);
  }

  private ensureFileExists() {
    if (!existsSync(this.filePath)) {
      writeFileSync(this.filePath, JSON.stringify([], null, 2));
    }
  }

  read(): T[] {
    this.ensureFileExists();
    const content = readFileSync(this.filePath, 'utf-8');
    return JSON.parse(content) as T[];
  }

  write(data: T[]) {
    writeFileSync(this.filePath, JSON.stringify(data, null, 2));
  }
}
```

Let's briefly go over what each method does in this class:

- `constructor(filename)`: Sets the file path where data will be stored—specifically inside `apps/devjobs-backend/data`.
- `ensureFileExists()`: Checks whether the file exists. If it doesn't, it creates an empty JSON file.
- `read()`: Loads and parses the JSON file into a JavaScript array.
- `write(data)`: Saves an updated array back to the file, replacing its contents.

This class gives us a simple way to persist arrays of objects without any external database. Also, it create a data directory at the root of your project:

```
mkdir apps/devjobs-backend/data
```

This is where we'll store our `.json` files (for users, companies, and jobs). Next, let's update our services starting with user services to use it.

## Step 2: Updating UsersService to persist data

Now, let's update our `UsersService` to use this new file-based storage instead of keeping users in memory. Replace the existing content of `users.service.ts` with the following:

```
import { Injectable } from '@nestjs/common';
import * as bcrypt from 'bcrypt';
import { randomUUID } from 'crypto';
import { FileStorage } from '../common/file-storage';

@Injectable()
export class UsersService {
  private storage = new FileStorage<any>('users.json');

  async register(user: any) {
    const users = this.storage.read();
    const hashedPassword = await bcrypt.hash(user.password, 10);

    const newUser = {
      id: randomUUID(),
      name: user.name,
      email: user.email,
      password: hashedPassword,
      role: user.role,
```

```
      companyId: user.companyId,
    };

    users.push(newUser);
    this.storage.write(users);

    const { password, ...userWithoutPassword } = newUser;
    return userWithoutPassword;
  }

  findByEmail(email: string) {
    const users = this.storage.read();
    return users.find((u) => u.email === email);
  }
}
```

Now, each time we register a user, we load the current users from the file and add the user, and then save the updated list. Your user data will persist between runs. You can restart your server and still log in with the same credentials; there is no need to recreate users each time. With user persistence in place, let's build out our `Companies` module.

## Companies module

Companies represent employers who can post jobs. We'll allow anyone to view companies, but only authenticated users with the company role can create them.

## Step 1: Scaffolding the module

Run the following commands:

```
npx nx g @nx/nest:module --path=apps/devjobs-backend/src/app/companies/companies
npx nx g @nx/nest:controller --path=apps/devjobs-backend/src/app/companies/
companies
npx nx g @nx/nest:service --path=apps/devjobs-backend/src/app/companies/companies
```

## Step 2: Defining the service

Add the following code to `companies.service.ts`:

```
import { Injectable } from '@nestjs/common';
import { randomUUID } from 'crypto';
import { FileStorage } from '../common/file-storage';
```

```
export interface Company {
  id: string;
  name: string;
  description: string;
  location: string;
}

@Injectable()
export class CompaniesService {
  private storage = new FileStorage<Company>('companies.json');

  findAll(): Company[] {
    return this.storage.read();
  }

  create(company: Omit<Company, 'id'>): Company {
    const companies = this.storage.read();
    const newCompany = { id: randomUUID(), ...company };
    companies.push(newCompany);
    this.storage.write(companies);
    return newCompany;
  }
}
```

Our company service contains two methods:

- `findAll()`: Loads and returns every company stored in `companies.json`
- `create()`: Generates a new unique ID, adds the new company, and writes it back to disk

With that in place, we can move on to the controller.

## Step 3: Defining the companies controller

Update `companies.controller.ts` to look like this:

```
import { Controller, Get, Post, Body, UseGuards, Request } from '@nestjs/common';
import { CompaniesService } from './companies.service';
import { AuthGuard } from '@nestjs/passport';

@Controller('companies')
export class CompaniesController {
  constructor(private readonly companiesService: CompaniesService) {}
```

```
  @Get()
  findAll() {
    // Public route: returns all company profiles
    return this.companiesService.findAll();
  }

  @UseGuards(AuthGuard('jwt'))
  @Post()
  create(@Body() body, @Request() req) {
    // Protected route: only users with 'company' role can create companies
    if (req.user.role !== 'company') {
      return { error: 'Only company accounts can create companies.' };
    }
    return this.companiesService.create(body);
  }
}
```

For our companies controller, there are basically two routes:

- `GET /companies`: Open to all users; retrieves all companies
- `POST /companies`: Protected; allows only authenticated users with the company role to create a profile

You can test this on Postman.

With our `Companies` module in place, let's move on add the final module, which is the `Jobs` module.

The approach to scaffolding the module is similar to the previous ones, so we will just jump into the actual code.

# Jobs module

The `Jobs` module lets companies post and manage job listings, while job seekers can browse and filter them.

## Step 1: Service – jobs.service.ts

Let's update the `jobs.service.ts` file.

```
import { Injectable } from "@nestjs/common";
import { randomUUID } from "crypto";
import { FileStorage } from "../common/file-storage";
```

```
import { Job } from "../../../../../libs/api-types/model";

@Injectable()
export class JobsService {
private storage = new FileStorage<Job>("jobs.json");

findAll(filters?: Partial<Job>): Job[] {
let jobs = this.storage.read();
if (filters) {
jobs = jobs.filter((job) =>
Object.entries(filters).every(([key, val]) =>
Val ? job[key as keyof Job]?.toString().includes(val.toString())
: true
)
);
}
return jobs;
}

create(job: Omit<Job, "id">): Job {
const jobs = this.storage.read();
const newJob = { id: randomUUID(), ...job };
jobs.push(newJob);
this.storage.write(jobs);
return newJob;
}
}
```

Our job service has two methods:

- `findAll(filters?)`: Reads all job postings and filters them by query params (such as location or technology)
- `create()`: Generates a unique ID, adds the job post, and saves the updated jobs list to `jobs.json`

With that in place, we can move on to the jobs controller.

## Step 2: Adding the jobs controller – jobs.controller.ts

Add the following code to your `jobs.controller.ts` file:

```
import { Controller, Get, Post, Body, Query, UseGuards, Request } from '@nestjs/
common';
import { JobsService } from './jobs.service';
import { AuthGuard } from '@nestjs/passport';

@Controller('jobs')
export class JobsController {
  constructor(private readonly jobsService: JobsService) {}

  @Get()
  findAll(@Query() query) {
    return this.jobsService.findAll(query);
  }

  @UseGuards(AuthGuard('jwt'))
  @Post()
  create(@Body() body, @Request() req) {
    if (req.user.role !== 'company') {
      return { error: 'Only company users can post jobs.' };
    }
    return this.jobsService.create({ ...body, companyId: req.user.sub });
  }
}
```

With that in place, we can now test the full flow of our backend application in the next subsection.

## Testing our devjobs backend full flow

To test our backend full flow, we go through the following steps:

1. Register a new user with the `company` role. See the following sample request:

```
curl --location --request POST 'http://localhost:3000/api/users' \
--header 'Content-Type: application/json' \
--data-raw '{
  "name": "Jane Doe Recruiter",
  "email": "janedoe@devjobs.com",
  "password": "password123",
```

```
    "role": "company",
    "companyId": "ffdba55c-78c2-44e3-9665-44d0582c1051"
}'
```

2. Log in and copy the JWT token from the response. See the following sample request:

```
curl --location --request POST 'http://localhost:3000/api/auth/login' \
--header 'Content-Type: application/json' \
--data-raw '{
    "email": "janedoe@devjobs.com",
    "password": "password123"
}'
```

3. Use the token in your request headers for subsequent requests:

```
Authorization: Bearer <token>
```

4. Create a company with a `POST` request to `/companies`:

```
curl --location --request POST 'http://localhost:3000/api/companies' \
--header 'Authorization: Bearer <add your token here... >' \
--header 'Content-Type: application/json' \
--data-raw '{
  "name": "jane-doe-recruitment-company",
  "website": "www.janedoerecruitement.com"
}'
```

5. Post a job under that company with a `POST` request to `/jobs`. See the following sample request:

```
curl --location --request POST 'http://localhost:3000/api/jobs'
--header 'Authorization: Bearer <add your token here...>'
--header 'Content-Type: application/json'
--data-raw ' {
"title": "Senior TypeScript Engineer",
"companyId": "d9d5927a-b327-4b09-80d3-ade23c4e547b", "location":
"Netherlands", "description": "We'''re seeking an exceptional Senior
TypeScript Engineer to join our team in the Netherlands. As a Senior
TypeScript Engineer, you will be responsible for developing, maintaining,
and extending our microservices platform, handling backend systems, and
collaborating on API-driven applications. You will work closely with our
```

```
engineering team to build scalable, efficient, and reliable software
solutions.\n\nKey Responsibilities:\n Develop high-quality software
solutions using TypeScript,....." } '
```

6. You can retrieve the jobs using `GET /jobs` with query parameters such as `?tech=typescript&location=remote`:

```
curl --location --request GET 'http://localhost:3000/api/jobs?
tech=typescript&location=Netherlands' \
--data-raw ''
```

Congratulations! We just went through the flow of our DevJobs backend. Our backend now supports the following:

 - JWT-based authentication and guards
 - Role-based access control
 - Persistent storage using JSON files
 - Modular APIs for users, companies, and jobs

In the next section, we'll move to the frontend and learn how to consume these endpoints using shared TypeScript types, completing the full stack workflow.

# Client-side TypeScript with React

With our type-safe backend in place, we are going to focus on building the frontend that consumes the API. I have opted to use React to keep things relatively straightforward, but the ideas and concepts learned here can be applied elsewhere. We are going to reuse the types we generated with Orval for our API contracts in the previous section while building.

We already used Orval to generate types for the backend. Now we'll configure it to generate React Query hooks that give us type-safe API calls with zero manual work.

`app.tsx` will be the root component where we'll set up routing, and `main.tsx` is the entry point where we'll configure React Query.

Before we proceed, let's install some frontend dependencies that we will need for our application.

## Installing frontend dependencies

Before we configure Orval, let's install the dependencies that we'll need. We're installing these now because Orval's configuration will reference some of these packages:

```
pnpm install react-router-dom @tanstack/react-query axios jwt-decode
pnpm install -D @types/react-router-dom
```

Here's why we need each:

- `react-router-dom`: For client-side routing (navigating between pages such as `/jobs`, `/login`, and `/post-job`)
- `@tanstack/react-query`: Manages server state and caching and provides the foundation for the hooks Orval will generate
- `axios`: HTTP client for making API requests to our backend
- `jwt-decode`: Decodes JWT tokens to extract user information (`userId` and `role`)

With the relevant packages installed, we can now move on to configuring Orval for our frontend. Orval is going to help us generate the hooks that we would use to query our backend. To do that, Orval needs to know that we're using React Query and Axios when it generates our hooks. This way, the generated code will be imported from the correct packages and use the right patterns. We also need to create an API client instance.

## Creating the API client instance

Before configuring Orval to generate hooks, we need to create an Axios instance that Orval will use. This instance will handle all our HTTP requests and is where we'll add authentication tokens.

First, if you haven't already, create the `api-client` library structure:

```
mkdir -p libs/api-client/src
```

Now create `./libs/api-client/src/axios.ts`:

Add the following code to the file:

```
import axios, { AxiosRequestConfig } from 'axios';

const instance = axios.create({
  baseURL: '/api',
});
```

```
// Add auth token to requests
instance.interceptors.request.use((config) => {
  const token = localStorage.getItem('access_token');
  if (token) {
    config.headers.Authorization = `Bearer ${token}`;
  }
  return config;
});

export const api = <T>(config: AxiosRequestConfig): Promise<T> => {
  return instance.request<T>(config).then((res) => res.data);
};
```

The code we've just added does three important things:

- **Creates an Axios instance** and uses `/api` as the base URL. All requests will be made relative to `/api`, for example, to retrieve jobs, `GET /api/jobs`, and to log in, `POST /api/auth/login`.
- **Adds an interceptor** that automatically reads the JWT from `localStorage` and attaches it as a `Bearer` token in the `Authorization` header on every request, so we don't have to manually configure authentication in each component.
- **Exports a custom API function** that Orval uses as its mutator for all generated requests. It unwraps the Axios response and returns only `res.data`, keeping our generated hooks simple and consistent.

> **Note**
>
> In this example, we store the JWT in `localStorage` for simplicity. In real-world applications, token storage is a security trade-off. While `localStorage` is easy to use, it can be vulnerable to XSS attacks if malicious scripts gain access to the page. Many production systems instead use secure, HTTP-only cookies to reduce this risk. The right choice depends on your application's security requirements and architecture.

Why create this now? Orval's configuration references this file as its mutator. When Orval generates hooks, it wraps all API calls with our `api` function, ensuring that requests automatically use the `/api` base path and include the `Authorization: Bearer <token>` header when available.

## Configuring Orval for frontend hooks

Now that we have our axios instance ready, let's configure Orval to generate React Query hooks. Open `orval.config.ts` at the root of your monorepo and update it:

```
export default {
  devjobs: {
    input: './apps/devjobs-backend/src/openapi.yml',
    output: {
      target: 'libs/api-client/src/generated', // folder for generated files
      client: 'react-query',
      mode: 'tags',          // separate file per tag
      override: {
        mutator: {
          path: './libs/api-client/src/axios.ts',
          name: 'api',
        },
      },
      prettier: true,
      index: true,
      clean: true,
    },
    hooks: {
      afterAllFilesWrite: [
        () => {
          console.log(' DevJobs API client generated successfully');
        },
      ],
    },
  },
};
```

Let's break down what each part does:

- `input`: Points to your OpenAPI specification, the same file that defines your backend API contract
- `mode: 'tags'`: Organizes generated files by OpenAPI tags (`users`, `auth`, `jobs`, and `companies`). Each tag gets its own file, making the generated code more maintainable.
- `target: './libs/api-client/src/generated'`: Where the generated hook files will be saved. This keeps the generated code separate from your custom code.

- `schemas: './libs/api-types/model'`: Where TypeScript types for your data models are saved (`User`, `Job`, `Company`, etc.).
- `client: 'react-query'`: This is the key setting. It tells Orval to generate React Query hooks (`useQuery` and `useMutation`) instead of plain fetch calls or other clients.
- `override.mutator`: Points to our custom API function in `libs/api-client/src/axios.ts`. This ensures all generated hooks use our authenticated HTTP client with the interceptor we set up.
- `index: true`: Generates a root `index.ts` file so we can import hooks cleanly from `@devjobs/api-client`.
- `clean: true`: Clears previously generated files before regeneration, preventing stale code.
- `hooks.afterAllFilesWrite`: Runs a small script after generation, in this case, logging a confirmation message so we know the client was rebuilt successfully.

After running `npx` orval, you'll see new files:

```
libs/api-client/src/generated/:
```

These files would contain the relevant hooks needed to communicate our backend app for example:

- `jobs.ts`: In this file, you will find hooks such as `useGetJobs`, `usePostJobs`, etc.
- `companies.ts`: In this file, you will find hooks such as `useGetCompanies`, `usePostCompanies`, and so on.
- `authentication.ts`: In this file, you will find the `usePostAuthLogin` hook.

If we focus on the `authentication.ts` file in `ch10/devjobs/libs/api-client/src/generated/authentication.ts` you'll find something like:

```
//... The rest of our code is above:
export const usePostAuthLogin = <TError = ErrorResponse,
    TContext =
unknown>(options?: { mutation?:UseMutationOptions<Awaited<ReturnType<typeof postAuthLogin>>, TErro
{data: LoginRequest}, TContext>, }
, queryClient?: QueryClient): UseMutationResult<
        Awaited<ReturnType<typeof postAuthLogin>>,
        TError,
        {data: LoginRequest},
```

```
      TContext
    > => {

    const mutationOptions = getPostAuthLoginMutationOptions(options);

    return useMutation(mutationOptions, queryClient);
  }
```

This means the following:

- `usePostAuthLogin` is just a thin wrapper around React Query's useMutation.
- It gives you a mutate or mutateAsync function to call the `/auth/login` endpoint.
- The types are fully generated, so you get type-safe input and output without writing them yourself.

In short, Orval generates a ready-to-use hook for every endpoint, wired to React Query and your custom Axios client. You can now focus on your components, not request plumbing.

These hooks are fully typed and ready to use.

You'll use these hooks throughout your React components. There is no need to write fetch calls or manage loading states manually—React Query handles it all.

Now, let's move on to setting up the React Query provider.

## Setting up the React Query provider

Before we can use the hooks that we generated in our components, we need to set up React Query's provider. This gives all components access to the query cache and configuration.

Update your `apps/devjobs-frontend/src/main.tsx`.

With everything in place, run Orval to generate your API hooks:

```
npx orval
```

Orval reads your OpenAPI spec and generates type-safe React Query hooks.

Update your `apps/devjobs-frontend/src/main.tsx`:

```
import { StrictMode } from "react";
import { BrowserRouter } from "react-router-dom";
import * as ReactDOM from "react-dom/client";
import { QueryClient, QueryClientProvider } from "@tanstack/react-query";
import App from "./app/app";
```

```
const queryClient = new QueryClient({
  defaultOptions: {
    queries: {
      refetchOnWindowFocus: false,
      retry: 1,
    },
  },
});

const root = ReactDOM.createRoot(
  document.getElementById("root") as HTMLElement
);

root.render(
  (
    <StrictMode>
      <QueryClientProvider client={queryClient}>
        <BrowserRouter>
          <App />
        </BrowserRouter>
      </QueryClientProvider>
    </StrictMode>
  ) as React.ReactNode
);
```

`QueryClient` is React Query's cache manager. Our configuration tells it the following:

- `refetchOnWindowFocus: false`: Don't automatically refetch queries when the user focuses the browser window. This prevents unnecessary API calls when users switch tabs.
- `retry: 1`: Only retry failed requests once instead of the default three times. This makes development faster and prevents hammering the backend with failed requests.

Now, any component inside `<App />` can use the generated hooks. React Query will handle caching, deduplication, background updates, and more. In the next step, we are going to start building the authentication flow.

# Building the authentication flow

Authentication is the foundation of our application. We need a way to manage authentication state globally. This simply means storing the state of our application in a place where every component has direct access to it; the global state would handle storing the JWT token, decoding it to get user information, and providing login/logout functionality to all components. There are several options, such as Zustand, Redux, and Recoil, but for this project, we are going to use React Context. This way, we don't have to install other libraries, and it just works.

## Creating the auth context

Create the directory structure and file:

```
mkdir -p apps/devjobs-frontend/src/contexts
```

Now, create `apps/devjobs-frontend/src/contexts/AuthContext.tsx`.

With our context file in place, let's start adding the piece of code that would make up our auth context.

We start by importing the relevant items and defining the basic interfaces/types that we would use in our auth context file:

```
import { createContext, useContext, useState, useEffect, ReactNode } from
'react'; import jwtDecode from 'jwt-decode';
interface DecodedToken {
sub: string;
role: string;
exp?: number;
}
interface AuthContextType {
  token: string | null;
  user: { userId: string; role: string } | null;
  login: (token: string) => void;
  logout: () => void;
  isAuthenticated: boolean;
}
```

`DecodedToken` represents the payload structure of our JWT, while `AuthContextType` defines what values and methods will be available to the rest of the app.

Now we create the context itself:

```
const AuthContext = createContext<AuthContextType | undefined>(undefined);
```

This gives us a globally accessible store for auth-related state.

With our context created, we can now create a provider component. This provider will hold our main logic for authentication state, decoding, and persistence.

Let's start with the state and initialization:

```
export function AuthProvider({ children }: { children: ReactNode }) {
    const [token, setToken] = useState<string | null>(null);
    const [user, setUser] = useState<{ userId: string; role: string } |
null>(null);

    // Load token from localStorage on mount
    useEffect(() => {
      const storedToken = localStorage.getItem('access_token');
      if (storedToken) {
        setToken(storedToken);
      }
    }, []);
}
```

The `token` state stores the JWT, while `user` stores the decoding info. We use `useEffect` to load any saved token when the app first mounts.

Next, let's decode the token whenever it changes:

```
  useEffect(() => {
    if (!token) {
      setUser(null);
      return;
    }

    try {
      const decoded = jwtDecode<DecodedToken>(token);

      // Optional: check if token is expired
      if (decoded.exp && decoded.exp * 1000 < Date.now()) {
        console.warn('JWT expired');
```

```
        logout();
        return;
      }

      setUser({ userId: decoded.sub, role: decoded.role });
    } catch (error) {
      console.error('Invalid token:', error);
      logout();
    }
  }, [token]);

  const login = (newToken: string) => {
    localStorage.setItem('access_token', newToken);
    setToken(newToken);
  };

  const logout = () => {
    localStorage.removeItem('access_token');
    setToken(null);
    setUser(null);
  };
```

In the `useEffect` hook we just provided, all authentication-related side effects are intentionally handled in one place, so state updates remain predictable and easy to reason about. The `jwtDecode` library is used to decode the JWT token's payload without verifying its signature, extracting key details such as the user ID (`sub`) and role. If no token is present, the user state is immediately cleared to `null`. Upon successful decoding, the code optionally validates expiration by checking whether the expiration claim, converted to milliseconds, is earlier than the current timestamp; if expired, it logs a warning and triggers logout to clear the token. Otherwise, it updates the user state with the decoded user ID and role. If any decoding error occurs, such as an invalid token format, it logs the issue and initiates a logout to maintain a safe authentication state.

For example, when a user logs in and a token is stored, this effect automatically runs, decodes the token, and updates the UI state so components can react immediately—such as showing admin controls for privileged users or redirecting unauthenticated users to a login page:

```
const login = useCallback((newToken: string) => {
    localStorage.setItem('access_token', newToken);
    setToken(newToken);
```

```
  }, []);

  const logout = useCallback(() => {
    localStorage.removeItem('access_token');
    setToken(null);
    setUser(null);
  }, []);
```

`login()` saves the token to both `localStorage` and the React state. `logout()` removes everything, effectively logging the user out. Finally, let's wrap up `AuthProvider`:

```
return (
    <AuthContext.Provider
      value={{
        token,
        user,
        login,
        logout,
        isAuthenticated: !!user && !!token,
      }}
    >
      {children}
    </AuthContext.Provider>
  );
```

Lastly, we'll add a simple helper for easier access to the context:

```
export const useAuth = () => {
  const context = useContext(AuthContext);
  if (!context) {
    throw new Error('useAuth must be used within an AuthProvider');
  }
  return context;
};
```

This ensures the following:

- Clean usage in components: `const { user, login, logout } = useAuth();`
- Clear error messages if the hook is used outside of its provider

For production apps, consider adding a refresh token mechanism that silently renews access tokens when they expire. We won't implement that here, but it's a good next step once basic authentication is working.

Lastly, make sure that in the `main.tsx` file, you wrap the entire application with `AuthProvider`, as follows:

```
// rest of you code above ...

    <AuthProvider>
        <BrowserRouter>
          <App />
        </BrowserRouter>
      </AuthProvider>
// rest of you code below ...
```

This is needed to make the login functionality work. With that in place, let's move on to building the login page.

## Login page

In this section, we'll build the login page for our frontend application. Rather than writing everything at once, we'll build it incrementally, adding one small piece at a time so it's always clear what changed and why.

We'll start simple, just rendering the page, then gradually add inputs, state, and form handling, and finally, wire everything to the backend using our generated API hooks.

### Step 1: Creating the login page and confirming that it renders

Let's start by creating the login page component. Create the following file:

```
apps/devjobs-frontend/src/pages/Login/index.tsx:
```

For now, we'll keep it intentionally minimal and just render some placeholder text:

```
export function Login() {
  return <div>Login Component</div>;
}
```

At this point, we're not adding any logic; we just want to confirm that the page renders correctly.

## Step 2: Adding the login page to the router

Next, we need to make this page reachable in our application.

Open `app.tsx` and update it to include the `Login` component:

```
import { Route, Routes } from 'react-router-dom';
import { Login } from './Login';

export function App() {
  return (
    <Routes>
      <Route path="/login" element={<Login />} />
    </Routes>
  );
}

export default App;
```

> **Note**
>
> We've removed the default boilerplate code that was generated when the frontend app was created. For now, we're keeping things intentionally minimal.

If you visit the root route (`/login`) in the browser, you should now see the following:

*Figure 11.3 — Showing the Login component*

Once you see this, you'll know that the page and routing are wired correctly.

## Step 3: Adding a basic page shell (minimal styling with Tailwind)

Now that the page renders, let's give it a small amount of structure. We'll add the following:

- A full-height wrapper
- A centered container
- A heading

There is no styling beyond layout and spacing. Update your `Login` component as follows:

```
export function Login() {
  return (
    <div className="min-h-screen flex items-center justify-center">
      <div className="w-full max-w-sm">
        <h1 className="text-xl font-semibold">Login</h1>
      </div>
    </div>
  );
}
```

At this point, we still don't have a form, just a visually structured page.

## Step 4: Adding the form and input fields (still no state)

With the page shell in place, we can now add the login form itself. Add the following *inside the existing wrapper div* from *Step 1*:

```
<form>
          <div className='flex flex-col space-y-1'>
            <label htmlFor='email' className='text-sm'>
              Email
            </label>
            <input
              id='email'
              type='email'
              className='border px-3 py-2 rounded'
            />
          </div>

          <div className='flex flex-col space-y-1'>
            <label htmlFor='password' className='text-sm'>
              Password
            </label>
            <input
              id='password'
              type='password'
              className='border px-3 py-2 rounded'
            />
          </div>
```

```
      <button type='submit' className='w-full border py-2 rounded'>
        Login
      </button>
    </form>
```

At this stage, the form renders correctly and the inputs accept text, but nothing happens when the user types or submits. See the following figure:

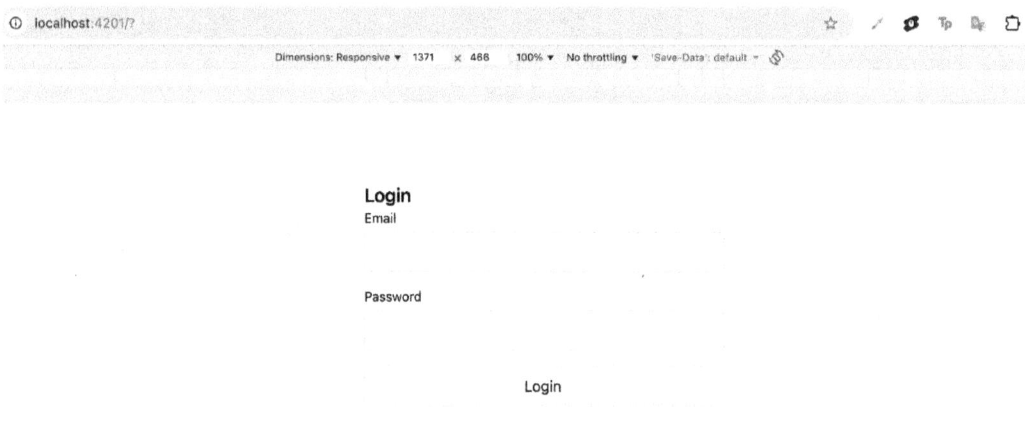


*Figure 11.4 — The state of the form*

## Step 5: Tracking input values with state

Next, we'll track the user's input using React state. First import `useState`:

```
import { useState } from 'react';
```

Then, add the state inside `Login`:

```
export function Login() {
  const [email, setEmail] = useState('');
  const [password, setPassword] = useState('');

  // rest of the component
}
```

Next, we make the inputs controlled by updating each input to reflect and update the state, as follows:

```
<input
  id='email'
  type='email'
  className='border px-3 py-2 rounded'
  onChange={(e) => setEmail(e.target.value)}/>

<input
  id='password'
  type='password'
  className='border px-3 py-2 rounded'
  onChange={(e) => setPassword(e.target.value)}/>
```

Now, whenever the user types, React updates the component state, and the input value always reflects that state.

## Step 6: Handling form submission (still no API call)

Before calling the backend, let's first handle form submission. Add a submit handler inside the component:

```
const handleSubmit = async (e: React.FormEvent) => {
  e.preventDefault();
  console.log('Attempting login with email:', email, 'and password:', password);
};
```

Then attach it to the form:

```
<form onSubmit={handleSubmit} className="space-y-4">
```

Now, when you type an email address and password, click **Login**, and check the browser console, you should see a log similar to the following:

```
Attempting login with email: user@example.com and password: yourpassword
```

This confirms that the form submits correctly and we have access to the user's input.

You may get an error with imports, as shown in the following figure:

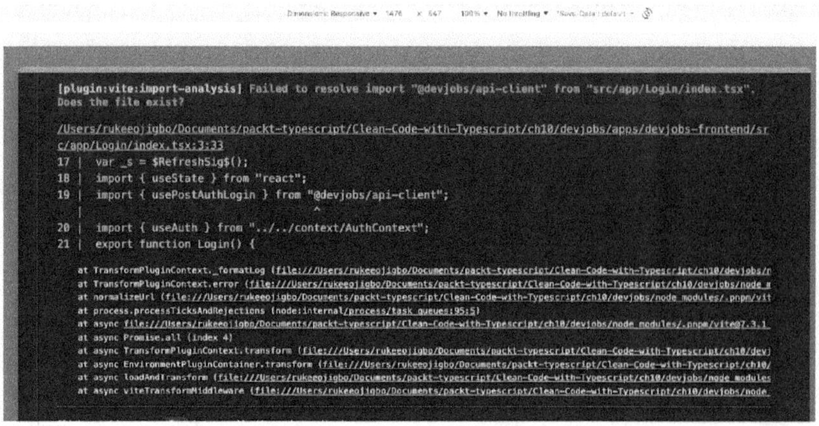


*Figure 11.5 — Handling Submission*

Check two main things. First, confirm that your alias exists in `tsconfig.base.join`:

```
{
  "compilerOptions":  {
{ "baseUrl": ".",
"paths": {
  "@devjobs/api-client": ["libs/api-client/index.ts"],
"@devjobs/api-client/*": ["libs/api-client/src/*"]
}
     }
 }
```

If that's present, then you need to check your `apps/devjobs-frontend/vite.config.ts` to confirm that the `nxViteTSPath` plugin is added:

```
import { nxViteTsPaths } from '@nx/vite/plugins/nx-tsconfig-paths.plugin';
```

Update your plugin array to be like this:

```
export default defineConfig({
  plugins: [react(), nxViteTsPaths()],
});
```

Restart the dev server after making the changes.

### Step 7: Calling the login API and storing the token

Now we'll connect the form to the backend. We'll start by importing the `usePostAuthLogin` we generated with Orval:

```
import { usePostAuthLogin } from '@devjobs/api-client';
```

Inside the `Login` component, we initialize the mutation as follows:

```
const loginMutation = usePostAuthLogin();
```

This hook was generated by Orval and internally uses React Query's `useMutation` to call our `/auth/login` endpoint.

### Step 8: Saving the token using AuthContext

Now, import the authentication context:

```
import { useAuth } from '../../context/AuthContext';
```

Then, initialize it in the component:

```
const { login } = useAuth();
const handleSubmit = async (e: React.FormEvent) => {
  e.preventDefault();
  if (!email || !password) return;

  const response = await loginMutation.mutateAsync({
    data: { email, password },
  });

  login(response.data.access_token);
};
```

Let's go over this quickly:

1. We submit the email address and password to the backend.
2. The backend returns an access token.
3. We store that token using our auth context.
4. The user is now authenticated across the app.

## Step 9: Displaying a friendly error message

In scenarios where something goes wrong, we need to handle errors and display a friendly message to the user. The React Query (TanStack query) mutation hook exposes an `IsError` Boolean, which lets us know if something went wrong. We can use this Boolean to conditionally render an error message, as follows:

```
{loginMutation.isError && (
            <p className='text-sm'>
              Login failed. Please check your email and password.
            </p>
)}
```

The preceding code simply checks whether `loginMutation.isError` is true, and if it is, it uses the logical `AND` operation (&&) to render the error message (within the `p` tag). If everything goes well, `isError` is false and we don't see an error message.

Beyond just displaying the message, you might want to do more in case of errors, such as logging the error or sending some custom message to an error monitoring tool that the devs or operation team monitors. To do this, as we discussed in previous chapters when we talked about error handling, you can introduce a `try/catch` block into the handle submit, as follows:

```
const handleSubmit = async (e: React.FormEvent) => {
    try {
      e.preventDefault();
      if (!email || !password) return;

      const response = await loginMutation.mutateAsync({
        data: { email, password },
      });

      login(response.data.access_token);
    } catch (error) {
        // you can use your custom Loggers here to handle the error in a better
way
        console.error('Login failed:', error); //
    }
  };
```

Now that we've seen how an error is handled, let's log in successfully.

## Step 10: Disabling the login button while the request is in progress

When a login request is in flight, the user can click the **Login** button multiple times. This can cause double submissions and multiple API calls, which may lead to confusing UI behavior (for example, multiple redirects or repeated error messages). React Query exposes an `isPending` flag on the mutation that tells us when the request is still running. We can use it to disable the button and optionally show a loading label.

Update your submit button like this:

```
<button

  type="submit"

  disabled={loginMutation.isPending} >

  {loginMutation.isPending ? 'Logging in...' : 'Login'}

</button>
```

Now, while the request is in progress, the button becomes disabled, and the user sees immediate feedback that the login is underway.

Now we should navigate to a home page (or jobs page).

Before doing this, we create a `Jobs` component in our jobs directory, something like this:

```
// ch10/devjobs/apps/devjobs-frontend/src/app/Jobs/index.tsx
export function Jobs() {
  return <div>Jobs Page</div>;
}
```

Then, add the route to `app.tsx`:

```
//
export function App() {
  return (
    <div>
      <Routes>
        <Route path='/login' element={<Login />} />
        <Route path='/jobs' element={<Jobs />} />
      </Routes>
```

```
    </div>
  );
}
```

Now we return our `Login` component and update it so that after a successful login, it navigates to the jobs page.

To make the navigation work, we make use of the hook from `react-router-dom`.

First, as before, we import the hook at the top of our `Login` file:

```
import { useNavigate } from 'react-router-dom';
```

Then, we instantiate the hook and assign it to a `navigate` variable within the `Login` component, as follows:

```
const navigate = useNavigate();
```

Now, inside our `handleSubmit` function, just under the point after the login, we call the `navigate` function to redirect to the jobs page:

```
const handleSubmit = async (e: React.FormEvent) => {
    try {
    // ... rest of your code
      navigate('/jobs')
    } catch (error) {
        // you can use your custom loggers here to handle the error in a better
way
        console.error('Login failed:', error); //
    }
  };
```

Now, when you log in successfully, it should navigate to the jobs page. This is a great step, but anyone can access the `/jobs` routes without logging in to the application first.

In the next subsection, we will look at protecting the route.

## Protected routes

In this step, we are going to create a protected route wrapper so that unauthenticated users can't access the application:

1. Create the following file: `devjobs/apps/devjobs-frontend/src/app/ProtectedRoute.tsx`.
2. Inside the file, add the following code:

```
import { Navigate } from 'react-router-dom';
import { useAuth } from '../context/AuthContext';

export function ProtectedRoute({ children }: { children: JSX.Element }) {
  const { isAuthenticated } = useAuth();

  if (!isAuthenticated) {
    return <Navigate to="/login" replace />;
  }

  return children;
}
```

`ProtectedRoute` is a small wrapper component that controls access to certain pages. It checks whether the user is authenticated using our `AuthContext`. If `isAuthenticated` is `false`, we redirect the user to the `/login` page. If `isAuthenticated` is `true`, we render the page passed in as children.

Why do we need this? Even though we redirect users to `/jobs` after login, nothing prevents someone from manually typing `/jobs` into the browser address bar. `ProtectedRoute` ensures the following:

- Only authenticated users can access protected pages
- Unauthenticated users are automatically redirected to `/login`

Finally, `Navigate` is a component from React Router that performs a redirect.

The `replace` prop ensures that the redirect does not leave the protected page in the browser's history stack.

To use the component we just created to protect our jobs route, we update our `app.tsx` as follows:

```
export function App() {
  return (
    <Routes>
      <Route path="/login" element={<Login />} />

      <Route
        path="/jobs"
        element={
          <ProtectedRoute>
            <Jobs />
          </ProtectedRoute>
        }
      />

      <Route path="/" element={<Navigate to="/jobs" replace />} />
    </Routes>
  );
}
```

In the preceding snippet, we are simply wrapping our `Jobs` component with `ProtectedRoute`, and using the `Navigate` component to enforce redirects from the home route to the `/jobs` route.

To test this, you can either clear the token from local storage or copy and paste the route for the job into an incognito browser, and you should be redirected to the login page every time.

## Building the jobs page

Now that our route is protected, we can move to building the page itself.

### Step 1: Starting with a simple jobs page shell

We start by adding a basic container for the page with Tailwind:

```
export function Jobs() {
  return (
    <div className="min-h-screen flex items-center justify-center">
      <div className="w-full max-w-2xl">
        <h1 className="text-xl font-semibold">Jobs</h1>
      </div>
```

```
    </div>
  );
}
```

This matches the same minimal Tailwind approach we used for the login.

## Step 2: Fetching jobs using useGetJobs

Import the hook:

```
import { useGetJobs } from '@devjobs/api-client';
```

Then call it inside the component:

```
const jobsQuery = useGetJobs();
```

Now your component knows how to fetch `/jobs`.

## Step 3: Adding loading and error states

In the following code, we are adding a minimal `<div` to handle the loading states:

```
if (jobsQuery.isLoading) {
  return <div className="p-4">Loading jobs...</div>;
}

if (jobsQuery.isError) {
  return <div className="p-4">Failed to load jobs.</div>;
}
```

This keeps the page beginner-friendly and avoids UI complexity.

## Step 4: Rendering the jobs list

In the following code, we are signing the jobs data:

```
const jobs = jobsQuery.data?.data ?? [];
```

Then, render it:

```
<ul className='space-y-2'>
          {jobs.map((job) => (
            <li key={job.id} className='border rounded p-3'>
              <div className='font-medium'>{job.title}</div>
```

```
          <div className='text-sm text-gray-600'>{job.location}</div>
          <p className='text-sm text-gray-700 line-clamp-2'>
            {job.description}
          </p>
        </li>
      ))}
    </ul>
```

In the previous code, we loop through the fetched jobs and display a clean and minimalist list, which shows each job's title, location, and a job description.

# Summary

In this chapter, we applied many of the core concepts covered earlier to building a full stack application in a more realistic, professional setting. We adopted a contract-first approach, using an OpenAPI specification as a shared source of truth between the frontend and backend.

From that contract, we generated a fully typed client and used it to power our React frontend, ensuring strong type safety across the entire stack. On the backend, we built out the necessary endpoints using NestJS, implementing authentication, protected routes, and job listing functionality.

On the frontend, we intentionally kept the UI minimal. In a production application, you would likely add input validation, richer error handling, pagination, filtering, and more refined UI states. However, the goal of this chapter was not visual polish; it was to demonstrate how the core pieces fit together: contract-driven development, type safety, authentication, route protection, and data fetching with React Query.

We now have a functioning full stack flow:

- Users can log in
- The authentication state is persisted
- Protected routes restrict access
- Authenticated users can fetch and view data

More importantly, we've established a way of thinking—one that prioritizes shared contracts, predictable architecture, and type-driven development across the stack.

In the next chapter, we'll take this foundation further by building an AI-backed full stack feature, exploring how to integrate a **Large Language Model** (**LLM**)-based chatbot into your applications in a clean, structured, and production-aware way.

## Get this book's PDF copy, code bundle, and more

Scan the QR code (or go to `packtpub.com/unlock`). Search for this book by name, confirm the edition, and then follow the steps on the page.

UNLOCK NOW

*Note: Have your invoice handy. Purchases made directly from the Packt website don't require an invoice.*

# 12

# TypeScript in Evolving Systems

Up to this point in the book, you've learned about the individual tools that make TypeScript effective in production applications. You've seen why late failures are expensive, why moving errors earlier matters, and how types can do more than annotate values. They can express intent, enforce structure, and shape how a system evolves. You've also seen these ideas applied in a clean, contract-first workflow where frontend and backend move together around shared definitions.

That approach works best when requirements are well understood early and teams evolve the system in a coordinated way.

This chapter explores how those same principles apply when requirements change, systems grow, and assumptions begin to shift over time. In this story, the system already works. A proof of concept has shipped. Users are happy. Then requirements change, more developers join, and assumptions begin to drift. That's when mistakes become easy to make, and expensive to discover, because the system feels "stable" right up until the moment it breaks in production-like conditions.

So, instead of introducing a new framework or a new syntax feature, this chapter follows one concrete narrative: a small full stack support chatbot that evolves under real-world pressure. We will intentionally experience runtime failures first, then progressively introduce TypeScript techniques that move those failures earlier from the browser and production to build time, where they are cheaper and easier to fix.

We will cover the following main topics:

- Starting with a fast proof of concept
- Detecting and handling contract drift
- Making the contract explicit

- The problem shared types don't solve by themselves
- Protecting the JSON boundary with a runtime gate
- Scaling the system without leaking vendor details
- Making variants explicit with discriminated unions
- Multiple endpoints without fragile casts
- The payoff: moving failures earlier, on purpose

# Technical requirements

All code for this chapter is available as a runnable Nx workspace, and each major milestone is tagged so you can jump to the exact state being discussed. You can download the example project and code for this book by following the instructions in the *Download the example code files* section in the *Preface* of this book.

This chapter's code files are included in the downloadable code bundle.

You'll see tags such as `ch12-01-poc`, `ch12-02-contract-drift`, and so on. Don't treat these tags as "versions you should copy." Treat them as snapshots in a story. The point is to feel how each small improvement changes what the system makes easy and what it makes difficult.

# Starting with a fast proof of concept

Imagine you're asked to build a simple AI support chatbot that lets users type questions in a browser, see the conversation history, and receive responses from a backend API. The frontend sends conversation history to a single endpoint, `POST /api/chat`, and the backend replies with a short answer.

At this stage, speed matters more than correctness. You don't design a perfect contract on day one. You let assumptions live in code because early momentum matters, and the goal is learning what users actually want.

On the backend, the handler reads untyped JSON and returns a simple response:

```
app.post('/api/chat', (req, res) => {
  const messages = req.body.messages; // untyped JSON
  const last = messages?.[messages.length - 1];

  res.json({
    reply: `You said: ${last?.content ?? ''}`,
  });
});
```

On the frontend, the response is treated as "whatever comes back," and messages are stored as `any[]`:

```
const [messages, setMessages] = useState<any[]>([]);

const data = await res.json();
setMessages([...updated, { role: 'assistant', content: data.reply }]);
```

The chatbot works. The demo succeeds. If you check out the `ch12-01-poc` tag and run the app, everything feels fine. But pause for a moment and ask yourself a subtle question: where is the contract for this endpoint written down?

In this version, it isn't. It exists only in the developer's head.

That sounds harmless when one person built both sides last week. It becomes dangerous the moment the system becomes collaborative or long-lived, because memory is not a scalable contract.

# Detecting and handling contract drift

A few days later, a realistic requirement shows up. The response can no longer be "just a string." It must become a structured object containing the assistant's message, a list of references, and a set of follow-up questions.

You update the backend first. The endpoint still returns a property called `reply`, but now `reply` is an object instead of a string. Conceptually, the backend moves from this:

```
{ "reply": "You said: hello" }
```

To something like this:

```
{
  "reply": {
    "message": { "role": "assistant", "content": "You said: hello" },
    "references": [],
    "followUps": []
  }
}
```

Before opening the browser, you build the frontend. The build passes.

This is the most dangerous part of the story. A passing build creates a false sense of safety. It feels like TypeScript "approved" the change. But TypeScript did not approve it. It simply had nothing meaningful to check, because the frontend opted out of typing at the boundary. `any[]` and `untyped res.json()` leave the compiler with nothing to enforce.

When you refresh the UI and send a message, React throws a runtime error because it tries to render an object where it expected a string. This is the exact failure mode we've been warning about: a mistake that should have been caught immediately instead surfaces late, in the browser, under production-like conditions.

If you check `ch12-02-contract-drift`, you can reproduce this failure yourself. The build succeeds. The runtime explodes.

That experience is intentional. You need to feel why this class of bug is so painful. It isn't just that it breaks. It's that it breaks *after* you have already been told "everything is fine."

# Making the contract explicit

The fix is not "more careful developers," and it's not scattered conditionals in the UI. The fix is to stop relying on memory and turn the implicit agreement into an explicit contract.

In earlier chapters, you saw a contract-first workflow where a formal contract is defined up front (often with OpenAPI) and types are generated. In this chapter, we are intentionally doing the opposite, starting with implicit assumptions, because that is how many real systems begin. The goal now is to claw our way back to safety without pretending we had perfect planning on day one.

So, we introduce a shared TypeScript library that defines the shapes of our chat messages, requests, and responses. Even if you eventually generate these types from OpenAPI, the idea is the same: make the contract real code, shared across the boundary.

Create a shared module—for example, `libs/chat-contract`—and define a minimal domain contract:

```
export interface ChatMessage {
  role: 'user' | 'assistant';
  content: string;
}

export interface ChatRequest {
  messages: ChatMessage[];
}

export interface ChatReference {
  title: string;
```

```
  url: string;
}

export interface FollowUpQuestion {
  question: string;
}

export interface ChatReply {
  message: ChatMessage;
  references: ChatReference[];
  followUps: FollowUpQuestion[];
}

export interface ChatResponse {
  reply: ChatReply;
}
```

Notice what we're doing here. We are not trying to model a vendor SDK. We are not trying to mirror raw OpenAI, Anthropic, or any other provider response. We are describing *our domain*: what our product needs to show a user. That distinction matters more as the system grows.

Now, both frontend and backend import these types. At this moment, the contract stops being an assumption. It becomes code.

On the frontend, you no longer store messages as `any[]`. You store them as the domain type:

```
const [messages, setMessages] = useState<ChatMessage[]>([]);
```

When you call the API, you stop treating JSON as "whatever comes back." You explicitly type the call:

```
async function postChat(request: ChatRequest): Promise<ChatResponse> {
  const res = await fetch('/api/chat', {
    method: 'POST',
    headers: { 'content-type': 'application/json' },
    body: JSON.stringify(request),
  });

  const data = (await res.json()) as ChatResponse;
  return data;
}
```

Even this simple shift changes the developer experience immediately. If you try to treat `reply` as a string now, TypeScript stops you during build. The same mistake that previously slipped through now fails before you even refresh the browser.

That is the first rescue moment. It is not "advanced TypeScript." It is basic TypeScript used at the correct boundary.

If you check `ch12-03-shared-contract` and repeat the earlier mistake, TypeScript blocks the build.

# The problem shared types don't solve by themselves

At this point, it's tempting to think you're done. You have shared types, so you have safety. But there is still one place where untyped data enters your system: JSON.

On the backend, that boundary is `req.body`. On the frontend, that boundary is `res.json()`. The correct mental model is simple: everything that crosses the network is unknown until proven otherwise.

Types do not magically validate runtime data. If the backend accidentally returns the wrong shape, if a proxy modifies responses, or if a bad deploy temporarily mixes versions, TypeScript cannot protect you from what it cannot see.

So, we add one more small but critical layer: a runtime gate.

# Protecting the JSON boundary with a runtime gate

We start by acknowledging reality. Incoming values are untrusted. They begin life as unknown and only become trusted after validation.

First, define a tiny helper:

```
export function isRecord(value: unknown): value is Record<string, unknown> {
  return typeof value === 'object'&&value!==null;
}
```

Then add type guards for your domain objects. You can keep this simple at first and deepen them as the contract grows:

```
import type { ChatMessage, ChatRequest, ChatResponse } from './chat-contract';

export function isChatMessage(value: unknown): value is ChatMessage {
  if (!isRecord(value)) return false;
  const role = value.role;
```

```
  return (
    (role === 'user' || role === 'assistant') &&
    typeof value.content === 'string'
  );
}

export function isChatRequest(value: unknown): value is ChatRequest {
  if (!isRecord(value)) return false;
  if (!Array.isArray(value.messages)) return false;
  return value.messages.every(isChatMessage);
}

export function isChatResponse(value: unknown): value is ChatResponse {
  if (!isRecord(value)) return false;
  if (!isRecord(value.reply)) return false;

  const reply = value.reply;

  if (!isRecord(reply.message)) return false;
  if (!isChatMessage(reply.message)) return false;

  if (!Array.isArray(reply.references)) return false;
  if (!Array.isArray(reply.followUps)) return false;

  return true;
}
```

Now, instead of trusting JSON, you treat it as unknown at the boundary. On the backend, that means validating `req.body` before using it:

```
import type { Request, Response } from 'express';
import type { ChatRequest, ChatResponse } from '@acme/chat-contract';
import { isChatRequest } from '@acme/chat-contract/guards';

app.post('/api/chat', (req: Request, res: Response) => {
  const body: unknown = req.body;

  if (!isChatRequest(body)) {
    res.status(400).json({ error: 'Invalid request body' });
    return;
  }
```

```
  const last = body.messages[body.messages.length - 1];

  const response: ChatResponse = {
    reply: {
      message: { role: 'assistant', content: `You said: ${last?.content ?? ''}` },
      references: [],
      followUps: [],
    },
  };

  res.json(response);
});
```

On the frontend, it means validating the response before trusting it:

```
import type { ChatRequest, ChatResponse } from '@acme/chat-contract';
import { isChatResponse } from '@acme/chat-contract/guards';

async function postChat(request: ChatRequest): Promise<ChatResponse> {
  const res = await fetch('/api/chat', {
    method: 'POST',
    headers: { 'content-type': 'application/json' },
    body: JSON.stringify(request),
  });

  const data: unknown = await res.json();

  if (!isChatResponse(data)) {
    throw new Error('Server returned an invalid ChatResponse shape');
  }

  return data;
}
```

This is not about building a heavyweight validation framework. It's about making the boundary honest. Once the data passes the gate, the rest of the system can rely on strong types. If it fails the gate, you fail fast with a clear error instead of letting corrupted data quietly poison your UI.

*This corresponds to the ch12-04-runtime-gate tag.*

## Scaling the system without leaking vendor details

The chatbot works again. The Product is happy. Then the next request arrives: support multiple LLM providers.

This is where many teams accidentally sabotage their own shared types. They do the right thing, introduce shared types, but they share the wrong thing. If your shared types mirror a vendor's raw response, every provider change becomes a frontend change, because you've baked vendor shape into your domain contract.

The key insight is that shared types should describe *your domain*, not a vendor.

So, instead of sharing `OpenAIResponse` or `AnthropicResponse`, we define a provider interface that returns our domain type:

```
import type { ChatMessage, ChatReply } from '@acme/chat-contract';

export interface LlmProvider {
  generateReply(messages: ChatMessage[]): Promise<ChatReply>;
}
```

Each provider adapts its SDK internally. This is where design patterns stop being academic and start being practical. The provider is effectively a strategy (we can swap implementations), and the provider wrapper is often an adapter (it converts vendor output into your domain shape). Your core application depends only on the interface, not on vendor-specific JSON.

A factory picks the provider at runtime:

```
export function createProvider(name: string): LlmProvider {
  switch (name) {
    case 'provider-a':
      return new ProviderA();
    case 'provider-b':
      return new ProviderB();
    default:
      throw new Error(`Unknown provider: ${name}`);
  }
}
```

Now the backend handler can remain stable. It calls `provider.generateReply()` and returns the domain response. Providers can evolve without forcing a coordinated frontend rewrite.

That is what "stable boundaries" looks like in practice: you isolate volatility behind an interface.

## Making variants explicit with discriminated unions

Another requirement appears. Sometimes the chatbot response includes citations. Sometimes it doesn't. It's still the same endpoint.

A common approach is to sprinkle optional fields everywhere. That feels flexible, but it quietly creates ambiguity: which combinations are valid? When are citations expected? When is it meaningless? Optional fields often turn your contract into "maybe everything exists," which is not the same as "only valid states exist."

This is where TypeScript becomes a modeling tool, not just a type annotator. Instead of describing one fuzzy shape, we describe the valid variants explicitly.

At this stage, we evolve our response type from a single interface into a discriminated union:

```
export interface Citation {
  sourceTitle: string;
  url: string;
}

export type ChatResponse =
  | { kind: 'answer'; reply: ChatReply }
  | { kind: 'answer-with-citations'; reply: ChatReply; citations: Citation[] };
```

Now, a response is always one of two valid shapes, and the `kind` field is the discriminator that makes narrowing natural. On the frontend, you stop guessing. You switch on `kind`:

```
switch (response.kind) {
  case 'answer':
    // render reply only
    break;

  case 'answer-with-citations':
    renderCitations(response.citations);
    break;

  default: {
    const _exhaustive: never = response;
    return _exhaustive;
```

```
    }
  }
```

That `never` line looks small, but it changes how the system behaves under change. If you add a third variant later, say `kind: 'rate-limited'`, and forget to handle it, the build fails. Correctness is enforced structurally.

This is what "type safety under change" actually means. It doesn't mean you never ship bugs. It means entire *classes* of bugs become difficult to ship because the type system forces you to update every place that must change.

**Why the never check works:** If a new variant is added to the union and the switch isn't updated, TypeScript detects that not all cases are handled. In that situation, the remaining unhandled type flows into the default branch, causing the assignment to never fail at compile time. This intentional error forces you to explicitly handle the new case, preventing incomplete logic from compiling.

# Multiple endpoints without fragile casts

As the system grows, endpoints multiply. Teams feel pressure to move fast, and a tempting shortcut appears: repeated `as SomeType` casts sprinkled across your API calls. Those casts look like type safety, but they silently disable it, because you are telling TypeScript, "Trust me," at the exact boundary where trust is most dangerous.

A better pattern is to define a mapping between endpoints and their types, and then build a small generic client where the endpoint literal determines the request and response types.

Here is one lightweight approach:

```
import type { ChatRequest, ChatResponse } from '@acme/chat-contract';

type ApiRoutes = {
  '/api/chat': {
    req: ChatRequest;
    res: ChatResponse;
  };
  '/api/health': {
    req: undefined;
    res: { ok: true };
  };
};
```

```
async function postJson<K extends keyof ApiRoutes>(
  path: K,
  body: ApiRoutes[K]['req']
): Promise<ApiRoutes[K]['res']> {
  const res = await fetch(path, {
    method: 'POST',
    headers: { 'content-type': 'application/json' },
    body: JSON.stringify(body),
  });

  return (await res.json()) as ApiRoutes[K]['res'];
}
```

With this pattern, you don't get to accidentally call the wrong endpoint and pretend it returns the shape you wanted. The mapping determines the type. The literal determines the type. The compiler enforces the agreement.

You can still combine this with runtime gates where appropriate, especially at boundaries where you cannot guarantee version alignment between deployments. But the biggest payoff here is eliminating the "silent type lie" of copy-pasted casts.

## The payoff: moving failures earlier, on purpose

At each step, the same pattern emerges. You start with code that works by convention. Then you change something realistic. Without contracts, failures appear late. With shared types, runtime gates, stable boundaries, and expressive modeling, failures move earlier.

The goal was never to write "advanced" TypeScript for its own sake. The goal was to make incorrect changes harder to ship.

When you build systems that evolve, systems where new teammates join, requirements shift, and vendor dependencies change, your real enemy is not complexity; it is invisible assumptions. TypeScript's best work happens when it turns those invisible assumptions into explicit structures that the compiler can enforce.

## Summary

In this chapter, you followed the lifecycle of a TypeScript system after its initial success. You began with a fast proof of concept where frontend and backend matched only by assumption. When the backend response evolved, the frontend broke at runtime because TypeScript had nothing concrete to enforce.

By introducing shared contracts, you transformed implicit agreements into explicit code. By adding a small runtime gate at the JSON boundary, you acknowledged that network data is unknown until validated, and prevented corrupted shapes from leaking into your system. As collaboration and complexity increased, you applied patterns to create stable boundaries and advanced TypeScript features to make valid states explicit. Provider interfaces prevented vendor details from leaking across layers. Discriminated unions replaced fragile optional fields and forced exhaustive handling as the contract evolved. Typed API clients eliminated unsafe casts and removed an entire category of invisible bugs.

TypeScript helped not because it was "advanced," but because it turned easy-to-make mistakes into hard-to-ship mistakes. That is the role TypeScript plays in long-lived systems: not as a set of annotations, but as a safety mechanism that evolves alongside your code as requirements change.

## Get this book's PDF copy, code bundle, and more

Scan the QR code (or go to `packtpub.com/unlock`). Search for this book by name, confirm the edition, and then follow the steps on the page.

UNLOCK NOW

*Note: Have your invoice handy. Purchases made directly from the Packt website don't require an invoice.*

# 13

# Unlock Your Exclusive Benefits

Your copy of this book includes the following exclusive benefits:

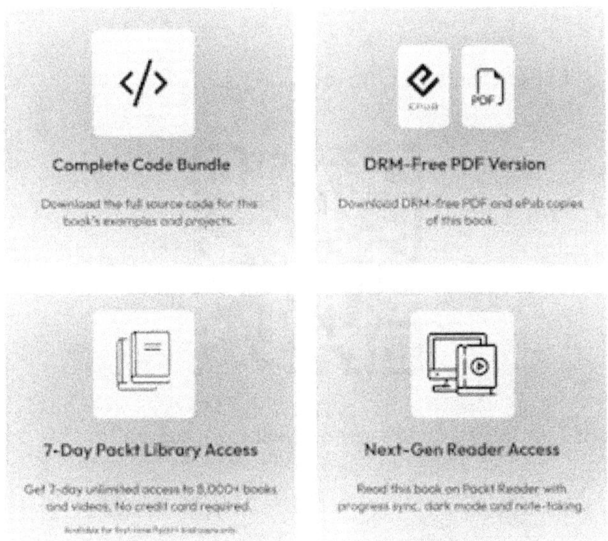


Follow the guide below to unlock them. The process takes only a few minutes and needs to be completed once.

# Unlock this Book's Free Benefits in 3 Easy Steps

## Step 1

Keep your purchase invoice ready for *Step 3*. If you have a physical copy, scan it using your phone and save it as a PDF, JPG, or PNG.

For more help on finding your invoice, visit `https://www.packtpub.com/en-us/unlock?step=1`.

> Note
>
> **Note**: If you bought this book directly from Packt, no invoice is required. After *Step 2*, you can access your exclusive content right away.

## Step 2

Scan the QR code or go to `packtpub.com/unlock`.

On the page that opens (similar to *Figure 13.1* on desktop), search for this book by name and select the correct edition.

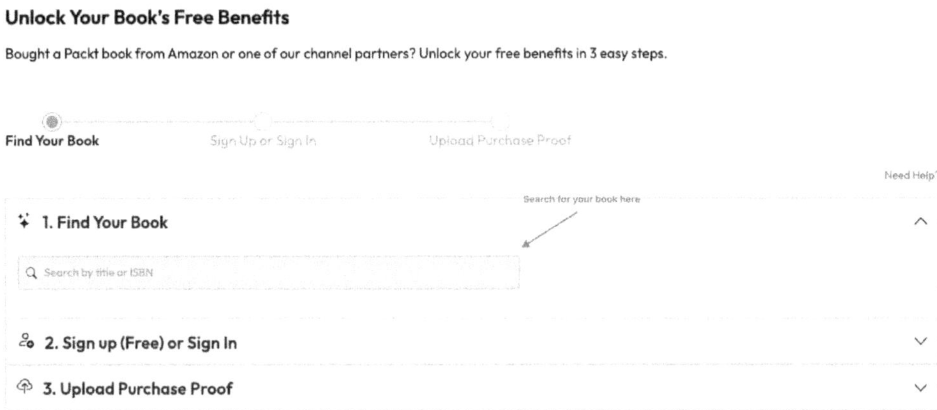


*Figure 13.1: Packt unlock landing page on desktop*

## Step 3

After selecting your book, sign in to your Packt account or create one for free. Then upload your invoice (PDF, PNG, or JPG, up to 10 MB). Follow the on-screen instructions to finish the process.

## Need Help

If you get stuck and need help, visit `https://www.packtpub.com/unlock-benefits/help` for a detailed FAQ on how to find your invoices and more. This QR code will take you to the help page.

Note

**Note**: If you are still facing issues, reach out to `customercare@packt.com`.

packtpub.com

Subscribe to our online digital library for full access to over 7,000 books and videos, as well as industry leading tools to help you plan your personal development and advance your career. For more information, please visit our website.

## Why subscribe?

- Spend less time learning and more time coding with practical eBooks and Videos from over 4,000 industry professionals
- Improve your learning with Skill Plans built especially for you
- Get a free eBook or video every month
- Fully searchable for easy access to vital information
- Copy and paste, print, and bookmark content

At www.packtpub.com, you can also read a collection of free technical articles, sign up for a range of free newsletters, and receive exclusive discounts and offers on Packt books and eBooks.

# Other Books You May Enjoy

If you enjoyed this book, you may be interested in these other books by Packt:

**Mastering TypeScript**

Nathan Rozentals

ISBN: 9781800564732

- Gain insights into core and advanced TypeScript language features
- Integrate with existing JavaScript libraries and third-party frameworks
- Build full working applications using JavaScript frameworks, such as Angular, React, Vue, and more
- Create test suites for your application with Jest and Selenium
- Apply industry-standard design patterns to build modular code
- Develop web server solutions using NodeJS and Express

**TypeScript 5 Design Patterns and Best Practices**

Theofanis Despoudis

ISBN: 9781835883228

- Understand the principles of design patterns and their role in TypeScript development
- Learn essential patterns, including creational, structural, and behavioral, with TypeScript
- Differentiate between patterns and design concepts and apply them effectively
- Gain hands-on experience implementing patterns in real-world TypeScript projects
- Explore advanced techniques from functional and reactive programming paradigms
- Write efficient, high-quality TypeScript code that enhances performance and flexibility

## Packt is searching for authors like you

If you're interested in becoming an author for Packt, please visit `authors.packt.com` and apply today. We have worked with thousands of developers and tech professionals, just like you, to help them share their insight with the global tech community. You can make a general application, apply for a specific hot topic that we are recruiting an author for, or submit your own idea.

## Share your thoughts

Now you've finished *Clean Code with TypeScript*, we'd love to hear your thoughts! Scan the QR code below to go straight to the Amazon review page for this book and share your feedback or leave a review on the site that you purchased it from.

*https://packt.link/r/1835889573*

Your review is important to us and the tech community and will help us make sure we're delivering excellent quality content.

# Index

# C

## H



## I



## J



## L

## M



## N



## O

## P



## R



## S

# T

www.ingramcontent.com/pod-product-compliance
Lightning Source LLC
LaVergne TN
LVHW060018210926
848481LV00013B/3742
* 9 7 8 1 8 3 5 8 8 9 5 6 5 *